A Charlton Standard Catalogue

STORYBOOK FIGURINES

ROYAL DOULTON
ROYAL ALBERT
BESWICK

Eighth Edition

By
Jean Dale

Introduction
by
Louise Irvine

W. K. Cross
Publisher

The Charlton Press

TORONTO, ONTARIO • PALM HARBOR, FLORIDA

Library and Archives Canada has catalogued this publication as follows:

Storybook figurines of Beswick, Royal Albert and Royal Doulton: a Charlton standard catalogue

Annual.
7th
Continues: Charlton standard catalogue of Royal Doulton Beswick
.   storybook figurines (1995)
ISSN 1706-7146
ISBN 0-88968-292-5 (8th ed.)

1. Porcelain figures--Prices--Catalogs. 2. Porcelain animals--Prices--Catalogues. 3. Royal Doulton figurines--Prices--Catalogs

NK4660.C5   738.8'2'0294   C2003-901662-5

EDITORIAL

Editor	Jean Dale
Editorial Assistant	Susan Cross
Graphic Technician	Davina Rowan
Photography	Marilyn and Peter Sweet

ACKNOWLEDGEMENTS

The Charlton Press wishes to thank those who have helped with the seventh edition of Storybook Figurines, Royal Doulton, Royal Albert, Beswick, (A Charlton Standard Catalogue).

Special Thanks

The publisher would like to thank:

Louise Irvine for writing the introduction to this edition. Louise is an independent writer and lecturer on Royal Doulton's history and products and is not connected with the pricing in this price guide.

Hank Corley for his extensive work on the understanding of the Beswick Beatrix Potter series and their backstamps.

Carolyn Baker for all her work on the Beatrix Potter series in previous editions.

Our thanks also go to the staff of Royal Doulton, who have helped with additional technical information, especially **Fiona Hawthorne**, General Manager, Director and Relationship Manager (U.K.); **Sara Williams**, Product Manager, Royal Doulton, (U.K.); **David Lovatt**, Marketing Communications Design Manager (U.K.); **Josie Hunt** and **Julie Tilestone**, Doulton & Company Doulton Direct (U.K.); **Julie Mountford**, International Collectors Club (U.K.); **Marion Proctor**, Marketing Manager (Canada); **Janet Drift**, Director of Retail Sales (U.S.A)

Contributors to the Eighth Edition

The publisher would also like to thank the following individuals and companies who graciously supplied photographs or information or allowed us access to their collections for photographic purposes: **Ted Crook**, Swansea, U.K.; **C. H. Crowley**, Essex, UK; **Simon Hadwick**, **Millennium Collectables**, U.K.; **William A. Haight**, Sarnia, Ontario; **David Hale Hand**, Fort Collins, CO; **Anita Hunter**; **Richard Kane**, Westlake, Ohio; **Judy Kula**, Flemington, New Jersey; **Mr. O'Neill**, U.K.; **Brenda and Ian Paterson**, Bedfordshire, UK; **Paul Watson**, Black Cat Collectables, U.K.

A SPECIAL NOTE TO COLLECTORS

We welcome and appreciate any comments or suggestions in regard to Storybook Figurines. If any errors or omissions come to your attention, please write to us, or if you would like to participate in pricing or supply previously unavailable data or information, please contact Jean Dale at (416) 488-1418, or e-mail us at chpress@charltonpress.com.

DISCLAIMER

While every care has been taken to ensure accuracy in the compilation of the data in this catalogue, the publisher cannot accept responsibility for typographical errors.

The Charlton Press

Editorial Office
P.O. Box 820, Station Willowdale B
North York, Ontario, M2K 2R1 Canada
Telephone (416) 488-1418 Fax: (416) 488-4656
Telephone (800) 442-6042 Fax: (800) 442-1542
www.charltonpress.com e-mail: chpress@charltonpress.com

HOW TO USE THIS PRICE GUIDE

THE PURPOSE

The sixth edition of this price guide covers the complete range of children's figures issued by Royal Doulton, Royal Albert and Beswick with the exception of the Bunnykins figurines which are included in The Charlton Standard Catalogue of Royal Doulton Bunnykins, Second Edition. In the process we have taken liberties with the name of this catalogue, for all figures listed are certainly not derived from storybook characters. However, the great majority are, and thus we have carried the name forward.

As with the other catalogues in Charlton's Royal Doulton reference and pricing library, this publication has been designed to serve two specific purposes. First, to furnish the collector with accurate and detailed listings that provide the essential information needed to build a rewarding collection. Second, to provide collectors and dealers with current market prices for Royal Doulton and Beswick storybook figures.

STYLES AND VERSIONS

STYLES: A change in style occurs when a major element of the design is altered or modified as a result of a deliberate mould change. An example of this is The Duchess With Flowers (style one) and The Duchess With a Pie (style two).

VERSIONS: Versions are modifications in a minor style element, such as the long ears becoming short ears on Mr. Benjamin Bunny.

VARIATIONS: A change in colour is a variation; for example, Mr. Jeremy Fisher's change in colourways from spotted to striped leggings.

THE LISTINGS

The Beatrix Potter figures are arranged alphabetically. At the beginning of the Beatrix Potter listings are seven pages graphically outlining backstamp variations. Backstamps are illustrated for eleven major varieties covering over fifty years of production. In the Beatrix Potter pricing charts, the reader will see Beswick and Doulton model numbers, backstamp numbers and market prices.

The Brambly Hedge figures are listed by their DBH numbers. There are no backstamp variations known.

The Snowman series is listed in numerical order by the DS numbers. There are no backstamp variations.

All of the above listings include the modeller, where known, the name of the animal figure, designer, height, colour, date of issue, varieties and series.

PRICING AND THE INTERNET

Over the past thirty years we have gathered pricing information from auctions, dealer submissions, direct mail catalogues and newsletters, all contributed prices on one of two levels, wholesale or retail. We, at Charlton Press, consider auctions basically a dealer affair, while price lists, naturally retail. To equate both prices, we needed to adjust the auction results upward, by a margin of 30% to 40%, allowing for dealer markups, before comparing and then looking for a consensus on a retail price.

The marketplace has changed, the Internet and on-line auctions are growing at such a rate that all other pricing sources we used are being completely overwhelmed by the sheer weight of the items being offered.

At a moment in time on August 13th 2004, under Storybook Characters on e-Bay, over 1,000 individual items were posted for sale. Assuming this is an average day, then for the week 7000 items are offered and for the year nearly 364,000 will be offered for sale. The "Economist," a weekly news magazine, put the on-line auctions with now over 100,000,000 registered users.

The impact the Internet will have on collectables has yet to be appreciated by collectors and dealers alike. All the old avenues such as fairs, shows, dealer stores, retail outlets, direct mail houses and auction rooms are being forced to change due to the extreme pressure of this new marketing force. Margins have come under pressure, wholesale and retail prices are starting to blend, and competition for the Collectors' budget will intensify. However, through it all one point remains, a price guide is just that, a guide, and the final say is between the buyer and the seller.

CONTENTS

INTRODUCTION
By Louise Irvine

THE HISTORY OF STORYBOOK CHARACTERS FROM THE ROYAL DOULTON, JOHN BESWICK AND ROYAL ALBERT STUDIOS

For over a century, the Royal Doulton Studios have entertained us with storybook characters, particularly animals endowed with human personalities. In Victorian times, a group of frogs enacting a well-known fable raised a smile in much the same way as the antics of the BRAMBLY HEDGE™ mice amuse us today. The tales of BEATRIX POTTER™, with lots of different animals acting and conversing as if they were human, are as popular now as when they were first written in the early 1900s. Obviously the idea of a creature simultaneously human and animal is deep rooted in our literary culture, and it is interesting to trace when it first became apparent in the Doulton world.

The Doulton factory was founded in London in 1815, but for the first 50 years production was confined to practical pottery. In the late 1860s, Sir Henry Doulton established an art studio, employing students from the Lambeth School of Art to decorate vases, jugs and plaques in fashionable Victorian styles. Some artists specialised in figurative sculpture, notably George Tinworth, who was the first to seek inspiration from well-known stories. The Bible provided him with most of his subject matter, but he also enjoyed reading the fables of Aesop and La Fontaine. These moralistic tales feature foxes, mice, lions and other creatures exemplifying human traits, and they fascinated the Victorians, particularly after the publication of Darwin's theory of evolution. Tinworth modelled several fables groups in the 1880s, including "The Fox and the Ape," "The Cat and the Cheese" and "The Ox and the Frogs." Later he produced mice and frog subjects, based on his own observations of human nature, which reflect his perceptive sense of humour.

Mr. Toad disguised as a washerwoman

The potential for dressed-up animals to disguise a deeper message soon led to their widespread use in children's literature, notably "Alice's Adventures in Wonderland" and Lear's nonsense poems. In 1908, Kenneth Grahame wrote "The Wind in the Willows" to comment on the behaviour of the English aristocracy, but the exciting adventures of Mr. Toad subtly conceal the author's critical stance. The dapper toad in his pinstripes and tails was modelled shortly afterwards by Lambeth artist Francis Pope, and a companion piece shows Mr. Toad disguised as a washerwoman in order to escape from prison.

Figures like these probably encouraged Beatrix Potter to approach the Lambeth studio in 1908 with a view to having her own animal characters immortalised in ceramic. Miss Potter published several illustrated stories about her favourite animals after the success of "The Tale of Peter Rabbit"™ in 1902, and some characters had already appeared as cuddly toys and decorative motifs on clothes, etc. Unfortunately an earlier contract with a German china firm made any arrangement with Doulton impossible, but she tried on a later occasion to have figures made of her characters at Grimwade's factory in Stoke-on-Trent. They suggested that Doulton's other factory in Burslem would be the best place to have the figures decorated, but again plans fell through. It was not until after Miss Potter's death that her dream was realised when the John Beswick factory in Longton began making little figures inspired by her books.

The John Beswick factory was founded in 1894 to produce ornamental jugs, vases and other decorative fancies. By the 1940s the Beswick artists had established a reputation for quality animal modelling, particularly portraits of famous horses by Arthur Gredington. In 1947, Gredington demonstrated his versatility when he modelled "Jemima Puddleduck" at the suggestion of Lucy Beswick, the wife of the managing director. She had been inspired by a visit to Beatrix Potter's Lake District home, where many of the tales are set. The success of this first study led to an initial collection of ten Beatrix Potter characters, including "Peter Rabbit," "Benjamin Bunny" and "Mrs. Tiggy-Winkle."

Launched in 1948, the new Beatrix Potter figures were welcomed with enthusiasm, and it was not long before Gredington was at work on another collection of character animals, this time from a British animated film. The "Lion" cartoon by David Hand was released in 1948, and "Zimmy Lion" became a new star for the Rank Film Organisation. Sequel cartoons introduced "Ginger Nutt," "Hazel Nutt," "Dinkum Platypus," "Loopy Hare," "Oscar Ostrich," "Dusty Mole" and "Felia Cat," all of which were modelled in 1949 as the DAVID HAND'S ANIMALAND™ series. David Hand had formerly worked for the Walt Disney studios, directing Mickey Mouse shorts, as well as the major films "Snow White" and "Bambi," and it was not long before these cartoons also inspired a collection of Beswick figures. Arthur Gredington modelled the little figures of "Snow White and the Seven Dwarfs" whilst Jan Granoska, a trainee modeller, was given the task of portraying Mickey Mouse and friends, plus some characters from "Pinocchio" and "Peter Pan." Although Miss Granoska was only at the Beswick studio for three years, she was responsible for some of their most desirable figures.

Music (of sorts!) is being played by the BEDTIME CHORUS™, a group of enthusiastic children accompanied by a singing cat and dog. These were amongst the first character figures to be modelled by Albert Hallam, who gradually took over responsibility for this area in the 1960s. As head mouldmaker, Hallam had made many of the production moulds for Gredington designs, so he was already familiar with the subject matter. He continued the Beatrix Potter collection, adding characters such as "Old Mr. Brown" and "Cecily Parsley," and in 1968 he launched a new Disney series based on their newest cartoon hit, "Winnie the Pooh and the Blustery Day."

The late 1960s was a time of transition for the company as Ewart Beswick was ready to retire but he had no heir for his successful business. Fortunately the Royal Doulton group was in the midst of an expansion programme and they acquired the Beswick factory in 1969. They soon benefited from Beswick's expertise in the field of character animals.

When Albert Hallam retired in 1975, Graham Tongue became the head modeller at the Beswick Studio under Harry Sales, the newly appointed design manager. Harry Sales was primarily a graphic artist and he dreamed up many new ideas for the Beatrix Potter range, which Graham Tongue and others modelled during the 1980s. This was becoming increasingly difficult as the most popular characters had already been modelled. Favourites, such as "Peter Rabbit" and "Jemima Puddleduck," were introduced in new poses, and he came up with the idea of double figures, for example "Mr Benjamin Bunny and Peter Rabbit" and "Tabitha Twitchet and Miss Moppet."

As well as developing the established figure collections, Harry Sales delved into lots of other children's books for inspiration. He re-interpreted the timeless characters from classic tales such as "Alice's Adventures in Wonderland" and "The Wind in the Willows," and he worked from contemporary picture books, notably Joan Walsh Anglund's "A Friend is Someone Who Likes You" and Norman Thelwell's "Angels on Horseback." Whenever possible, Harry liaised closely with the originators of the characters he portrayed. He spent many happy hours of research at Thelwell's studio, studying his cartoons of shaggy ponies with comical riders, and he also worked with Alfred Bestall, the illustrator of the Rupert Bear adventures in the "Daily Express" newspaper before embarking on this series in 1980.

With their outstanding reputation for developing character animals, it is not surprising that Royal Doulton artists were invited to work on the publishing sensation of the 1980s, the Brambly Hedge stories by Jill Barklem. Within three years of their launch the "Spring," "Summer," "Autumn" and "Winter" stories had been reprinted 11 times, translated into ten languages, and had sold in excess of a million copies. Readers young and old were captivated by the enchanting world of the Brambly Hedge mice, as indeed was Harry Sales, whose job it was to recreate the characters in the ceramic medium. In his own words, "The first time I read the books and studied the illustrations I felt that I was experiencing something quite unique. Over a period of many years designing for the pottery industry one develops an awareness, a feeling for that something special. Brambly Hedge had this."

Ideas flowed quickly and eight leading characters were chosen from the seasonal stories for the initial collection, which was launched in 1983. Such was the response that they were soon joined by six more subjects, making a total of 14 by 1986, when Harry left the company. Graham Tongue succeeded him as design manager and continued to add new Brambly Hedge figures from the original stories. Miss Barklem's later titles, The Secret Staircase, The High Hills and The Sea Story, provided inspiration for some of his figures; for example, Mr and Mrs Saltapple who supply the Brambly Hedge community with salt in The Sea Story.

Encouraged by the amazing success of the Brambly Hedge collection, Royal Doulton's marketing executives were soon considering other new storybook characters. Like millions of TV viewers, they were spellbound by the magical film, The Snowman, which was first screened in 1982. Based on the illustrated book of the same name by Raymond Briggs, the animated film about a snowman who comes to life has become traditional Christmas entertainment in many parts of the world. The absence of words

gives the tale a haunting quality, and there is hardly a dry eye in the house when the little boy, James, awakes to find his Snowman friend has melted away after an exciting night exploring each other's worlds. Fortunately the SNOWMAN™ lives on in more durable form in the Royal Doulton collection. Again Harry Sales was given the challenge of transforming this amorphous character into ceramic, whilst remaining faithful to Briggs' original soft crayon drawings. He succeeded in this difficult task by adding additional curves to the contours of the figures which gives them a life-like appearance. The first four figures were ready and approved by Raymond Briggs in 1985, and the collection grew steadily until 1990, latterly under the direction of Graham Tongue.

The 1990s saw Graham Tongue and his team of artists develop the Beatrix Potter collection for the 100th birthday of "Peter Rabbit" and, in 1994, the centenary of the Beswick factory was marked with the launch of the "Pig Promenade," featuring a special commemorative backstamp.

This series is just one of three new collections of novelty figures, and it is refreshing to see this traditional type of Beswick ware being revitalised by a new generation of artists. Amanda Hughes-Lubeck and Warren Platt created the LITTLE LOVABLES™, a series of cute clowns with special messages, such as "Good Luck" and "Congratulations," and they also worked with Martyn Alcock on the collection of ENGLISH COUNTRY FOLK™, which has been very well received.

The collecting of Beatrix Potter and Brambly Hedge figures has reached epidemic proportions in recent years, and there is now a growing awareness of the desirability of all their storybook cousins, hence the need for this much expanded price guide.

COLLECTING BEATRIX POTTER FIGURES

A number of factors have combined recently to make Beatrix Potter figures the "hottest" collectables of the day. The 100th birthday of "Peter Rabbit" was celebrated amidst a storm of publicity in 1993, and the centenary of the John Beswick factory in 1994 focused a lot of collector attention on its products. 1997 saw more celebrations as Beatrix Potter figures had been in continuous production at Beswick for fifty years.

A group of Beatrix Potter books with the figures beside

The market has been stimulated by regular withdrawals from the range and prices are rocketing for the early discontinued figures. Most collectors will need a bank loan to purchase "Duchess with Flowers," the first Beatrix Potter figure to be retired, if indeed they are lucky enough to find one for sale.

Ever since the Beswick factory launched their Beatrix Potter collection in 1948, most of the figures have been bought as gifts for children. However, many young fans have grown up to find they have some very valuable figures, with early modelling and backstamp variations, and they have begun collecting in earnest to fill the gaps and find the rarities. Figures marked with a Beswick backstamp are most in demand, as this trademark was replaced with the Royal Albert backstamp in 1989. The Royal Albert factory, another famous name in the Doulton group, produces all the Beatrix Potter tableware, and the change of backstamps was made for distribution reasons. The most desirable Beswick marks are the gold varieties, which predate 1972, and these are often found on early modelling or colour variations, which also attract a premium price, for example "Mrs Rabbit" with her umbrella sticking out and "Mr Benjamin Bunny" with his pipe protruding.

As well as seeking out discontinued figures and rare variations, it is advisable to keep up to date with new models as they are introduced. A complete Beatrix Potter figure collection will encompass more than 100 of the standard-size models, around three inches tall, and thirteen large models, which are about twice the size. "Peter Rabbit," the first of these large size models, was launched in 1993 with a special commemorative backstamp from the John Beswick studio, and it changed in 1994 to a Royal Albert mark. The Royal Albert mark was used on most Beatrix Potter figures between 1989 and 1998 when new John Beswick backstamps were introduced.

If owning all the Beatrix Potter figures is beyond the realms of possibility, whether for financial or display limitations, then why not focus on particular types of animals or characters from your favourite tales. There are twenty mice figures to find, a dozen cat characters and more than twenty rabbits, half of which feature "Peter Rabbit." There are also discontinued character jugs, relief modelled plaques and a ceramic display stand to look out for, so happy hunting.

COLLECTING BRAMBLY HEDGE FIGURES

Since their introduction in 1983, the Brambly Hedge mice have overrun households in many parts of the world. They are scurrying about the shelves as Royal Doulton figures and even climbing up the walls on decorative plates. Far from being undesirable, these particular mice are considered indispensable members of the family. Children frequently receive them as gifts from doting grandparents, but adults have also been seduced by the cosy, timeless mouse world which Jill Barklem has created. The mood of rustic nostalgia has all been painstakingly researched. The interiors of the field mice homes are of the sort common in English farmhouses at the end of the 19th century, and the food served is genuine country fare, based on old recipes and tested in Jill Barklem's kitchen. The Brambly Hedge residents were all expertly drawn with the aid of her two mouse models, a keen understanding of zoology and a knowledge of historical costume.

The same attention to detail went into the Royal Doulton figures designed by Harry Sales. As he explains, "One important feature in the concept was that I chose poses which, when the figures are together, appear to be reacting to one another. I can imagine the fun children and the young at heart will have arranging the figures in conversational situations." Essentially this sums up the collectability of the Brambly Hedge mice, and as there are only 25 figures in the first series, they can all be displayed effectively together on one shelf. There are, however, a couple of unusual

modelling variations to look out for as "Mr Toadflax's" tail was altered shortly after its introduction, plus some colour variations. Royal Doulton retired the first Brambly Hedge collection in 1997, but a new collection of figures was introduced in 2000 to celebrate the 20th anniversary of Brambly Hedge.

COLLECTING SNOWMAN FIGURES

Initially, the seasonal appeal of the Snowman tended to limit his collectability, as most purchases were made around Christmas time, and he was more popular in areas which regularly experience snow. Having said this, for some fans the wintry connotations were overshadowed by the inherent quality and humour of the models and there are now keen collectors in sunny Florida as well as in Australia, where beach barbecues are typical Christmas celebrations.

Between 1985 and 1990, young children regularly received the new Snowman models in their Christmas stockings, and the characters have been widely used as holiday decorations. Like the Brambly Hedge models, they were designed to interact, and the little figure of James, gazing up in wonder, can be positioned with various Snowman characters, whilst the band works very well as a separate display grouping. There are 19 figures and two musical boxes to collect in the first series, and as the range was withdrawn in 1994, they can now be quite difficult to locate. In fact, prices have been snowballing, particularly for the figures that were not in production for long, notably "The Snowman Skiing." The antics of the Snowman were revived in 1999 for a limited edition collection commissioned by Lawleys By Post.

COLLECTING STORYBOOK CHARACTERS

The Beatrix Potter, Brambly Hedge and Snowman stories have already been discussed in some detail, as there are so many figures to collect in each of the categories. However, the Beswick artists have also sought inspiration in other children's stories, some better known than others.

The American author-illustrator, Joan Walsh Anglund, enjoyed quite a vogue in the 1960s following the publication of "A Friend is Someone Who Likes You" (1958). Three of her drawings of cute children with minimal features were modelled by Albert Hallam for the Beswick range in 1969, but they were withdrawn soon after, making them extremely hard to find today.

The bizarre cast of characters from Alice's Adventures in Wonderland has offered a lot more scope for collectors. First published in 1865, this classic tale has entertained generations of young readers and inspired many artistic interpretations. In the early 1900s, Doulton's Lambeth artists modelled some fantastic creatures from the tale, notably the pig-like "Rath" from the "Jabberwocky" poem. The Burslem studio designed an extensive series of nursery ware and, more recently, a collection of character jugs based on the original illustrations by Sir John Tenniel, who firmly fixed the appearance of the Wonderland characters in the public imagination. Harry Sales also consulted the Tenniel illustrations in 1973 when designing Beswick's ALICE IN WONDERLAND™.

Curiously the figures inspired by another great children's classic, The Wind in the Willows, did not have the same appeal. Christina Thwaites, a young book illustrator, was commissioned to produce designs for a collection of wall plates and tea wares, and her watercolours of "Mr Toad," "Ratty," "Mole," "Badger" and others were interpreted by the Beswick modellers. Four figures were launched in 1987 and two more in 1988 as part of a co-ordinated giftware range with the Royal Albert backstamp, but they were withdrawn in 1989. Consequently "Portly and Weasel," the later introductions, were only made for one year, and will no doubt prove particularly hard to find in the future. Royal Doulton has recently embarked on a new Wind in the Willows collection, which is distributed by Lawleys by Post in a limited edition of 2,000.

With the WIND IN THE WILLOWS™ collection, the Royal Doulton artists have come full circle, reflecting the enthusiasm of their predecessors at Lambeth, notably Francis Pope who modelled two superb figures of "Mr Toad" shortly after the book was published. Obviously storybook characters, particularly animals in human guises, have timeless appeal.

COLLECTING CARTOON CHARACTERS

Cartoon characters, whether they be from animated films or comic book strips, are becoming a popular field for collectors. A major reference book on the subject, together with introductions such as the Hanna Barbera and Disney collections have already generated even more interest. Now is the time to start collecting, if you have not already done so.

The characters from David Hand's Animaland are virtually unknown today, but following their film debut in 1948, they were sufficiently well known to inspire Beswick's first series of cartoon figures. Modelled in 1949 and withdrawn in 1955, "Zimmy the Lion" and his seven friends now have a different kind of notoriety, stealing the show when they come up for auction.

In contrast, Mickey Mouse is the best known cartoon character in the world. Within a year of his 1928 screen debut in "Steamboat Willie," his image was being used to endorse children's products, and by the 1950s there were more than 3,000 different Mickey Mouse items, including plates, dolls, watches and clothes. With all this merchandising activity, it is not surprising that the Beswick studio sought a license for portraying Mickey and his friends in ceramic.

A range of nursey ware was launched in 1954, along with figures of "Mickey" and his girlfriend "Minnie," "Pluto" his dog and his crazy friends "Goofy" and "Donald Duck." Characters from some of Walt Disney's feature-length cartoons completed the original WALT DISNEY CHARACTERS™ set of 12 figures. "Peter Pan," the newest Disney hit in 1953, inspired four characters, "Peter" himself, "Tinkerbell," "Smee" and "Nana," whilst the classic "Pinocchio" (1940) provided the puppet hero and his insect conscience "Jiminy Cricket." Surprisingly only "Thumper" was modelled from another favourite film, "Bambi" (1942), although the fawn appears on the tableware designs. The response to the initial Disney collection encouraged the Beswick factory to launch a second set the following year, featuring "Snow White and the Seven Dwarfs" from Disney's first feature symphony. All the Disney characterisations are superb, making them extremely desirable amongst collectors of Beswick and Disneyana and they are all hard to find, even though they were produced until 1967.

The 1960s saw the rise of a new Disney star, Winnie the Pooh, who became a very popular merchandising character after his cartoon debut in 1966. The Beswick factory was quick off the mark, launching an initial collection of six characters from the film in 1968, followed by two more in 1971. "The Bear of Little Brain" originated in bedtime stories about nursery toys told by A. A. Milne to his son Christopher Robin in the 1920s, and he was visualised in the resulting books by the illustrator E. H. Shepard. To celebrate the 70th anniversary of the first "Winnie the Pooh" book, Royal Doulton launched a second series of figures in 1996 and these have been a great success. Royal Doulton continue to work closely with the Walt Disney company today and they have launched two exciting figurine collections featuring Disney "Princesses" and "Villains" exclusively for sale in the Disney stores. The other new Disney collections have been distributed through specialist china shops, notably the "101 Dalmatians" series, which was inspired by the live action film, and the second series of "Snow White and the Seven Dwarfs," which was prompted by the 60th anniversary of the film. A new Disney series featuring Mickey Mouse and his gang, was launched during 1998 so don't miss the opportunity to add these to your cartoon collection.

The massive marketing campaigns for Disney characters have made them household names all over the world. British cartoon characters, by comparison, are less well known internationally. The "Daily Express" newspaper was slow to capitalise on the success of "Rupert the Bear," who has been the star of their children's comic strip since 1920. Originated by Mary Tourtel, the Rupert stories were enlivened by Alfred Bestall who took over the daily drawings in 1935. Rupert enjoys the most extraordinary adventures with his friends Bill the Badger, Algy Pug and Pong-Ping, always returning safely to his comfortable family home in Nutwood. Rupert Bear annuals sold in millions from the mid 1930s, and his exploits were adapted for TV in the 1970s, but his following is essentially British. No doubt it was for this reason that the five figures in the original RUPERT THE BEAR™ collection, designed by Harry Sales in 1980, were relatively short lived. However, the second Rupert Bear collection, launched in 1998, is proving very popular with Lawleys By Post customers.

A similar fate befell the NORMAN THELWELL™ figures, which were in production from 1981 to 1989. Norman Thelwell was a humorous illustrator for "Punch" magazine, who made his reputation with comical observations of young riders and their mounts. "Angels on Horseback," published in 1957, was the first compilation of his successful cartoons, and many other popular books followed. Thelwell worked closely with Harry Sales to create the most effective figures, both in ceramic and resin, and the results are guaranteed to raise a smile without breaking the bank.

After a gap of nearly 15 years, famous British cartoon characters are back on the drawing board at the Royal Doulton studios once again. "Denis the Menace" and "Desperate Dan," stars of the long-established children's comics, "The Beano" and "The Dandy," have been immortalised as character jugs. This is the first time large-size character jugs have been used for portraying cartoons, although there are similarities to the set of six THUNDERBIRDS™ busts modelled by jug designer Bill Harper to celebrate the 30th anniversary of this children's TV show in 1992.

COLLECTING CHARACTER ANIMALS

In the 1880s Doulton's first artist, George Tinworth, was modelling groups of mice engaged in popular human pastimes, and nearly a century later Kitty MacBride did much the same thing with her "Happy Mice." The appeal of these anthropomorphic creatures is timeless, and collectors have responded with enthusiasm from Victorian times to the present day. Admittedly, developing a taste for Tinworth's sense of humour will prove very expensive, with models costing several hundreds of pounds each, but the KITTY MACBRIDE™ whimsical mice are still relatively affordable.

Kitty MacBride was a writer and illustrator who began to model little clay figures of mice in 1960. Initially they were sold through a London dealer, but when she could not keep up with the demand she asked the Beswick factory to produce 11 of them commercially, which they did between 1975 and 1983.

The Beswick studio has had a considerable reputation for character animals since the launch of the Beatrix Potter collection in 1948. However, the modellers have not only interpreted illustrations from famous books, from time to time they have envisaged their own comical creatures. Albert Hallam was responsible for a succession of animals with human expressions in the late 1960s. Similar humanising traits can be found in the LITTLE LIKEABLES™ collection, which was produced briefly in the mid

1980s. Robert Tabbenor's animals play up the humour of their situation, notably the carefree frog, "Watching the World Go By," whilst Diane Griffiths takes a more sentimental approach, using human feelings to describe her cartoon-like animals.

The fun has continued in recent years with a collection of "Footballing Felines," produced in 1999, and the on-going series of "English Country Folk," depicting appropriate animals with human manners and costumes. However, the last laugh is reserved for the "Pig Promenade." The absurdity of nine different breeds of pigs playing musical instruments makes this one of the most hilarious series of character animals.

MAKING STORYBOOK CHARACTERS

All the current storybook characters are made at the John Beswick factory in Longton, which became part of the Royal Doulton group in 1969. They have over fifty years' experience in the production of humorous figures and character animals, and essentially the methods have not changed since the earliest days of the Beatrix Potter figures.

First of all the designer has to familiarise himself thoroughly with the character to be portrayed, reading the story and studying the illustration. Having chosen the most suitable pose for interpretation in ceramic, he will produce reference drawings for the modeller. Often he can only see one side of the character in the original illustration, so he has to improvise for his three-dimensional model.

In consultation with the designer, the modeller will create the figure in modelling clay, and if satisfactory, a set of master moulds will be made in plaster of Paris. The number of mould parts will depend on the complexity of the figure, and sometimes the head and arms have to be moulded separately. Two or three prototype figures will be cast from the master mould for colour trials and subsequent approval by the original artist or his agent.

In the case of the Beatrix Potter figures, all the models are scrutinised by the licensing agents, Copyrights, working on behalf of Miss Potter's original publishers, Frederick Warne. Raymond Briggs, who was responsible for the Snowman, is generally quite relaxed about letting experts in other media interpret his drawings. He thought Royal Doultons models were marvellous and really captured the spirit of the story, although he maintained he would "jolly well say so" if he thought they had got it wrong! Jill Barklem, the creator of Brambly Hedge, likes to get very involved in the licensing of her characters, and design manager Harry Sales spent a lot of time working with her on the finer points of detail. Sometimes slight modifications need to be made to the model or the colour scheme before the figure is approved by all concerned.

The next stage is to produce plaster of Paris working moulds from the master, and supplies are sent to the casting department. An earthenware body is used to cast all the character figures produced at the John Beswick studio, and it is poured into the mould in liquid form, known as slip. The moisture in the slip is absorbed into the plaster of Paris moulds and a "skin" of clay forms the interior.

Once the clay has set to the required thickness, the excess clay is poured out and the mould is carefully dismantled. Any separate mould parts, such as projecting arms, will be joined on at this stage using slip as an adhesive, and the seams will be gently sponged away. The figure is then allowed to dry slowly before it goes for its first firing. The high temperature in the kiln drives out the moisture in the body and the figure shrinks by about 1/12th of its original size, forming a hard "biscuit" body.

Skilled decorators will paint the figure, using special under-glaze ceramic colours. They work from an approved colour sample and great care is taken to match the colours to the original book illustrations. A second firing hardens on the colour before the figure is coated with a solution of liquid glaze. When the figure is fired in the glost kiln, it emerges with a shiny transparent finish which enhances and permanently protects the vibrant colours underneath. After a final inspection, the figures are dispatched to china shops all over the world where they will capture the hearts of collectors young and old.

RESIN FIGURES

Several collectables manufacturers began experimenting with new sculptural materials in the 1980s and developed different types of resin bodies that allow more intricately modelled detail than conventional ceramic processes. Royal Doulton launched its new "bonded ceramic body" in 1984, and two storybook collections were included in its Beswick Studio Sculptures, as the range was known. Seven subjects were chosen from the "Tales of Beatrix Potter" and two from the Thelwell series. Production was short-lived, despite the minute detailing of the animals' fur and the tiny pebbles and grasses in their habitat, which would have been impossible to achieve in traditional earthenware. Royal Doulton ceased production of resin at the end of 1985, but designs have been commissioned from resin specialists, notably the "Paddington Bear" and "St. Tiggywinkles series."

YEAR CYPHERS

Beginning in 1998 a cypher was added to the base of each figurine. The cypher for 1998 was an umbrella, for 1999 the Top Hat as worn by Sir Henry Doulton, for 2000 a fob watch, for 2001 a waistcoat, for 2002 a boot for 2003 a pair of gloves and for 2004 a Bottle Oven

1998 Umbrella   1999 Top Hat   2000 Fob Watch   2001 Waistcoat

2002 Boot   2003 Gloves   2004 Bottle Oven

THE DOULTON MARKETS

INTERNATIONAL COLLECTORS CLUB

Founded in 1980 The Royal Doulton International Collectors Club provides an information service on all aspects of the company's products, past and present. A Club magazine, "Gallery," is published four times per year with information on new products and current events that will keep the collector up-to-date on the happenings in the world of Royal Doulton. Upon joining the club, each new member will receive a free gift and invitations to special events and exclusive offers throughout the year. To join the Royal Doulton Collectors Club, please contact the club directly by writing to the address opposite or calling the appropriate number.

INTERNATIONAL COLLECTORS CLUB
Sir Henry Doulton House
Forge Lane, Etruria
Stoke-on-Trent, Staffordshire
ST1 5NN, England
Telephone:
U.K.: 8702 412696
Overseas: +44 (0) 1782 404045
On-line at www.doulton-direct.co.uk
E-mail: icc@royal-doulton.com

WEBSITE AND E-MAIL ADDRESS

Websites
www.royal-doulton.com
www.doulton-direct.com.au
www.royal-doulton-brides.com

E-mail:
Consumers Enquiries: enquiries@royal-doulton.com
Museum Curator: heritage@royal-doulton.com
Doulton-Direct: direct@royal-doulton.com

DOULTON CHAPTERS IN NORTH AMERICA

Detroit Chapter
Ronald Griffin, President
629 Lynne Avenue
Ypsilanti, MI. 48198-3829

Edmonton Chapter
Mildred's Collectibles
6813 104 Street,
Edmonton, AB Canada

New England Chapter
Lee Piper, President
Meridith Nelson, Vice President
Michael Lynch, Secretary
Scott Reichenberg, Treasurer
E-mail: doingantiq@aol.com

Northern California Chapter
Edward L. Khachadourian, President
P. O. Box 214, Moraga, CA 94556-0214
Tel.: (925) 376-2221
Fax: (925) 376-3581
E-mail: khach@pacbell.net

Northwest, Bob Haynes Chapter
Alan Matthew, President
15202 93rd Place NE, Bothell
WA 98011 Tel.: (425) 488-9604

Rochester Chapter
Judith L. Trost, President
103 Garfield Street, Rochester
NY 14611 Tel.: (716) 436-3321

Ohio Chapter
Reg Morris
5556 Whitehaven Avnue
North Olmstead, Ohio 44070
Tel.: (216) 779-5554

Western Pennsylvania Chapter
John Re, President
9589 Parkedge Drive
Allison Park, PA 15101
Tel.: (412) 366-0201
Fax: (412) 366-2558

THE DOULTON MARKETS

LAND AUCTIONS

AUSTRALIA

Goodman's

7 Anderson Street
Double Bay, Sydney, 2028, N.S.W., Australia
Tel.: +61 (0) 2 9327 7311; Fax: +61 (0) 2 9327 2917
Enquiries: Suzanne Brett
www.goodmans.com.au
E-mail: info@goodmans.com.au

Sotheby's

1180122 Queen Street, Woollahra
Sydney, 2025, N.S.W., Australia
Tel.: +61 (0) 2 9362 1000; Fax: +61 (0) 2 9362 1100

CANADA

Empire Auctions

Montreal

5500 Paré Street, Montreal, Quebec H4P 2M1
Tel.: (514) 737-6586; Fax: (514) 342-1352
Enquiries: Isadore Rubinfeld
E-mail: montreal@empireauctions.com

Ottawa

1380 Cyrville Road, Gloucester, Ontario
Tel.: (613) 748-5343; Fax: (613) 748-0354
Enquiries: Elliot Melamed
E-mail: ottawa@empireauctions.com

Toronto

165 Tycos Drive
Toronto, Ontario, M6B 1W6
Tel.: (416) 784-4261; Fax: (416) 784-4262
Enquiries: Michael Rogozinsky
www.empireauctions.com
E-mail: toronto@empireauctions.com

Maynards Industries Ltd.

415 West 2nd Avenue, Vancouver, BC, V5Y 1E3
Tel.: (604) 876-1311; Fax: (604) 876-1323
www.maynards.com
E-mail: antiques@maynards.com

Ritchie's

288 King Street East, Toronto, Ontario M5A 1K4
Tel.: (416) 364-1864; Fax: (416) 364-0704
Enquiries: Caroline Kaiser
www.richies.com
E-mail: auction@richies.com

Waddingtons

111 Bathurst Street, Toronto, Ontario M5V 2R1
Tel.: (416) 504-9100; Fax: (416) 504-0033
Enquiries: Bill Kime
www.waddingtonsauctions.com
E-mail: info@waddingtonsauctions.com

UNITED KINGDOM

BBR Auctions

Elsecar Heritage Centre, Nr. Barnsley
South Yorkshire, S74 8HJ, England
Tel.: +44 (0) 1226 745156; Fax: +44 (0) 1226 351561
Enquiries: Alan Blakeman
www.bbauctions.co.uk
E-mail: sales@bbauctions.com

Bonhams

Bond Street

101 New Bond Street, London W15 1SR, England

Chelsea

65-69 Lots Road, Chelsea, London SW10 0RN, England

Knightsbridge

Montpelier Street, Knightsbridge, London, SW7 1HH
Tel.: +44 (0) 20 7393 3900; Fax: +44 (0) 20 7393 3905
Enquiries:
Decorative Arts; Joy McCall
Tel.: +44 (0) 20 7393 3942
Contemporary Ceramics: Gareth Williams
Tel.: +44 (0) 20 7393 3941
Doulton Beswick Wares: Mark Oliver
Tel.: +44 (0) 20 7468 8233
www.bonhams.com
E-mail: info@bonhams.com

Christie's

London

8 King Street, London, SW1, England
Tel.: +44 (0) 207-839-9060; Fax: +44 (0) 20 7839-1611

South Kensington

85 Old Brompton Road, London SW7 3LD, England
Tel.: +44 (0) 20 7581 7611; Fax: +44 (0) 20 7321-3321
Enquiries:
Decorative Arts: Michael Jeffrey
Tel.: +44 (0) 20 7321 3237
www.christies.com; E-mail: info@christies.com

Potteries Specialist Auctions

271 Waterloo Road, Cobridge, Stoke-on-Trent
Staffordshire, ST6 6HR, England
Tel.: +44 (0) 1782 286622
Fax: +44 (0) 1782 213777
Enquiries: Stella Ashbrooke
www.potteriesauctions.com
E-mail: enquiries@potteriesauctions.com

Sotheby's

London

34-35 New Bond Street, London W1A 2AA, England
Tel.: +44 (0) 20 7293 5000; Fax: +44 (0) 20 7293 5989

Olympia

Hammersmith Road, London, W14 8UX, England
Tel.: +44 (0) 20 7293 5555; Fax: +44 (0) 20 7293 6939

Sotheby's (cont.)

Sussex
Summers Place, Billingshurst, Sussex
RH14 9AF, England
Tel.: +44 (0) 1403 833500
Fax: +44 (0) 1403 833699
www.sothebys.com
E-mail: info@sothebys.com

Louis Taylor
Britannia House
10 Town Road, Hanley
Stoke-on-Trent, Staffordshire, England
Tel.: +44 (0) 1782 214111
Fax: +44 (0) 1782 215283
Enquiries: Clive Hillier

Thomson, Roddick & Laurie
60 Whitesands
Dumfries DG1 2RS
Scotland
Tel.: +44 (0) 1387 279879
Fax: +44 (0) 1387 266236
Enquiries: C. R. Graham-Campbell

Peter Wilson Auctioneers
Victoria Gallery, Market Street
Nantwich, Cheshire CW5 5DG, England
Tel.: +44 (0) 1270 610508
Fax: +44 (0) 1270 610508
Enquiries: Peter Wilson

UNITED STATES

Christie's East
219 East 67th Street, New York, NY 10012
Tel.: +1 212 606 0400
Enquiries: Timothy Luke
www.christies.com

William Doyle Galleries
175 East 87th Street, New York, NY 10128
Tel.: +1 212 427-2730
Fax: +1 212 369 0892

Sotheby's Arcade Auctions
1334 York Avenue, New York, NY 10021
Tel.: +1 212 606 7000
Enquiries: Andrew Cheney
www.sothebys.com

VIRTUAL AUCTIONS

Amazon.com ® Auctions
Main site: www.amazon.com
Plus 4 International sites

AOL.com Auctions ®
Main site: www.aol.com
Links to − E-bay.com
        − U-bid.com

E-BAY ® The Worlds On-Line Market Place™
Main site: www.ebay.com
Plus 20 International sites

YAHOO! Auctions ®
Main site: www.yahoo.com
Plus 15 International auction sites

FAIRS, MARKETS AND SHOWS

AUSTRALIA

Royal Doulton and Antique Collectable Fair
Marina Hall, Civic Centre
Hurstville, Sydney

CANADA

Christie Antique Show
Christie Conservation Park
Highway 5
near Dundas, Ontario
usually May and September
Gadsden Promotions Ltd.
P.O. Box 490, Shelburne, ON. LON 1S0
Tel.: (800) 667-0619
Fax: (519) 925-6498
Website: www.craftshoes.canada.com

UNITED KINGDOM

20th Century Fairs
266 Glossop Road, Sheffield S10 2HS, England
Usually in May or June
For information on times and dates:
Tel.: +44 (0) 114 275 0333
Fax: +44 (0) 114 275 4443

Doulton and Beswick Collectors Fair
National Motorcycle Museum, Meriden
Birmingham
Usually March and August
For information on times and dates:
Doulton and Beswick Dealers Association
Tel.: +44 (0) 181 303 3316

DMG Antiques Fairs Ltd.
Newark, the largest in the UK with usually six fairs
annually. For information on times and dates for this
and many other fairs contact:
DMG
Newark, P.O. Box 100, Newark
Nottinghamshire NG2 1DJ
Tel.: +44 (0) 1636 702326
Fax: +44 (0) 1636 707923
www.antiquesdirectory.co.uk

U.K. Fairs
Doulton and Beswick Fair for Collectors
River Park Leisure Centre, Winchester
Usually held in October.
For information on times and dates contact:
Enquiries U.K. Fairs; Tel.: +44 (0) 20 8500 3505
www.portia.co.uk
E-mail: ukfairs@portia.co.uk

LONDON MARKETS

Alfie's Antique Market
13-25 Church Street, London; Tuesday - Saturday

Camden Passage Market
London; Wednesday and Saturday

New Caledonia Market
Bermondsey Square, London; Friday morning

Portobello Road Market
Portobello Road, London; Saturday

UNITED STATES

Atlantique City
Atlantic City Convention Centre
Atlantic City, NJ

International Gift and Collectible Expo
Donald E. Stephens Convention Centre
Rosemont, Illinois

For information on the above two shows contact:

Krause Publications
700 East State Street, Iola, WI 54990-9990
Tel.: (877) 746-9757
Fax: (715) 445-4389
www.collectibleshow.com
E-mail: iceshow@krause.com

Doulton Convention and Sale International
Fort Lauderdale, Florida, U.S.A.
Usually February.
For information on times and dates:

Pascoe & Company
575 S.W. 22nd Ave., Miami, Florida 33135
Tel.: (305) 643-2550; Fax: (305) 643-2123
www.pascoeandcompany.com
E-mail: sales@pascoeandcompany.com

Royal Doulton Convention & Sale
Cleveland, Ohio
Usually August. For information on times and dates:
Colonial House Productions
182 Front Street, Berea, Ohio 44308
Tel.: (440) 826-4169; Fax: (440) 826-0839
www.Colonial-House-Collectibles.com
E-mail: yworrey@aol.com

FURTHER READING

Storybook Figurines

Beatrix Potter Figures and Giftware edited by Louise Irvine
Beswick Price Guide by Harvey May
Brambly Hedge Collectors Book by Louise Irvine
Bunnykins Collectors Book by Louise Irvine
Cartoon Classics and other Character Figures, by Louise Irvine
Charlton Standard Catalogue of Bunnykins by Jean Dale and Louise Irvine
Charlton Standard Catalogue of Border Fine Arts Storybook Figurines, by Marylin Sweet
Royal Doulton Bunnykins Figures by Louise Irvine

Animals, Figures and Character Jugs

Character Jug Collectors Handbook by Kevin Pearson
Charlton Standard Catalogue of Beswick Animals by Callows and Sweets
Charlton Standard Catalogue of Royal Doulton Animals by Jean Dale
Charlton Standard Catalogue of Royal Doulton Figurines by Jean Dale
Charlton Standard Catalogue of Royal Doulton Jugs by Jean Dale
Collecting Character and Toby Jugs by Jocelyn Lukins
Collecting Doulton Animals by Jocelyn Lukins
Doulton Figure Collectors Handbook by Kevin Pearson
Doulton Flambé Animals by Jocelyn Lukins
Royal Doulton Figures by Desmond Eyles, Louise Irvine and Valerie Baynton

General

Charlton Standard Catalogue of Beswick Pottery by Diane and John Callow
Discovering Royal Doulton by Michael Doulton
Doulton Burslem Advertising Wares by Jocelyn Lukins
Doulton Burslem Wares by Desmond Eyles
Doulton for the Collector by Jocelyn Lukins
Doulton Kingsware Flasks by Jocelyn Lukins
Doulton Lambeth Advertising Ware by Jocelyn Lukins
Doulton Lambeth Wares by Desmond Eyles
Doulton Story by Paul Atterbury and Louise Irvine
George Tinworth by Peter Rose
Hannah Barlow by Peter Rose
John Beswick: A World of Imagination. Catalogue reprint (1950-1996)
Limited Edition Loving Cups by Louise Irvine and Richard Dennis
Phillips Collectors Guide by Catherine Braithwaite
Royal Doulton by Julie McKeown
Royal Doulton by Jennifer Queree
Royal Doulton Series Ware by Louise Irvine (Vols. 1-5)
Sir Henry Doulton Biography by Edmund Gosse

Magazines and Newsletters

Beswick Quarterly (Beswick Newsletter) Contact Laura J. Rock-Smith: 10 Holmes Ct., Sayville, N.Y. 11782-2408, U.S.A. Tel./Fax 516-589-9027
Collecting Doulton Magazine, Contact Barry Hill, Collecting Doulton, P.O. Box 310, Richmond, Surrey, TW10 7FU, England
Cottontails (Newsletter of Bunnykins Collectors' Club), Contact Claire Green: 6 Beckett Way Lewes, East Sussesx, BN7 2EB, U.K.: E-mail: claireg@btinternet.com
Rabbitting On (Bunnykins Newsletter) Contact Leah Selig: 2 Harper Street, Merrylands 2160, New South Wales, Australia. Tel./Fax: 61 2 9637 2410 (International), 02 637 2410 (Australia)

2004 Brambly Hedge – "In The Brambles" DBH 65.

ALICE IN WONDERLAND

EARTHENWARE SERIES 1973-1983
RESIN SERIES 1997-1997
EARTHENWARE SERIES 1998-2000

ALICE IN WONDERLAND
EARTHENWARE SERIES 1973-1983

2476
ALICE™
Style One

Designer:	Albert Hallam and Graham Tongue
Height:	4 ¾", 12.1 cm
Colour:	Dark blue dress, white apron with red trim
Issued:	1973 - 1983
Series:	Alice
U.S.	**$450.00**
Can.	**$600.00**
U.K.	**£250.00**
Aust.	**$650.00**

2477
WHITE RABBIT™
Style One

Designer:	Graham Tongue
Height:	4 ¾", 12.1 cm
Colour:	White rabbit wearing a brown coat and yellow waistcoat
Issued:	1973 - 1983
Series:	Alice
U.S.	**$500.00**
Can.	**$650.00**
U.K.	**£275.00**
Aust.	**$800.00**

2478
MOCK TURTLE™

Designer:	Graham Tongue
Height:	4 ¼", 10.8 cm
Colour:	Browns and grey
Issued:	1973 - 1983
Series:	Alice
U.S.	**$325.00**
Can.	**$425.00**
U.K.	**£175.00**
Aust.	**$450.00**

2479
MAD HATTER™
Style One

Designer:	Albert Hallam
Height:	4 ¼", 10.8 cm
Colour:	Burgundy coat, yellow and blue check trousers, yellow and red bowtie, grey hat
Issued:	1973 - 1983
Series:	Alice
U.S.	**$325.00**
Can.	**$425.00**
U.K.	**£175.00**
Aust.	**$450.00**

2480
CHESHIRE CAT™
Style One

Designer:	Albert Hallam and Graham Tongue
Height:	1 ½", 3.8 cm
Colour:	Tabby cat
Issued:	1973 - 1982
Series:	Alice
U.S.	**$575.00**
Can.	**$775.00**
U.K.	**£325.00**
Aust.	**$825.00**

2485
GRYPHON™

Designer:	Albert Hallam
Height:	3 ¼", 8.3 cm
Colour:	Browns and greens
Issued:	1973 - 1983
Series:	Alice
U.S.	**$175.00**
Can.	**$250.00**
U.K.	**£100.00**
Aust.	**$275.00**

2489
KING OF HEARTS™

Designer:	Graham Tongue
Height:	3 ¾", 9.5 cm
Colour:	Burgundy, yellow, white, blue and green
Issued:	1973 - 1983
Series:	Alice
U.S.	**$150.00**
Can.	**$200.00**
U.K.	**£ 85.00**
Aust.	**$225.00**

2490
QUEEN OF HEARTS™
Style One

Designer:	Graham Tongue
Height:	4", 10.1 cm
Colour:	Blue, green, yellow, white and burgundy
Issued:	1973 - 1983
Series:	Alice
U.S.	**$150.00**
Can.	**$200.00**
U.K.	**£ 85.00**
Aust.	**$225.00**

ALICE SERIES
"Dodo"
BESWICK
MADE IN ENGLAND
© ROYAL DOULTON TABLEWARE LTD. 1975
REGISTRATION APPLIED FOR.

ALICE SERIES
"Fish Footman"
BESWICK
MADE IN ENGLAND
© ROYAL DOULTON TABLEWARE LTD 1975
REGISTRATION APPLIED FOR

ALICE SERIES
"Frog Footman"
BESWICK
MADE IN ENGLAND
© ROYAL DOULTON TABLEWARE LTD 1975
REGISTRATION APPLIED FOR

2545
DODO™
Style One

Designer:	David Lyttleton
Height:	4", 10.1 cm
Colour:	Browns and greens
Issued:	1975 - 1983
Series:	Alice
U.S.	**$350.00**
Can.	**$475.00**
U.K.	**£200.00**
Aust.	**$500.00**

2546
FISH FOOTMAN™

Designer:	David Lyttleton
Height:	4 ¾", 14.6 cm
Colour:	Blue, gold, white and brown
Issued:	1975 - 1983
Series:	Alice
U.S.	**$450.00**
Can.	**$600.00**
U.K.	**£250.00**
Aust.	**$650.00**

2547
FROG FOOTMAN™

Designer:	David Lyttleton
Height:	4 ¼", 10.8 cm
Colour:	Maroon jacket with yellow trim, blue trousers
Issued:	1975 - 1983
Series:	Alice
U.S.	**$450.00**
Can.	**$600.00**
U.K.	**£250.00**
Aust.	**$650.00**

ALICE IN WONDERLAND
RESIN SERIES 1997-1997

The Alice in Wonderland resin series does not carry a backstamp. It was sold as a set through Lawleys By Post.

ALICE™
Style Two

Modeller:	Adrian Hughes
Size:	4", 10.1 cm
Colour:	Pale blue, white, red and green
Issued:	1997 - 1997
U.S.	**$35.00**
Can.	**$50.00**
U.K.	**£20.00**
Aust.	**$55.00**

CHESHIRE CAT™
Style Two

Modeller:	Adrian Hughes
Size:	4", 10.1 cm
Colour:	Ginger, blue, red, and brown
Issued:	1997 - 1997
U.S.	**$35.00**
Can.	**$50.00**
U.K.	**£20.00**
Aust.	**$55.00**

DODO™
Style Two

Modeller:	Adrian Hughes
Size:	4", 10.1 cm
Colour:	White, blue, yellow and black
Issued:	1997 - 1997
U.S.	**$35.00**
Can.	**$50.00**
U.K.	**£20.00**
Aust.	**$55.00**

MAD MATTER™
Style Two

Modeller:	Adrian Hughes
Size:	4", 10.1 cm
Colour:	Brown, green, and blue
Issued:	1997 - 1997
U.S.	**$35.00**
Can.	**$50.00**
U.K.	**£20.00**
Aust.	**$55.00**

QUEEN OF HEARTS™
Style Two

Modeller:	Adrian Hughes
Size:	4", 10.1 cm
Colour:	Red, white and black
Issued:	1997 - 1997
U.S.	**$35.00**
Can.	**$50.00**
U.K.	**£20.00**
Aust.	**$55.00**

WHITE RABBIT™
Style Two

Modeller:	Adrian Hughes
Size:	4", 10.1 cm
Colour:	White, brown and green
Issued:	1997 - 1997 edition of 2,500
U.S.	**$35.00**
Can.	**$50.00**
U.K.	**£20.00**
Aust.	**$55.00**

ALICE IN WONDERLAND
EARTHENWARE SERIES 1998-2000

LC 1
THE MAD HATTER'S TEA PARTY™

Modeller:	Martyn Alcock
Size:	5" x 8 ½", 12.7 x 21.6 cm
Colour:	Green, yellow, red and blue
Issued:	1998 in a limited edition of 1,998
Series:	1. Alice's Adventures
	2. Tableau

Beswick Number	Price			
	U.S. $	Can. $	U.K. £	Aust. $
LC 1	250.00	350.00	145.00	375.00

Note: Issued to commemorate the centenary of Lewis Carroll's death.

LC 2
ALICE™
Style Three

Modeller:	Martyn Alcock
Size:	4 ½", 11.9 cm
Colour:	Pink and white
Issued:	1999 in a limited edition of 2,500
Series:	Alice's Adventures

U.S.	**$115.00**
Can.	**$155.00**
U.K.	**£ 65.00**
Aust.	**$170.00**

Note: Issued, numbered, sold as a pair with the Cheshire Cat.

LC 3
CHESHIRE CAT™
Style Three

Modeller:	Martyn Alcock
Size:	3 ½", 8.9 cm
Colour:	Ginger striped cat
Issued:	1999 in a limited edition of 2,500
Series:	Alice's Adventures

U.S.	**$115.00**
Can.	**$155.00**
U.K.	**£ 65.00**
Aust.	**$170.00**

Note: Issued, numbered and sold as a pair with Alice.

LC 4
QUEEN OF HEARTS™
Style Three

Modeller:	Martyn Alcock
Size:	5 ¼", 13.3 cm
Colour:	Red, dark blue, yellow and pink
Issued:	2000 in a limited edition of 2,500
Series:	Alice's Adventures

U.S.	**$ 90.00**
Can.	**$120.00**
U.K.	**£ 50.00**
Aust.	**$135.00**

BEATRIX POTTER
FIGURINES

NOTES ON COLLECTING BESWICK BEATRIX POTTER FIGURES

by Frank W. Corley

The key to serious collecting of Beswick Beatrix Potter figures is making sense of the somewhat confusing series of changes to many of the original figures that took place between 1970 and 1975. In retrospect, these changes portray a particularly turbulent transition period during which the old Beswick corporate culture was being supplanted by that of Royal Doulton, the new owners as of 1969. Although the changes were little noticed by customers and collectors at the time, in later years they have had the effect of shifting the emphasis in Beswick Beatrix Potter collecting to the changes rather than the original figures. The many versions, variations and multiple associated backstamps of many of those thirty-seven original figures apparently were the consequence of well-intended management steps to improve the production side of things at Royal Doulton's newly-acquired Stoke-on-Trent plant. While we do not have an insider's account of the rationales underlying the then-new management's initiatives, the evidence that came off the production line in that period strongly suggests that major decisions were made in several areas, though unevenly implemented.

Decision 1: do something about the untidy plethora of gold oval backstamps:

* the lettering on the gold oval backstamps, which had replaced the gold circle (and gold parallel lines) in 1955, had evolved into a rather sloppy assortment of styles — large script, small script, large block letters, hand-made block letters, reverse slant script and two more styles of smaller size block letters. While the gold oval was a constant, the lettering style was associated only with figures introduced in a particular year, rather than with the whole range of production. It seems as if whenever new figues were introduced someone was told to go off in a corner, speak to no one, and design a new lettering format; that format was then used for that/those figure(s) from then on. Perhaps the grossest example involves the three 1955 figures (Duchess [with flowers], Pigling Bland, and Tommy Brock), with their very crude hand-made block letters.

* In any event, Beswick went off the gold standard at the end of 1972 in favour of a new, standardized brown-lettered backstamp, the initial version of which, like all its gold predecessors, did not carry a copyright date (the Charlton BP-3a).

* a copyright date was added in 1975, a decision that probably was driven by legal considerations (the BP-3b).

Decision 2: improve production efficiency for certain figures by simplyfying their moulds:

* at the expense of a loss in aesthetic appeal Benjamin Bunny's shoes, Mrs. Rabbit's umbrella and Mr. Benjamin Bunny's pipe were moulded to their bodies to reduce susceptibility to damage in the production process and to improve yields; also, the top of Tommy Brock's spade handle was eliminated and a minor change made to the tip of the bottle in Appley Dappley's basket for similar reasons.

Decision 3: simplify the decoration process and improve the eye-appeal of certain figures by lightening the colours:

* the colours of Squirrel Nutkin's coat and nut were lightened, Little Pig Robinson's striped tunic was replaced with a blue textured one, Pigling Bland's and Mr. Benjamin Bunny's dark maroon coats were changed to lilac, the top of Tabitha Twitchett's striped dress and the patterned dress of Goody Tiptoes became plain, and, Mr. Jackson's skin became brown instead of green.

Decision 4: standardise hand painting to improve quality control and decrease the range of hand painting variation:

* broad 'discretion' in the hand painting phase, which had been a Beswick hallmark since the Beatrix Potter line was introduced, was curtailed. This discretion had resulted in strikingly different variations of some figures in the same time frames. For example, Timmy Tiptoes was produced with both red and pink jackets; the pattern of Mrs. Tiggy-winkle's dress was sometimes diagonal, sometimes square; Mr. Jeremy Fisher usually had spots on his legs but sometimes had stripes; and, Miss Moppet was sometimes mottled, sometimes striped and sometimes in between. Although the catalogues mistakenly continue to describe "variation one" as ending and "variation two" as originating in the 1972-1975 time frame, in fact, what happened was that the standardisation process simply eliminated one of the two existing variations, with the surviving version labeled as the second despite the fact that it had existed all along. Thus, Timmy Tiptoes'

red jacket, Mrs. Tiggy-winkle's diagonal dress pattern, Mr. Jeremy Fisher's spots and Miss Moppet's mottled fur were eliminated, apparently in the interests of standardisation.

* the size of Tommy Brock's eye patch is in a category similar to the above. For the sixteen or so years prior to the transition period the size of Tommy Brock's eye patches varied within fairly small limits – mainly half-way between the two now familiar extremes, and alway curling inward towards the centre of his forehead with a somewhat feathery appearance; they all had open spade handles. Those differences in eye patch size would probably have gone unnoticed except that during the transition an initial decision was made to use a very small eye patch as well as a closed spade handle. A year or two later, the eye patch part of the decision was reversed in favour of a very large eye patch. Both of the new styles are readily recognisable by their exaggerated sizes – one small, one large – crisp rather than fuzzy appearance and the fact that they point in a straight line towards the ears rather than curling inward towards the centre of the forehead. In the actual production process, the patch changes, the spade handle change and the backstamp change were uncoordinated, resulting in multiple combinations of eye patch styles, spade handle configurations and backstamps.

* a number of less obvious colour standardisation changes were made to address long-time variations not much noticed by the collecting world until recent years:

    * Timmy Tiptoe's brown and grey fur variations became grey only;

    * Benjamin Bunny's light tan/light green jacket variations changed to a rich dark brown during the transition– and then to a luxurious cream in the later years of the Royal Albert period;

    * Other changes: Mrs. Rabbit (dress colours), Goody Tiptoes (dress colour, pattern and a longer base), Old Mr. Brown (colour of squirrel), Amiable Guinea Pig (jacket colour), Aunt Petitoes (dress colour), Pigwig (skin and dress colours), and, Sir Isaac Newton (jacket colour, scarf pattern).

* in addition to the foregoing colour standardisation changes, but several years later, the dark blues of the following figures were changed to a light blue: Peter Rabbit, Tom Kitten, The Old Woman Who Lived in a Shoe, Anna Maria, Cecily Parsley, and, Mrs. Flopsy Bunny. The reason for this is not clear but it has been suggested that it was done out of paint formulae considerations. But, curiously, the dark blue of Mrs. Rabbit and the Bunnies was not changed. Distressingly, all these light blues evolved into sickly pale blues during the Royal Albert period.

It would appear that undertaking to tune-up the entire range of Beatrix Potter production, while probably successful from a management point of view, resulted in some figures being produced in multiple versions, variations and backstamps before things settled down. In particular, for figures undergoing both a mould change and a decorating change synchronisation of the two changes was not in the cards. The result is a collector's dream: multiple mould, colour, pattern and design changes with up to three backstamp possibilities – BP-2, BP-3a and BP-3b.

Changes to the gold circle (BP-1a) backstamps prior to the 1955 introduction of the gold oval (BP-2):

* The 1955 change to the gold oval backstamp to accommodate small base figures was preceded by a gold parallel lines style with the words Beswick and England one atop the other in tiny gold block letters. When Tailor of Gloucester was introduced in 1949 there were obvious problems in accommodating the Beswick-England gold circle, plus the other backstamp information, in the limited space available on Tailor of Gloucester's small base. Beswick's solution was to create what Charlton calls the BP-1b backstamp. An unknown, but small, quantity of Tailor of Gloucester, first version, may have been produced with the gold circle but the new backstamp quickly replaced it. Several of the original ten 1948 figures also have shown up with the BP-1b design but Tailor of Gloucester is the only one on which it was used with any consistency. Use of the BP-1b backstamp was discontinued in 1951.

* The gold oval modification. Beswick was presented with a similar small base problem in 1951 when Mrs. Rabbit was introduced. However instead of using the rather unattractive gold parallel line design a gold oval modification of the original gold circle, now known as the Charlton BP-2 backstamp, was developed. An unknown but small quantity of Mrs. Rabbit, first version, were produced with the gold circle.

* In 1954, another small base figure, Johnny Town-Mouse, was introduced and relative scarcity of that figure with the gold circle suggests that the new gold oval was used early-on, despite the fact that it – the BP-2 – did not become official for all standard range figures until a year later.

* The relative scarcity of gold circles for the other three 1954 figures (Miss Moppet, Flopsy, Mopsy and Cottontail and Foxy Whiskered Gentleman) suggests that in addition to the gold circle the gold oval was heavily used prior to 1955.

* While general use of the gold oval (BP-2) for all standard range figures did not begin until 1955, it seems probable that use of the BP-1b for Tailor of Gloucester was ended in 1951 in favour of the new gold oval.

Other notes:

* The metamorphoses of Benjamin Bunny are of particular collector interest: leaving aside the shoe and ear mould changes the early catalogue descriptions had version one wearing a pale green jacket, version two a brown jacket and version three a light tan jacket; the pompon on the tam was orange with red stripes. In fact: version one varied between pale green, light tan and in between; version two started out the same as version one, but very quickly changed to brown, with a solid orange pompon; version three started out as brown and remained that colour until it became cream sometime in the Royal Albert period. In sum, three mould versions, three backstamp possibilties, two pompon colour schemes, and, three jacket colours overlapping and occurring within a span of about three years! Are there exceptions to the above? Of course, that's what hand painting is all about!

* Mrs. Tiggy-Winkle: while there are dress pattern differences in the early years they seem minor and insufficient to justify a version one vs. version two distinction.

* Timmy Willie: the multicoloured base on some of the early figures − mainly BP-1's − is very attractive and is an example of desirable decorator discretion. The multicoloured base variation is a must for the serious collector!

* Sally Henny Penny: some of the BP-3a's and early BP-3b's have red hearts rather than checks on the breast feathers, and, a tiny red tongue in an open mouth. Note: the open mouth appears to be a matter of whether the mould used was new and clean or clogged from repeated use; in any event, there are definitely open mouth versions.

* Louise Irvine B1 and B3 backstamps: when brown backstamps were introduced in 1973 the Beswick designers of the five latest figures at that time − Appley Dappley, Pickles, Pig-Wig, Mr. Alderman Ptolemy and Sir Isaac Newton − had apparently anticipated the change over and had produced slightly different variations of the new brown backstamp design. The first three figures were similar to the new design in all respects except that the figure names are all in capital letters; this anomaly, Irvine's B-1 category, applies to all of the no copyright date figures (BP-3a's) as well as some copyright date figures (BP-3b's). The last two figures also used the new brown lettering format except that the words "made in England" are used versus the single word "England"; this is Irvine's B-3 category and again the anomaly applies to both no copyright date and copyright date versions. The B1/B3 anomalies disappeared sometime after 1975.

SCARCEST BESWICK BEATRIX POTTER FIGURES
THE RAREST OF THE RARE

Abbreviated Relative Scarcity Lists of Beswick and
Royal Albert Beatrix Potter Figures/Versions

To arrive at a comfortable perspective on scarcity and value of Beswick/Royal Albert Beatrix Potter figures a collector needs to acquire a data base of the relative number of each figure, version and variation produced. The lists which follow are shortened versions of complete lists that were created as tools for estimating relative scarcity, which is the key to value. In the form presented they represent raw data based on presumed years in production broken down not only by figure, version and variation but also by backstamp.

The data are considered raw because years-in-production is only the starting point in determining relative value. Years- in-production does not mean equal numbers of different figures produced the same number of years. For example, Duchess (with flowers) was in production for thirteen years, Duchess (with pie) for four; yet, the first Duchess appears to be the scarcer figure – although, it may not be, And, Peter Rabbit in a given year surely was produced in far greater quantities then, say, Mrs. Flopsy Bunny.

The term scarcity is used in preference to rarity because, while the difference between the terms may be minimal in an academic sense, scarcity seems more data driven and to connote a number, whereas rarity tends to imply a judgment of the collector community, hence connoting value.

The term value, while related to scarcity, is related to the number of active collectors in search of a particular figure at a particular time; it is inherently relative, reflecting a judgment of the collecting community at a particular time, or, in a particular auction. Also, even though a figure might be quite scarce in an absolute sense its value will decrease as the number of collectors possessing it increases: supply and demand, pure and simple.

In the real world, collectors searching for items being resold in various secondary markets see scarcity as a reflection of what is appearing in the markets they see, with the number of a particular figure likely to appear in a particular secondary market at a particular time related, in a broad sense, to the actual number originally produced. Many other factors contribute to local scarcity: geographic distribution when initially marketed; susceptibility of particular figures to breakage, changes in the kinds of things people collect; the age factor where old figures simply disappear, etc.

Although hard data to determine scarcity is not available, the auction sites have compensated to a degree by vastly increasing the number and variety of figures available on the secondary market. How? By simply pulling out of attics, basements, closets, shoe boxes, etc. figures that otherwise would remain unavailable to collectors. In its short lifespan eBay has done a remarkably efficient job of matching up the relatively limited pool of collectors with an increased quantity of available figures. As a result prices/values have decreased substantially. Assuming willing-buyer, willing-seller transactions are the final arbiter of true value, tracking eBay transactions can provide a serious collector with an authoritative range of a figure's current value.

Except: Except that sometimes there may be an intrinsic value based on real scarcity that escapes the perception of the collecting community as well as that of dealers and investors. For example, Mr. Jackson, variation one (green frog) is easily among the scarcest Beswick Beatrix Potter variations yet its price is relatively modest.

Except: Except that different collectors collect different parts of the Beswick figure/version/variation/backstamp spectrum. That is, many Beswick Beatrix Potter collectors collect only a portion of the figures available, or, ignore the different versions and variations and backstamps.

Except: Except that there are overlapping collector communities that distort availability of certain type figures. For example, cat collectors search out Ginger and Simpkin, mouse collectors search out Anna Maria and rabbit collectors collect Peter, Benjamin etc. – all to the exclusion of the full range of Beatrix Potter figures.

Except: Except that auction sales prices seem to vary seasonally: a high value figure listed without reserve during a holiday period might sell for a deceptively low price.

Except. Except that scarce figures tend to have greater value than scarce versions or variations which, in turn, tend to have greater vakue than scarce backstamps – all other thinks being equal:

* figure scarcity – figures which have appeared in only one version or variation are inherently of greater value than multi-version/variation figures because many collectors do not collect multiple versions/variations.

* version/variation scarcity – the appeal and collectability of individual versions or variations of multiple version/variation figures is related to unique discernable differences – something that can be seen by a viewer. Thus, for example, a version two or version three Benjamin Bunny is collectable in its own right because the differences can be seen,

* backstamp scarcity – since different backstamps can be detected only through handling, the appeal of a figure having a short run with a particular backstamp tends to be esoteric and limited

to a smaller segment of the collector community. Nonetheless, scarce backstamps, particularly the first backstamp used on a figure/version/variation, are highly collectable. It is just that there are few collectors willing to pay the price scarcity might otherwise command. This abbreviated list shows mainly backstamps with one year of less production.

Caveat: in using auction prices as a guide to value, take the long view, because auction prices can vary widely from one week to the next.

In the absence of better data, using the number of years a particular figure/version/variation was in production is a reasonable starting point for estimating the number of figures that exist in a global, collecting sense. Hence, a good clue to current relative scarcity. Another caveat: unsuccessful figures such as Duchess (with flowers) never in their best years were produced in numbers comparable to, say, Peter Rabbit in his worst year, sales-wise.

Following is an abbreviated listing of the scarcest figures/versions/variations, plus the old Beswick figures retired early. Parts I to III are abbreviated listings of original Beswick, Royal Albert and new Beswick figures and major versions/variations thereof, in descending order of scarcity. Part IV is a combined listing and Part V lists scarce backstamps.

Ideally there should be a separate (and later) step in which the raw data would be "massaged" to take account of (1) different levels of production of individual figures, (2) individual figure susceptibility to damage and (3) an "age factor" where over a time a number of figures simply disappear beyond the reach of collectors. Such an effort would result in more accurate final scarcity rankings.

Corley's Short List of Scarce Beswick/Royal Albert Beatrix Potter Figures

I – OLD BESWICK

Figure	Version/Variation	Years in production
Mr. Benjamin Bunny	v 1b	<1 (rare)
Mr. Jeremy Fisher Digging		1
Mr. Tod		1
Johnny Town-Mouse with Bag		1
Mr. Jackson (green frog)	v 1	1
Little Pig Robinson Spying		2
Tom Kitten and Butterfly		2
Tom Thumb		2
Mr. Benjamin Bunny	v 2a	2
Benjamin Bunny	v 2	2 – maybe as many as 4
Tommy Brock	v 3	2 – maybe as many as 3
Cecily Parsley	v 2	3
Benjamin Bunny Sat on a Bank	v 1	3
Benjamin Bunny Sat on a Bank	v 2	3

Plus, the 12 old Beswick figures retired early:

Duchess (with Pie)	4
Old Mr. Pricklepin	6
Susan	6
Ginger	7
Thomasina Tittlemouse	8
Simpkin	9
Pig-Wig	11
Pickles	12
Sir Isaac Newton	12
Duchess (with flowers)	13
Amiable Guinea Pig	17
Anna Maria	21

II – ROYAL ALBERT

Note: bold face type = originally issued as old Beswick

Figure	Years
Susan	<1 (small handful)
Thomasina Tittlemouse	<1 (scarce)
Old Mr. Pricklepin	<1 (scarce)
Mrs. Rabbit and Peter	2
Peter with Postbag	3
Peter with Daffodils	3

III — NEW BESWICK

Note: bold face type = originally issued as old Beswick or Royal Albert

Figure	Version/Variation	Years in Production
Peter Ate a Radish		>0 (tiny handful)
And This Pig Had None		>0
Benjamin Ate a Lettuce Leaf		>0
Mrs. Flopsy Bunny		>0
Pigling Bland	v 2	>0
Peter and the Red Pocket Handkerchief		<1
Peter with Daffodils		<1
Mrs. Rabbit Cooking		<1
Jemima Puddle-Duck and Foxy Whiskered Gentleman		<1
Old Mr Brown		<1
Jeremy Fisher Catches a Fish	v 1	<1
Tom Kitten	v 2	<1
Two Gentleman Rabbits		1
Mrs. Tiggy-Winkle Buys Provisions		1
Head Gardener		1
Little Pig Robinson	v 2	1*
Peter Rabbit Gardening		>1
Hunca Munca		>1
Lady Mouse		<2
Ribby		<2
Mr. Drake Puddle-Duck		<2
Rebeccah Puddle-Duck		<2*
Squirrel Nutkin	v 2	<2
Mrs. Tiggy-Winkle	v 2	<2
Mr. Benjamin Bunny	V 2b	<2*
Hunca Munca		2
Peter Rabbit Digging		2
Hunca Munca Sweeping		2*
Mrs. Rabbit and Peter		2
Mr. Jeremy Fisher	v 2	2

Note: the four asterisked figures were re-issued in the closing months of 2002 with new "P" numbers and with BP-11 John Beswick signature backstamps. All four were originally old Beswick figures which also had been produced as Royal Albert and as new Beswick figures; they had been discontinued after varying periods of production with the Beswick BP-10 series backstamps.

IV – COMBINED : OLD BESWICK< ROYAL ALBERT AND NEW BESWICK

Figure	Old Beswick Years	Royal Albert Years	New Beswick Years	O/A Total Years
Jeremy Fisher Catches a Fish (v-1)	0	0	<1	<1
Two Gentlemen Rabbits	0	0	<1	<1
Mrs. Tiggy-Winkle Buys Provisions	0	0	<1	<1
Head Gardener	0	0	<1	<1
Mr. Benjamin Bunny (v 1b)	1	0	0	<1
Mr. Jackson (green frog) (v 1)	1	0	0	1
Mr. Peter Rabbit Gardening	0	0	>1	>1
Hunca Munca, style two	0	0	2	2
Peter Rabbit Digging	0	0	2	2
Mr. Benjamin Bunny (v 2a)	2	0	0	2
Benjamin Bunny (v 2)	2	0	0	2
Mrs. Tiggy-Winkle Washing	0	0	<3	<3
Tom Kitten in the Rockery	0	0	3	3
Johnny Town-Mouse Eating Corn	0	0	3	3
Yock-Yock in the Tub	0	0	3	3
Timmy Willie Fetching Milk	0	0	3	3
Farmer Potatoes	0	0	3	3
Mrs. Tittlemouse, style two	0	0	3	3
Amiable Guinea Pig, style two	0	0	3	3
Tommy Brock (v 3)	3	0	0	3
Benjamin Bunny Sat on a Bank (v 1)	3	0	0	3
Peter with Daffodils	0	3	<1	<4
Jeremy Fisher Catches a Fish (v 2)	0	0	4	4
Fierce Bad Rabbit (v 1)	4	0	0	4

Plus, the 12 old Beswick figures retired early:

Figure	Old Beswick Years	Royal Albert Years	New Beswick Years	O/A Total Years
Duchess (with pie)	4	0	0	4
Susan	6	<1	0	<7
Old Mr. Pricklepin	6	<1	0	<7
Ginger	7	0	0	7
Thomasina Tittlemouse	8	<1	0	<9
Simpkin	9	0	0	9
Pig-Wig	11	0	0	11
Pickles	12	0	0	12
Sir Isaac Newton	12	0	0	12
Duchess (with flowers)	13	0	0	13
Amiable Guinea Pig	17	0	0	17
Anna Maria	21	0	0	21

V - BACKSTAMP SCARCITY

BP-1a (gold circle) backstamps

Figure	Version/Variation	Years Produced
Duchess (with flowers)		<1 (tiny handful)
Tommy Brock	v 1 and v 2	<1 (tiny handful)
Pigling Bland	v 1	<1 (tiny handful)
Tailor of Gloucester		<1* (very rare)
Johnny Town-Mouse		<1* (very rare)
Mrs. Rabbit	v 1	<1* (rare)
Miss Moppet	v 1 and v 2	1 (very scarce)
Flopsy, Mospy and Cottontail, style one		1 (very scarce)
Foxy Whiskered Gentleman		1 (very scarce)

* Difficulties with fitting the gold circle on small base figures first surfaced in 1949 with Tailor of Gloucester and led to the ultra small-type (and unattractive) gold parallel lines backstamp. A similar problem arose in 1951 with the introduction of Mrs. Rabbit, which led to the so-called "flattened circle" (oval) modification of the gold circle. In 1955 this special oval backstamp became standard and is now known as the BP-2. Another small base figure, Johnny Town-Mouse, apparently began using the gold oval soon after its introduction in 1954; its gold circle version is very rare.

BP-1b (gold parallel lines) backstamps

Figure	Version/Variation	Years Produced
Tailor of Gloucester		2 (scarce)

BP-2 (gold oval) backstamps

Figure	Version/Variation	Years Produced
Pig-Wig		<1 (tiny handful)
Benjamin Bunny	v 2	<1 (rare)

BP-3a (brown no copyright date) backstamps

Figure	Version/Variation	Years Produced
Mr. Benjamin Bunny	vers. 2 / var. 2	1
Sally Henny Penny		1
Sir Isaac Newton		2
Mr. Alderman Ptolemy		2

BP-5 (gold backstamp Royal Albert) backstamps

Figure	Version/Variation	Years Produced
Jemima Puddle-Duck		1 (scarce)
Peter Rabbit	v 2	1 (scarce)
Benjamin Bunny	v 3	1 (scarce)
Hunca Munca, style one		1 (scarce)
Flopsy, Mopsy and Cottontail, style one		1 (scarce)
Mrs. Rabbit and Bunnies		1 (scarce)

BP-6 (brown Royal Albert) backstamps

Figure	Version/Variation	Years Produced
Susan		<1 (small handful)
Thomasina Tittlemouse		<1 (scarce)
Old Mr. Pricklepin		<1 (scarce)

BP-8a (Beswick Ware) backstamps

Figure	Version/Variation	Years Produced
Jemima and Her Ducklings		<1 (tiny handful)
Mrs. Tiggy-Winkle Washing		<1 (about 1700)

BP-10a/b/c (Beswick) backstamps

Note: excepting Peter Rabbit Gardening all of these figures were introduced as either old Beswick or Royal Albert figures.

Figure	Version/Variation	Years Produced
Peter Ate a Radish (10b)		>0 (tiny handful)
And This Pig Had None (10a)		>0
Benjamin Ate a Lettuce Leaf		>0
Mrs. Flopsy Bunny (10b)		>0
Pigling Bland (10c)	v 2	>0
Peter / Red Pocket Handkerchief (10a)		<1
Mrs. Rabbit Cooking (10b)		<1
Tom Kitten (10c)	v 2	1
Old Mr. Brown (10a)		1
Jemima Puddle-Duck and Foxy Whiskered Gentleman (10b)		1
Peter with Daffodils (10b)		1
Peter Rabbit Gardening (10b)		>1

BP-11 (Beswick) backstamps (Oct.-Dec. 2002 reissues)

Figure	Version/Variation	Years Produced
Little Pig Robinson	v 2	<1 (3 months)
Mr. Benjamin Bunny	v 2b	<1 (3 months)
Hunca Munca Sweeping		<1 (3 months)
Rebeccah Puddle-Duck		<1 (3 months)

BEATRIX POTTER BACKSTAMPS

BP-1

BESWICK GOLD CIRCLE AND BESWICK GOLD PARALLEL LINES ISSUED 1948 TO 1954

The Beswick-England gold circle backstamp (BP-1a) was the primary backstamp used from the introduction of the first ten figures in 1948 through 1954. However, three small base figures introduced during that period could not easily accommodate the full gold circle and forced changes in the backstamp design.

The first small base figure, Tailor of Gloucester, introduced in 1949, resulted in the creation of a special backstamp especially for that figure – the BP-1b gold parallel lines backstamp which has the words Beswick and England in very small type. While the BP-1b was used in small quantities on several other figures, such usage was likely simply a matter of production line convenience.

The second figure presenting problems for the full gold circle was Mrs. Rabbit, introduced in 1951. In this instance instead of using the unattractive BP-1b parallel lines design the gold circle was "modified" into a gold oval – which is now called the BP-2. In addition, it appears likely that use of the BP-1b on Tailor of Gloucester was discontinued at this time in favour of the gold oval.

The third small base figure, Johnny Town-Mouse, introduced in 1954, apparently used the new gold oval almost from the start of production and probably led to the decision to simplify the backstamp situation by using the gold oval (BP-2) design for all figures starting in 1955. This much is clear: there are only a tiny handful of gold circle backstamps on the three small base figures introduced prior to 1955 – and all of these are probably pre-production prototypes produced prior to the start of the regular production.

It should be noted that a tiny handful of each of the three figures introduced in 1955 – Tommy Brock, Duchess with Flowers, and Pigling Bland – were produced with the gold circle backstamp. In all likelihood, all of these are pre-production prototypes produced in 1954 for marketing purposes.

BP-1a (gold circle). The first variety has the words "Beswick" and "England" forming a circle; the word "copyright" may or may not appear. While this variety was used on a total of 24 figures plus one variation, it is found only in miniscule quantities on six of these:

- Duchess with Flowers
- Johnny Town-Mouse
- Mrs. Rabbit
- Pigling Bland
- Tailor of Gloucester
- Tommy Brock

BP-1a Beswick Gold Circle

The following is a list of the 18 figures which regularly used the BP-1a backstamp:

- Benjamin Bunny, first version
- Flopsy, Mopsy and Cottontail, style one
- Foxy Whiskered Gentleman, first version, first variation
- Hunca Munca, style one
- Jemima Puddle-Duck, first version, first variation
- Lady Mouse
- Little Pig Robinson, first variation
- Miss Moppet, first variation
- Mr. Jeremy Fisher, first version, first and second variations
- Mrs. Tiggy-Winkle, first version, first variation
- Mrs. Tittlemouse, style one
- Peter Rabbit, first version, first variation
- Ribby
- Samuel Whiskers
- Squirrel Nutkin, first version, first variation
- Timmy Tiptoes, first variation
- Timmy Willie
- Tom Kitten, first version, first variation

BP-1b (gold parallel lines). The second variety has the words "Beswick" and "England" arranged in parallel lines, one atop the other; the word "Copyright" appears in script. This variety was created for use on Tailor of Gloucester but was used in error on several other figures incuding:

BP-1b Beswick Gold Parallel Lines

- Benjamin Bunny, first version
- Little Pig Robinson, first variation
- Peter Rabbit, first version, first variation
- Samuel Whiskers
- The Tailor of Gloucester, first version
- Timmy Tiptoes, first variation
- Tom Kitten, first version, first variation

Note: There also may be some, or all, of the other three 1948 figures.

BP-2   **BESWICK GOLD OVAL**
ISSUED 1955 TO 1972

BP-2a The gold oval was in use for 18 years, between 1955 and 1972, on 38 figures plus 4 versions/variations. The last gold oval figure, "Pig-Wig," was introduced in late 1972. The tiny number of gold oval Pig Wig's produced suggests that they were the usual pre-production prototypes and that, because plans to introduce the brown line backstamp in 1973 were at full throttle, all 1972 regular production Pig-Wig's received the no-copyright-date variety of the new backstamps. The following is a list of figures that can found with a BP-2 backstamp:

BP-2 Beswick Gold Oval

Amiable Guinea-Pig, style one
Anna Maria
Apply Dappley, first version
Aunt Pettitoes
Benjamin Bunny, first and second versions
Cecily Parsley, first version
Cousin Ribby
Duchess, style one (with flowers)
Flopsy, Mopsy and Cottontail, style one
Foxy Whiskered Gentleman, first version, first variation
Goody Tiptoes
Hunca Munca, style one
Jemima Puddle-Duck, first version, first variation
Johnny Town-Mouse
Lady Mouse
Little Pig Robinson, first variation
Miss Moppet, first variation
Mr. Benjamin Bunny, first version
Mr. Jeremy Fisher, first version, first variation
Mrs. Flopsy Bunny
Mrs. Rabbit, first version
Mrs. Tiggy-Winkle, first version, first and second variations
Mrs. Tittlemouse, style one
Old Mr. Brown
Old Woman Who Lived in a Shoe, The
Peter Rabbit, first version, first variation
Pickles
Pigling Bland, first variation
Pig-Wig
Ribby
Samuel Whiskers
Squirrel Nutkin, first version, first variation
Tabitha Twitchit, first variation
Tailor of Gloucester, first version
Timmy Tiptoes, first and second variations
Timmy Willie From Johnny Town-Mouse
Tom Kitten, first version, first variation
Tommy Brock, first version, first and second variations

BP-2b   **Transitional Gold/Brown**
Issued 1971 - 1972

BP-2b Between BP-2 and BP-3 there exist transitional backstamps. These appear on a very limited number of figures. The backstamp is part gold and part brown line; usually "Beatrix Potter" and the figure's name appear in gold with the last three lines in brown.

Part gold, part brown line backstamp

The following is a list of figures known to carry the transitional backstamp:

Flopsy, Mopsy and Cottontail
Mr. Benjamin Bunny, first version
Mr. Benjamin Bunny, second version
Mrs. Tittlemouse, style one
Peter Rabbit, first version, first variation
Squirrel Nutkin, first version, first variation
Timmy Tiptoes, first variation

BP-3   **BESWICK BROWN LINE**
ISSUED 1973 TO 1988

BP-3a Potter's, no date, issued 1973 to 1974
(no copyright date)
Used on 41 figures, plus 9 versions/varieties

The overall BP-3 category groups eight minor backstamp varieties into three major categories, as set forth below. In each category, the words "Beswick" and "England" appear in brown lettering either in a straight line or with "Beswick" atop "England," depending on the size or shape of the base. Over a period of 16 years BP-3 category backstamps were used on a total of 70 figures plus 27 versions/variations.

Note: The eight minor varieties are described in Louise Irvine's "Beatrix Potter Figures," 2nd edition, pp74-75. Three of the varieties (B1, B3 abd B4) are included in BP-3a; three (B2, B5 and B6) are included in BP-3b; and two (B7 and B8) are included in BP-3c. Similarly, there are two varieties (B9 and B10) included in BP-4."

BP-3b Potter's, date, issued 1974 to 1985
(copyright date)
Used on 63 figures, plus 16 versions/varieties

BP-3c Potter, date, issued 1985 to 1988
(no "s" on Potter)
Used on 63 figures, plus 16 versions/varieties

BP-4　　　　BESWICK SIGNATURE
ISSUED 1988 TO 1989

BP-4 Beswick Signature
Used on a total of 29 figures

This era saw the Beswick backstamp converted to the Royal Doulton backstamp. The connection with Beswick was kept by the addition of the John Beswick signature to the backstamp. In use for a year to a year and a half, this is one of the shortest time periods for a backstamp.

BP-5　　　　ROYAL ALBERT GOLD CROWN
ISSUED 1989

BP-5 Royal Albert Gold Crown

The gold backstamp was reinstituted for 1989 to mark the change from the Doulton/Beswick backstamps to Royal Albert. It was used on only the following six figures:

Benjamin Bunny, third version, first variation
Flopsy, Mopsy and Cottontail, style one
Hunca Munca, style one
Jemima Puddleduck, first version, first variation
Mrs. Rabbit and Bunnies
Peter Rabbit, first version, second variation

BP-6　　　　ROYAL ALBERT BROWN CROWN
ISSUED 1989 TO 1998

BP-6a Small brown crown　　BP-6b Large brown crown

This backstamp was issued in two sizes. A small version was used on the standard figures with a larger size for the large size figures. The small size was issued in 1989 and was used on 90 figures. The large size was issued in 1993 and was used on 10 figures. A variation of the small size exists without the crown for small base figures.

BP-7   **BESWICK BROWN OVAL**
ISSUED 1993

BP-7 Brown Oval

Issued only on the large size Peter Rabbit to commemorate the 100th anniversary of Peter Rabbit 1893-1993.

BP-8   **BESWICK WARE BROWN SCRIPT**
ISSUED 1994 TO 1998

"Beswick Ware England" or the mark that followed, "Beswick Ware Made in England" is the earliest printed backstamp of the J. W. Beswick, Baltimore Works, Longton, and it was for the Beswick Centenary that the Beswick Ware logo was reinstated as the primary backstamp of the John Beswick Studio of Royal Doulton.

BP-8a   General Backstamp Issue 1998

BP-8a Beswick Ware Brown Script

Issued as a general backstamp for a very short period of time in 1998, the brown script may turn out to be the rarest of the Beatrix Potter backstamps. It is found on only 2 figures.

Jemima and her Ducklings
Mrs. Tiggy-Winkle Washing

BP-8b   50th Anniversary of Production of
Beatrix Potter Figures at Beswick, Issued 1997

BP-8b Beswick 50th Anniversary

1997 was the 50th anniversary of production of Beatrix Potter figurines at the John Beswick Studios in Longton. This backstamp was in use only during 1997.

BP-8c   Limited Edition Backstamp

BP-8c Beswick Ware Brown Script
Limited Edition Backstamp

BP-8c is a modification of BP-8a and designed for a limited edition figurines.

The following is a list of figures that can be found with a BP-8c backstamp:

Hiding From the Cat
Mittens, Tom Kitten and Moppet
Peter and Benjamin Picking Up Onions

BP-9   BESWICK WARE GOLD SCRIPT
ISSUED 1997 TO 1999

A gold Beswick Ware script backstamp was coupled with the anniversary, limited edition, gold or platinum highlighted figurines. There are three varieties of this backstamp.

BP-9a   100th Anniversary of
John Beswick Studios, Issued 1994

BP-9a Beswick Centenary

Issued to commemorate the 100th anniversary of the founding of the Beswick studios. This backstamp was available only on Jemima Puddle-Duck.

BP-9b   General Backstamp
1997-1998

BP-9b Beswick Gold Script

The following small size figures issued with gold accents are coupled with gold Beswick Ware backstamps:

Benjamin Bunny, third version, second variation
Hunca Munca Sweeping, first version, second variation
Jemima Puddle-Duck, first version, second variation
Mrs. Tiggy-Winkle, first version, third variation
Peter Rabbit, first version, third variation
Tom Kitten, first version, third variation

BP-9c   Limited Edition Backstamp

BP-9c Beswick Ware Gold Script
Limited Edition

This backstamp, a modification of BP-9b, appears on 12 large size figurines issued by Lawleys By Post between 1997-1999. They were issued in pairs except for "Mrs. Rabbit and Peter" (1999) and "Tabitha Twitchet and Miss Moppet" (2000).

Issued in pairs:
1. Benjamin Bunny, fourth version, second variation
   Peter Rabbit, second version, second variation
2. Jemima Puddle-Duck, second version, second var.
   Mrs. Tiggy-Winkle, second version, second variation
3. Mr. Jeremy Fisher, second version, second variation
   Tom Kitten, second version, second variation
4. Foxy Whiskered Gentleman, second version,
      second variation
   Mrs. Rabbit, third version, second variation
5. Peter and the Red Pocket Handkerchief, second
      version, second variation
   Tailor of Gloucester, second version, second var.
6. Hunca Munca Sweeping, second version
   Squirrel Nutkin, second version

Issued singly (double figures):
1. Mrs. Rabbit and Peter, second version
   (Single issue-double figure)
2. Tabitha Twitchit and Moppet, second version

BP-9d   Peter Rabbit and Friends
Limited Editions

BP-9d Peter Rabbit and Friends
Limited Editions

This backstamp is a modification of BP-9b and is found on limited edition figures with gold accents issued by Peter Rabbit and Friends.

Duchess and Ribby
Ginger and Pickles
Mrs. Tiggy-Winkle and Lucie
Peter and the Red Pocket Handkerchief, first version,
   second variation
This Pig Had a Bit of Meat

BP-10   BESWICK BLACK CREST
ISSUED 1998 TO DATE

In 1998 the Beswick backstamp was redesigned and the Beswick crest, first seen in 1968-1969, was re-introduced for the Beswick line of Storybook figurines. There are three varieties of this backstamp.

BP-10a

General Backstamp Issue

BP-10a Beswick Black Crest

This backstamp, now in general use, will be found on the following Beatrix Potter figurines:

Amiable Guinea-Pig, style two
And This Pig Had None
Appley Dapply, second version
Benjamin Ate a Lettuce Leaf
Farmer Potatoes
Foxy Whiskered Gentleman, first version, first variation
Hunca Munca Sweeping, first version, first variation
Jemima and her Ducklings
Jemima Puddle-Duck, first version, first variation
Jemima Puddle-Duck with Foxy Whiskered Gentleman
Jeremy Fisher Catches a Fish
Johnny Town-Mouse Eating Corn
Lady Mouse
Mr. Jeremy Fisher, first version, second variation
Mrs. Tiggy-Winkle Takes Tea
Mrs. Tiggy-Winkle Washing
Mrs. Tittlemouse, style two
Old Mr. Brown
Peter and the Red Pocket Handkerchief, first version, first variation
Peter in Bed
Peter in the Watering Can
Squirrel Nutkin, first version, second variation
The Old Woman Who Lived in a Shoe Knitting
Timmy Willie Fetching Milk
Tom Kitten in the Rockery
Tommy Brock, second version, second variation
Yock-Yock in the Tub

BP-10b

Beswick Black Arch

BP-10b A modification of backstamp BP-10a

This backstamp is a modification of BP-10a and can be found on the following figurines. The modification was necessary due to base restriction.

Hunca Munca, style one
Miss Moppet, second variation
Mr. Benjamin Bunny, second version
Mr. Drake Puddle-Duck
Mr. McGregor
Mrs. Flopsy Bunny
Mrs. Rabbit and Peter, first version
Mrs. Rabbit Cooking
Peter Ate a Raddish
Peter Rabbit, first version, second variation
Peter Rabbit Gardening
Peter with Daffodils
Peter with Postbag
Rebeccah Puddle-Duck

BP-10c

Beswick Black Circle

BP-10c A modification of backstamp BP-10a

This backstamp is a modification of BP-10a. Its modification is also due to base restriction. It can be found on the following figurines:

Benjamin Bunny, third version, first variation
Little Pig Robinson, second variation
Mrs. Rabbit, second version
Mrs. Tiggy-Winkle, first version, second variation
Pigling Bland, second variation
Ribby
Tailor of Gloucester, first version
Tom Kitten, first version, second variation

BP-10d

Peter Rabbit and Friends Limited Editions

BP-10d Beswick Gold Crest

At the time of publication BP-10d was found only on Sweet Peter Rabbit, a limited edition figurine commissioned by Peter Rabbit and Friends. This backstamp is a gold version of BP-10a

BP-11   **JOHN BESWICK SIGNATURE**
                        ISSUED 2001 TO 2002

Beginning in 2001 all standard range figures and limited/special edition figures carry a "John Beswick" signature in lieu of the word "Beswick". In addition, the Doulton "P" number for each figure is included for all limited/special edition figures beginning in 2001 and for the standard range figures beginning in 2002.

BP-11a   **General Backstamp Issue**

BP-11a John Beswick Signature

Standard range figures:

Head Gardener, The
Hunca Munca, style two
Hunca Munca Sweeping
Little Pig Robinson
Mr. Benjamin Bunny
Mrs. Tiggy-Winkle Buys Provisions
Peter Rabbit Digging
Rebeccah Puddle-duck
Two Gentlemen Rabbits

Satin glaze figures:

Benjamin Bunny, third version, third variation
Foxy Whiskered Gentleman, first version, second variation
Jemima Puddle-duck, first version, third variation
Mr. Jeremy Fisher, first version, third variation
Mrs. Tiggy-Winkle, first version, fourth variation
Peter Rabbit, first version, fourth variation

Note: In addition to the normal BP-11a backstamp these six figures have the words "SATIN FINISH" arranged in a circle on a paper sticker.

BP-11b   **Limited/Special Edition Backstamp**

BP-11b John Beswick Signature

Limited/special edition figures:

Flopsy and Benjamin Bunny
Flopsy, Mopsy and Cottontail, style two
Kep and Jemima
My Dear Son Thomas
Peter and Benjamin Picking Apples
Peter on his Book

AMIABLE GUINEA-PIG™
Style One

Modeller:	Albert Hallam
Height:	3 ½", 8.9 cm
Colour:	Tan jacket, white waistcoat, yellow trousers
Issued:	1967 - 1983

Back Stamp	Beswick Number	Doulton Number	Price U.S. $	Can. $	U.K. £	Aust. $
BP-2	2061	P2061	550.00	725.00	300.00	775.00
BP-3a			275.00	350.00	150.00	375.00
BP-3b			275.00	350.00	150.00	375.00

Note: The colour of the coat varies from tan to brown.

AMIABLE GUINEA-PIG™
Style Two

Modeller:	Warren Platt
Height:	4 ¼", 10.8 cm
Colour:	Brown jacket and waistcoat, beige trousers and hat, blue bowtie and book
Issued:	2000 - 2002

Back Stamp	Beswick Number	Doulton Number	Price U.S. $	Can. $	U.K. £	Aust. $
BP-10a	4031	P4031	100.00	135.00	55.00	150.00

AND THIS PIG HAD NONE™

Modeller:	Martyn Alcock
Height:	4", 10.1 cm
Colour:	Mauve dress, mottled burgundy and green shawl, brown hat
Issued:	1992 - 1998

Back Stamp	Beswick Number	Doulton Number	Price U.S. $	Can. $	U.K. £	Aust. $
BP-6a	3319	P3319	55.00	70.00	30.00	75.00
BP-10a			55.00	70.00	35.00	75.00

ANNA MARIA™

Modeller:	Albert Hallam
Height:	3", 7.6 cm
Colour:	Blue dress and white apron
Issued:	1963 - 1983

BEATRIX POTTER'S
Anna Maria
F. WARNE & CO. LTD.
COPYRIGHT
BESWICK
ENGLAND

Back Stamp	Beswick Number	Doulton Number	Price			
			U.S. $	Can. $	U.K. £	Aust. $
BP-2	1851	P1851	400.00	550.00	225.00	575.00
BP-3a			225.00	300.00	125.00	325.00
BP-3b			225.00	300.00	125.00	325.00

Note: Dress is bright blue in earlier versions and pale blue in later versions.

APPLEY DAPPLY™

Modeller:	Albert Hallam
Height:	3 ¼", 8.3 cm
Colour:	Brown mouse, white apron, blue trim, blue bow, yellow basket, tray of jam tarts

BEATRIX POTTER'S
APPLEY DAPPLY
F. WARNE & CO. LTD.
COPYRIGHT
BESWICK
ENGLAND

FIRST VERSION: BOTTLE OUT

Issued:	1971 - 1975

Back Stamp	Beswick Number	Doulton Number	Price			
			U.S. $	Can. $	U.K. £	Aust. $
BP-2	2333/1	P2333/1	350.00	475.00	200.00	500.00
BP-3a			225.00	300.00	125.00	325.00
BP-3b			225.00	300.00	125.00	325.00

First version: Bottle out

BEATRIX POTTER'S
"APPLEY DAPPLY"
F. Warne & Co.Ltd.
© Copyright 1971
BESWICK
ENGLAND

SECOND VERSION: BOTTLE IN

Issued:	1975 - 2002

Back Stamp	Beswick Number	Doulton Number	Price			
			U.S. $	Can. $	U.K. £	Aust. $
BP-3b	2333/2	P2333/2	70.00	95.00	40.00	100.00
BP-3c			70.00	95.00	40.00	100.00
BP-6a			45.00	60.00	25.00	65.00
BP-10a			45.00	60.00	25.00	65.00

BEATRIX POTTER

AMIABLE GUINEA-PIG
Style One

AMIABLE GUINEA-PIG
Style Two

AND THIS PIG HAD NONE

ANNA MARIA

APPLEY DAPPLY
Bottle Out

APPLEY DAPPLY
Bottle In

AUNT PETTITOES

BABBITTY BUMBLE

BENJAMIN ATE A
LETTUCE LEAF

BENJAMIN BUNNY
Small Size
Ears Out, Shoes Out

BENJAMIN BUNNY
Small Size
Ears Out, Shoes In

BENJAMIN BUNNY
Small Size
Ears In, Shoes In, Brown Shoes

BEATRIX POTTER

BENJAMIN BUNNY
Small Size, Ears In, Shoes In
Gold Shoes

BENJAMIN BUNNY
Small Size, Satin Finish

BENJAMIN BUNNY
Large Size, Brown Shoes

BENJAMIN BUNNY
SAT ON A BANK
Head Looks Down

BENJAMIN BUNNY
SAT ON A BANK
Head Looks Up

BENJAMIN WAKES UP

CECILY PARSLEY
Head Down, Bright Blue Dress

CECILY PARSLEY
Head Up, Pale Blue Dress

CHIPPY HACKEE

CHRISTMAS STOCKING

COTTONTAIL

COUSIN RIBBY

BEATRIX POTTER

DIGGORY DIGGORY DELVET

DUCHESS
Style One (Holding Flowers)

DUCHESS
Style Two (Holding a Pie)

FARMER POTATOES

FIERCE BAD RABBIT
Feet Out

FIERCE BAD RABBIT
Feet In

FLOPSY, MOPSY AND
COTTONTAIL, Style One

FOXY READING
COUNTRY NEWS

FOXY WHISKERED
GENTLEMAN
Small Size, Gloss Finish

FOXY WHISKERED
GENTLEMAN
Small Size, Satin Finish

FOXY WHISKERED
GENTLEMAN
Large Size, Green buttons

GENTLEMAN MOUSE
MADE A BOW

BEATRIX POTTER

GINGER

GOODY AND TIMMY TIPTOES

GOODY TIPTOES

HEAD GARDENER

HUNCA MUNCA
Style One

HUNCA MUNCA
Style Two

HUNCA MUNCA
SPILLS THE BEADS

HUNCA MUNCA SWEEPING
Small Size, Brown Dustpan

HUNCA MUNCA SWEEPING
Small Size, Gold Dustpan

HUNCA MUNCA SWEEPING
Large Size, Gold Dustpan
and Broom Handle

JEMIMA AND HER DUCKLINGS

JEMIMA PUDDLE-DUCK
Small Size, Yellow Scarf Clip

BEATRIX POTTER

JEMIMA PUDDLE-DUCK
Small Size, Gold Scarf Clip

JEMIMA PUDDLE-DUCK
Small Size, Satin Finish

JEMIMA PUDDLE-DUCK
Large Size, Yellow Scarf Clip

JEMIMA PUDDLE-DUCK
MADE A FEATHER NEST

JEMIMA PUDDLE-DUCK WITH
FOXY WHISKERED GENTLEMAN

JEREMY FISHER
CATCHES A FISH

JOHN JOINER

JOHNNY TOWN-MOUSE

JOHNNY TOWN-MOUSE
EATING CORN

JOHNNY TOWN-MOUSE
WITH BAG

LADY MOUSE

LADY MOUSE MADE
A CURTSY

BEATRIX POTTER

LITTLE BLACK RABBIT

LITTLE PIG ROBINSON
Blue Striped Dress

LITTLE PIG ROBINSON
Blue Checked Dress

LITTLE PIG
ROBINSON SPYING

MISS DORMOUSE

MISS MOPPET
Mottled Brown Cat

MISS MOPPET
Brown Striped Cat

MITTENS AND MOPPET

MOTHER LADYBIRD

MR. ALDERMAN PTOLEMY

MR. BENJAMIN BUNNY
Pipe Out, Dark Maroon Jacket

MR. BENJAMIN BUNNY
Pipe In, Lilac Jacket

BEATRIX POTTER

MR. BENJAMIN BUNNY
AND PETER RABBIT

MR. DRAKE PUDDLE-DUCK

MR. JACKSON
Green Toad

MR. JACKSON
Brown Toad

MR. JEREMY FISHER
Small Size, Spotted Legs

MR. JEREMY FISHER
Small Size, Striped Legs

MR. JEREMY FISHER
Large Size, Lilac Buttons

MR. JEREMY FISHER
DIGGING

MR. McGREGOR

MR. TOD

MRS. FLOPSY BUNNY

MRS. RABBIT
Small Size, Umbrella Out

BEATRIX POTTER

MRS. RABBIT
Small Size
Umbrella Moulded To Dress

MRS. RABBIT
Large Size
Gold Umbrella Point and Handle

MRS. RABBIT
AND BUNNIES

MRS. RABBIT AND PETER
Large Size

MRS. RABBIT COOKING

MRS. TIGGY-WINKLE
Small Size, Diagonal Striped Dress

MRS. TIGGY-WINKLE
Small Size, Plaid Dress

MRS. TIGGY-WINKLE
Small Size, Platinum Iron

MRS. TIGGY-WINKLE
Small Size, Satin Finish

MRS. TIGGY-WINKLE
Large Size
Creamy-brown Iron

MRS. TIGGY-WINKLE
Large Size, Platinum Iron

MRS. TIGGY-WINKLE
BUYS PROVISIONS

AUNT PETTITOES™

Modeller:	Albert Hallam
Height:	3 ¾", 9.5 cm
Colour:	Blue dress and white cap with blue polka dots
Issued:	1970 - 1993

Back Stamp	Beswick Number	Doulton Number	Price			
			U.S. $	Can. $	U.K. £	Aust. $
BP-2	2276	P2276	350.00	475.00	200.00	500.00
BP-3a			100.00	135.00	55.00	150.00
BP-3b			90.00	120.00	50.00	135.00
BP-3c			80.00	110.00	45.00	125.00
BP-6a			80.00	110.00	45.00	125.00

Note: The dress is light blue in earlier versions and bright blue in later versions.

BABBITTY BUMBLE™

Modeller:	Warren Platt
Height:	2 ¾", 7.0 cm
Colour:	Black and gold
Issued:	1989 - 1993

Back Stamp	Beswick Number	Doulton Number	Price			
			U.S. $	Can. $	U.K. £	Aust. $
BP-6a	2971	P2971	350.00	475.00	200.00	500.00

BENJAMIN ATE A LETTUCE LEAF™

Modeller:	Martyn Alcock
Height:	4 ¾", 11.9 cm
Colour:	Brown, white and yellow
Issued:	1992 - 1998

Back Stamp	Beswick Number	Doulton Number	Price			
			U.S. $	Can. $	U.K. £	Aust. $
BP-6a	3317	P3317	55.00	70.00	30.00	75.00
BP-10a			60.00	85.00	35.00	90.00

First version: Ears out, shoes out

Second version: Ears out, shoes in

Third version: Ears in, shoes in

BENJAMIN BUNNY™

Modeller:	Arthur Gredington
Height:	4", 10.1 cm
Size:	Small

FIRST VERSION: EARS OUT, SHOES OUT

Colour:	Variation No. 1 Pale green jacket
	Variation No. 2 Tan jacket
Issued:	1948 - 1974

Back Stamp	Beswick Number	Colour Variation	Price U.S. $	Can. $	U.K. £	Aust. $
BP-1a	1105/1	Pale green	550.00	725.00	300.00	775.00
BP-1a		Tan	550.00	725.00	300.00	775.00
BP-1b		Pale green		Rare		
BP-2a		Pale green	350.00	475.00	200.00	525.00
BP-2a		Tan	350.00	475.00	200.00	525.00
BP-3a		Pale green	325.00	425.00	175.00	475.00
BP-3b		Tan	325.00	425.00	175.00	475.00

SECOND VERSION: EARS OUT, SHOES IN

Colour:	Variation No. 1 Pale green jacket, yellow and orange pompon
	Variation No. 2 Tan jacket, yellow and orange pompon
	Variation No. 3 Brown jacket, solid orange pompon
Issued:	1972 - c.1980

Back Stamp	Beswick Number	Colour Variation	Price U.S. $	Can. $	U.K. £	Aust. $
BP-2	1105/2	Pale green		Very rare		
BP-3a		Pale green	325.00	425.00	175.00	475.00
BP-3a		Tan	325.00	425.00	175.00	475.00
BP-3b		Pale green	275.00	350.00	150.00	375.00
BP-3b		Tan	275.00	350.00	150.00	375.00

THIRD VERSION: EARS IN, SHOES IN
FIRST VARIATION: BROWN OR TAN SHOES

Colour:	Variation No. 1 Brown jacket, green beret / solid orange pompon, tan shoes
	Variation No. 2 Light tan jacket and shoes
Issued:	c.1980 - 2000

Back Stamp	Beswick Number	Colour Variation	Price U.S. $	Can. $	U.K. £	Aust. $
BP-3b	1105/3	Brown	80.00	110.00	45.00	115.00
BP-3c		Brown	80.00	110.00	45.00	115.00
BP-4		Brown	90.00	120.00	50.00	130.00
BP-5		Brown	110.00	150.00	60.00	165.00
BP-6a		Brown	45.00	60.00	25.00	65.00
BP-6a		Light tan	45.00	60.00	25.00	65.00
BP-10c		Light tan	45.00	60.00	25.00	65.00

THIRD VERSION: EARS IN, SHOES IN
SECOND VARIATION: GOLD SHOES

Colour:	Brown jacket, green beret with orange pompon, gold shoes
Issued:	1998 - 1998

Back Stamp	Beswick Number	Doulton Number	Price U.S. $	Can. $	U.K. £	Aust. $
BP-9b	1105/4	PG1105	90.00	120.00	50.00	135.00

THIRD VERSION: EARS IN, SHOES IN
THIRD VARIATION: BROWN SHOES, SATIN FINISH

Colour:	Pale brown jacket, green beret with solid orange pompon, dark brown shoes
Issued:	2001 - 2002

Back Stamp	Beswick Number	Doulton Number	Price U.S. $	Can. $	U.K. £	Aust. $
BP-11a	1105/5	PS1105	450.00	600.00	250.00	650.00

BENJAMIN BUNNY™

Modeller: Martyn Alcock
Height: 6 ¼", 15.9 cm
Size: Large

FOURTH VERSION: LARGE SIZE, EARS IN, SHOES IN
FIRST VARIATION: BROWN SHOES

Colour: Tan jacket, green beret with orange pompon
Issued: 1994 - 1997

Back Stamp	Beswick Number	Doulton Number	Price			
			U.S. $	Can. $	U.K. £	Aust. $
BP-6b	3403/1	P3403	80.00	110.00	45.00	125.00

FOURTH VERSION: LARGE SIZE, EARS IN, SHOES IN
SECOND VARIATION, GOLD SHOES

Issued: 1997 in a limited edition of 1,947
Series: Gold edition

Back Stamp	Beswick Number	Doulton Number	Price			
			U.S. $	Can. $	U.K. £	Aust. $
BP-9c	3403/2	PG3403	110.00	150.00	60.00	165.00

Note: Issued, numbered and sold as a pair with Peter Rabbit, second version, second variation.

Benjamin Bunny, large size, gold shoes

BENJAMIN BUNNY SAT ON A BANK™

Modeller: David Lyttleton
Height: 3 ¾", 9.5 cm

FIRST VERSION: HEAD LOOKS DOWN

Colour: Brown jacket
Issued: 1983 - 1985

Back Stamp	Beswick Number	Doulton Number	Price			
			U.S. $	Can. $	U.K. £	Aust. $
BP-3b	2803/1	P2803/1	175.00	250.00	100.00	275.00
BP-3c			145.00	190.00	80.00	210.00

First version: Head looks down

SECOND VERSION: HEAD LOOKS UP

Colour: Golden brown jacket
Issued: 1983 - 1997

Back Stamp	Beswick Number	Doulton Number	Price			
			U.S. $	Can. $	U.K. £	Aust. $
BP-3b	2803/2	P2803/2	115.00	155.00	65.00	170.00
BP-3c			150.00	200.00	85.00	220.00
BP-6a			60.00	85.00	35.00	100.00

Second version: Head looks up

BENJAMIN WAKES UP™

Modeller: Amanda Hughes-Lubeck
Height: 2 ¼", 5.7 cm
Colour: Green, white and orange
Issued: 1991 - 1997

Back Stamp	Beswick Number	Doulton Number	Price			
			U.S. $	Can. $	U.K. £	Aust. $
BP-6a	3234	P3234	60.00	85.00	35.00	100.00

CECILY PARSLEY™

Modeller: Arthur Gredington
Height: 4", 10.1 cm

FIRST VERSION: HEAD DOWN, BRIGHT BLUE DRESS

Colour: Bright blue dress, white apron, brown pail
Issued: 1965 - 1985

Back Stamp	Beswick Number	Doulton Number	Price			
			U.S. $	Can. $	U.K. £	Aust. $
BP-2	1941/1	P1941/1	225.00	300.00	125.00	325.00
BP-3a			110.00	150.00	60.00	175.00
BP-3b			110.00	150.00	60.00	175.00
BP-3c			150.00	200.00	85.00	225.00

First version: Head down

SECOND VERSION: HEAD UP, PALE BLUE DRESS

Colour: Pale blue dress, white apron
Issued: 1985 - 1993

Back Stamp	Beswick Number	Doulton Number	Price			
			U.S. $	Can. $	U.K. £	Aust. $
BP-3c	1941/2	P1941/2	125.00	170.00	70.00	185.00
BP-6a			125.00	170.00	70.00	185.00

Note: Cecily Parsley was issued with both a dark and a light blue dress.

Second version: Head up

CHIPPY HACKEE™

Modeller: David Lyttleton
Height: 3 ¾", 9.5 cm
Colour: Pale green blanket, white handkerchief, green foot bath
Issued: 1979 - 1993

Back Stamp	Beswick Number	Doulton Number	Price			
			U.S. $	Can. $	U.K. £	Aust. $
BP-3b	2627	P2627	150.00	200.00	85.00	225.00
BP-3c			145.00	190.00	80.00	210.00
BP-6a			350.00	475.00	200.00	500.00

Note: The colour of the blanket may range from pale green to pale yellow.

CHRISTMAS STOCKING™

Modeller: Martyn Alcock
Height: 3 ¼", 8.3 cm
Colour: Brown mice, red and white striped stocking
Issued: 1991 - 1994

Back Stamp	Beswick Number	Doulton Number	Price			
			U.S. $	Can. $	U.K. £	Aust. $
BP-6a	3257	P3257	450.00	600.00	250.00	650.00

COTTONTAIL™

Modeller: David Lyttleton
Height: 3 ¾", 9.5 cm
Colour: Blue dress, brown chair
Issued: 1985 - 1996

Back Stamp	Beswick Number	Doulton Number	Price			
			U.S. $	Can. $	U.K. £	Aust. $
BP-3b	2878	P2878	80.00	110.00	45.00	120.00
BP-3c			110.00	150.00	60.00	165.00
BP-4			115.00	155.00	65.00	170.00
BP-6a			60.00	85.00	35.00	90.00

BEATRIX POTTER'S
Cousin Ribby
F. WARNE & CO. LTD.
COPYRIGHT
BESWICK
ENGLAND

COUSIN RIBBY™

Modeller:	Albert Hallam
Height:	3 ½", 8.9 cm
Colour:	Pink skirt and hat, green apron, blue shawl, yellow basket
Issued:	1970 - 1993

Back Stamp	Beswick Number	Doulton Number	Price			
			U.S. $	Can. $	U.K. £	Aust. $
BP-2	2284	P2284	500.00	650.00	275.00	675.00
BP-3a			110.00	150.00	60.00	160.00
BP-3b			80.00	110.00	45.00	120.00
BP-3c			80.00	110.00	45.00	120.00
BP-6a			135.00	175.00	75.00	185.00

BEATRIX POTTER
"Diggory Diggory Delvet"
© Frederick Warne & Co. 1982
Licensed by Copyrights
BESWICK ENGLAND

DIGGORY DIGGORY DELVET™

Modeller:	David Lyttleton
Height:	2 ¾", 7.0 cm
Colour:	Grey mole
Issued:	1982 - 1997

Back Stamp	Beswick Number	Doulton Number	Price			
			U.S. $	Can. $	U.K. £	Aust. $
BP-3b	2713	P2713	115.00	155.00	65.00	165.00
BP-3c			135.00	175.00	75.00	185.00
BP-6a			70.00	95.00	40.00	100.00

BEATRIX POTTER
DUCHESS
WARNE & CO. L.
L. 16. COPY
BESWICK
ENGLAND

DUCHESS™
Style One (Holding Flowers)

Modeller:	Graham Orwell
Height:	3 ¾", 9.5 cm
Colour:	Black dog, multicoloured flowers
Issued:	1955 - 1967

Back Stamp	Beswick Number	Doulton Number	Price			
			U.S. $	Can. $	U.K. £	Aust. $
BP-1a	1355	P1355			Extremely Rare	
BP-2			2,875.00	3,850.00	1,600.00	4,000.00

DUCHESS™
Style Two (Holding a Pie)

Modeller:	Graham Tongue
Height:	4", 10.1 cm
Colour:	Black dog, blue bow, light brown pie
Issued:	1979 - 1982

Back Stamp	Beswick Number	Doulton Number	Price			
			U.S. $	Can. $	U.K. £	Aust. $
BP-3b	2601	P2601	625.00	850.00	350.00	900.00

For **Duchess and Ribby** see the Tableaux Section, page 84.

FARMER POTATOES™

Modeller:	Shane Ridge
Height:	5", 12.7 cm
Colour:	Tan jacket, brown trousers, yellow shirt, blue hat and lantern
Issued:	2000 - 2002

Back Stamp	Beswick Number	Doulton Number	Price			
			U.S. $	Can. $	U.K. £	Aust. $
BP-10a	4014	P4014	90.00	120.00	50.00	135.00

First version: Feet out

Second version: Feet in

FIERCE BAD RABBIT™

Modeller: David Lyttleton
Height: 4 ¾", 12.1 cm

FIRST VERSION: FEET OUT

Colour: Dark brown and white rabbit,
             red-brown carrot, green seat
Issued: 1977 - 1980

Back Stamp	Beswick Number	Doulton Number	Price			
			U.S. $	Can. $	U.K. £	Aust. $
BP-3b	2586/1	P2586/1	175.00	250.00	100.00	275.00

BEATRIX POTTER'S
"Fierce Bad Rabbit"
F. Warne & Co.Ltd.
© Copyright 1977
BESWICK ENGLAND

SECOND VERSION: FEET IN

Colour: Light brown and white rabbit,
             red-brown carrot, green seat
Issued: 1980 - 1997

Back Stamp	Beswick Number	Doulton Number	Price			
			U.S. $	Can. $	U.K. £	Aust. $
BP-3b	2586/2	P2586/2	135.00	175.00	75.00	190.00
BP-3c			110.00	150.00	60.00	160.00
BP-4			125.00	170.00	70.00	180.00
BP-6a			70.00	95.00	40.00	100.00

BEATRIX POTTER
"Fierce Bad Rabbit"
© Frederick Warne & Co. 1977
Licensed by Copyrights
BESWICK ENGLAND

For **Flopsy and Benjamin Bunny** see the Tableaux Section, page 84.

FLOPSY, MOPSY AND COTTONTAIL™
Style One

Modeller:	Arthur Gredington
Height:	2 ½", 6.4 cm
Colour:	Brown/white rabbits wearing rose-pink cloaks
Issued:	1954 - 1997

Back Stamp	Beswick Number	Doulton Number	Price			
			U.S. $	Can. $	U.K. £	Aust. $
BP-1a	1274	P1274	725.00	950.00	400.00	1,00000
BP-2			225.00	300.00	125.00	325.00
BP-3a			110.00	150.00	60.00	160.00
BP-3b			100.00	135.00	55.00	145.00
BP-3c			90.00	120.00	50.00	130.00
BP-4			110.00	150.00	60.00	160.00
BP-5			225.00	300.00	125.00	325.00
BP-6a			70.00	95.00	40.00	100.00

Note: Colour variations of the cloaks exist. Angle of bunnies heads may vary.

For **Flopsy, Mopsy and Cottontail**, Style Two, see the Tableaux Section, page 84.

FOXY READING COUNTRY NEWS™

Modeller:	Amanda Hughes-Lubeck
Height:	4 ¼", 10.8 cm
Colour:	Brown and green
Issued:	1990 - 1997

Back Stamp	Beswick Number	Doulton Number	Price			
			U.S. $	Can. $	U.K. £	Aust. $
BP-6a	3219	P3219	90.00	120.00	50.00	130.00

FOXY WHISKERED GENTLEMAN™

Modeller: Arthur Gredington

FIRST VERSION: SMALL
FIRST VARIATION: GLOSS FINISH

Height: 4 ¾", 12.1 cm
Size: Small
Colour: Pale green jacket and trousers, pink waistcoat
Issued: 1954 - 2002

Back Stamp	Beswick Number	Doulton Number	Price			
			U.S. $	Can. $	U.K. £	Aust. $
BP-1a	1277/1	P1277	725.00	950.00	400.00	1,000.00
BP-2			150.00	200.00	85.00	225.00
BP-3a			90.00	120.00	50.00	130.00
BP-3b			90.00	120.00	50.00	130.00
BP-3c			90.00	120.00	50.00	130.00
BP-4			110.00	150.00	60.00	160.00
BP-6a			45.00	60.00	25.00	65.00
BP-10a			45.00	60.00	25.00	65.00

Note: 1. Variations occur with the head turned either right or left.
2. Gentleman is spelled as "Gentlemen" on all BP-1a and BP-2 backstamps

Small size, gloss finish

FIRST VERSION: SMALL
SECOND VARIATION: SATIN FINISH

Height: 4 ¾", 12.1 cm
Size: Small
Colour: Pale green jacket and trousers,
             pink waistcoat
Issued: 2001 - 2002

Back Stamp	Beswick Number	Doulton Number	Price			
			U.S. $	Can. $	U.K. £	Aust. $
BP-11a	1277/2	PS1277	450.00	600.00	250.00	650.00

SECOND VERSION: LARGE
FIRST VARIATION: GREEN BUTTONS

Height: 7 ½", 19.1 cm
Size: Large
Colour: Pale green jacket and trousers, pink waistcoat
Issued: 1995 - 1997

Back Stamp	Beswick Number	Doulton Number	Price			
			U.S. $	Can. $	U.K. £	Aust. $
BP-6b	3450/1	P3450	70.00	95.00	40.00	100.00

Small size, satin finish

SECOND VERSION: LARGE
SECOND VARIATION: GOLD BUTTONS

Height: 7 ½", 19.1 cm
Size: Large
Colour: Pale green jacket and trousers, pink waistcoat, gold buttons
Issued: 1998 in a limited edition of 1,947
Series: Gold edition

Back Stamp	Beswick Number	Doulton Number	Price			
			U.S. $	Can. $	U.K. £	Aust. $
BP-9c	3450/2	PG3450	110.00	150.00	60.00	165.00

Note: The gold edition was issued, numbered and sold as a pair with Mrs. Rabbit, third version, first variation.

Large size

GENTLEMAN MOUSE MADE A BOW™

Modeller:	Ted Chawner
Height:	3", 7.6 cm
Colour:	Brown, blue and white
Issued:	1990 - 1996

Back Stamp	Beswick Number	Doulton Number	Price			
			U.S. $	Can. $	U.K. £	Aust. $
BP-6a	3200	P3200	70.00	95.00	40.00	100.00

GINGER™

Modeller:	David Lyttleton
Height:	3 ¾", 9.5 cm
Colour:	Green, white and brown
Issued:	1976 - 1982

Back Stamp	Beswick Number	Doulton Number	Price			
			U.S. $	Can. $	U.K. £	Aust. $
BP-3b	2559	P2559	550.00	725.00	300.00	750.00

Note: The jacket colour varies from light to dark green.

For **Ginger and Pickles** see the Tableaux Section, page 85.

GOODY AND TIMMY TIPTOES™

Modeller:	David Lyttleton
Height:	4", 10.1 cm
Colour:	Timmy - rose coat Goody - pink overdress with green and biege underskirt, green umbrella
Issued:	1986 - 1996

Back Stamp	Beswick Number	Doulton Number	Price			
			U.S. $	Can. $	U.K. £	Aust. $
BP-3c	2957	P2957	325.00	425.00	175.00	450.00
BP-6a			100.00	135.00	55.00	145.00

GOODY TIPTOES™

Modeller:	Arthur Gredington
Height:	3 ½", 8.9 cm
Colour:	Grey squirrel wearing pink dress and white apron, brown sack with yellow nuts
Issued:	1961 - 1997

Back Stamp	Beswick Number	Doulton Number	Price			
			U.S. $	Can. $	U.K. £	Aust. $
BP-2	1675	P1675	275.00	350.00	150.00	375.00
BP-3a			115.00	155.00	65.00	165.00
BP-3b			90.00	120.00	50.00	130.00
BP-3c			90.00	120.00	50.00	130.00
BP-6a			55.00	70.00	30.00	75.00

Note: This model has two different bases and the dress comes in various shades of pink.

HEAD GARDENER™

Modeller:	Shane Ridge
Height:	3 ½", 8.9 cm
Colour:	Brown and green
Issued:	2002 - 2002

Back Stamp	Beswick Number	Doulton Number	Price			
			U.S. $	Can. $	U.K. £	Aust. $
BP-11a	P4236	P4236	350.00	475.00	200.00	500.00

For **Hiding From the Cat** see the Tableaux Section, page 85.

HUNCA MUNCA™
Style One

Modeller:	Arthur Gredington
Height:	2 ¾", 7.0 cm
Colour:	Blue dress, white apron, pink blanket and straw cradle
Issued:	1951 - 2000

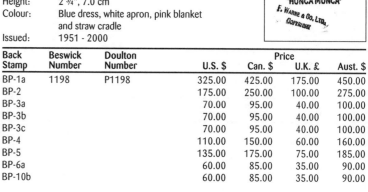

Back Stamp	Beswick Number	Doulton Number	Price			
			U.S. $	Can. $	U.K. £	Aust. $
BP-1a	1198	P1198	325.00	425.00	175.00	450.00
BP-2			175.00	250.00	100.00	275.00
BP-3a			70.00	95.00	40.00	100.00
BP-3b			70.00	95.00	40.00	100.00
BP-3c			70.00	95.00	40.00	100.00
BP-4			110.00	150.00	60.00	160.00
BP-5			135.00	175.00	75.00	185.00
BP-6a			60.00	85.00	35.00	90.00
BP-10b			60.00	85.00	35.00	90.00

HUNCA MUNCA™
Style Two

Modeller:	Shane Ridge
Height:	4 ¼", 10.8 cm
Colour:	Mauve dress, white apron, grey pans
Issued:	2001 - 2002

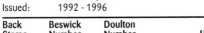

Back Stamp	Beswick Number	Doulton Number	Price			
			U.S. $	Can. $	U.K. £	Aust. $
BP-11a	P4074	P4074	80.00	110.00	45.00	120.00

HUNCA MUNCA SPILLS THE BEADS™

Modeller:	Martyn Alcock
Height:	3 ¼", 8.3 cm
Colour:	Brown mouse, blue and white rice jar
Issued:	1992 - 1996

Back Stamp	Beswick Number	Doulton Number	Price			
			U.S. $	Can. $	U.K. £	Aust. $
BP-6a	3288	P3288	80.00	110.00	45.00	120.00

HUNCA MUNCA SWEEPING™

Modeller:	David Lyttleton
Height:	3 ½", 8.9 cm
Size:	Small

BEATRIX POTTER'S
"Hunca Munca Sweeping"
F. Warne & Co.Ltd.
© Copyright 1977
BESWICK ENGLAND

FIRST VERSION: SMALL SIZE
FIRST VARIATION: LIGHT BROWN DUSTPAN

Colour:	Mauve patterned dress with white apron, green broom handle
Issued:	1977 - 2002

Back Stamp	Beswick Number	Doulton Number	Price			
			U.S. $	Can. $	U.K. £	Aust. $
BP-3b	2584/1	P2584	90.00	120.00	50.00	130.00
BP-3c			90.00	120.00	50.00	130.00
BP-4			90.00	120.00	50.00	130.00
BP-6a			60.00	85.00	35.00	90.00
BP-10a			55.00	70.00	30.00	75.00
BP-11a			60.00	85.00	35.00	90.00

Green broom handle

FIRST VERSION: SMALL SIZE
SECOND VARIATION: GOLD DUSTPAN

Colour:	Mauve patterned dress, white apron, green broom handle, gold dustpan
Issued:	1998 - 1998

Back Stamp	Beswick Number	Doulton Number	Price			
			U.S. $	Can. $	U.K. £	Aust. $
BP-9b	2584/2	PG2584	60.00	85.00	35.00	90.00

Gold dustpan

SECOND VERSION: LARGE SIZE, GOLD DUSTPAN AND BROOM HANDLE

Modeller:	Amanda Hughes-Lubeck
Height:	5 ¼", 13.3 cm
Size:	Large
Colour:	Mauve patterned dress, white apron, gold dustpan and broom handle
Issued:	1999 in a limited edition of 1,947
Series:	Gold edition

Back Stamp	Beswick Number	Doulton Number	Price			
			U.S. $	Can. $	U.K. £	Aust. $
BP-9c	3894	PG3894	110.00	150.00	60.00	160.00

Note: Issued, numbered and sold as a pair with Squirrel Nutkin, large size.

Gold dustpan and broom handle

JEMIMA AND HER DUCKLINGS™

Modeller: Martyn Alcock
Height: 4 ¼", 10.5 cm
Colour: Mauve shawl
Issued: 1998 - 2002

Beswick Ware
MADE IN ENGLAND
Jemima and Her Ducklings
Beatrix Potter
© F. WARNE & CO. 1998
© 1998 ROYAL DOULTON

Back	Beswick	Doulton	Price			
Stamp	Number	Number	U.S. $	Can. $	U.K. £	Aust. $
BP-8a	3786	P3786	625.00	850.00	350.00	900.00
BP-10a			60.00	85.00	35.00	90.00

Note: Very few examples of BP-8a are known

JEMIMA PUDDLE-DUCK™

Modeller: Arthur Gredington
Height: 4 ¾", 12.1 cm
Size: Small

FIRST VERSION: SMALL SIZE
FIRST VARIATION: GLOSS FINISH, YELLOW SCARF CLIP

Colour: Mauve or pink shawl, light blue
bonnet, yellow scarf clip
Issued: 1948 - 2002

BEATRIX POTTER'S
Jemima Puddleduck
copyright
BESWICK ENGLAND
5

Back	Beswick	Doulton	Price			
Stamp	Number	Number	U.S. $	Can. $	U.K. £	Aust. $
BP-1a	1092/1	P1092	275.00	350.00	150.00	375.00
BP-2			150.00	200.00	85.00	225.00
BP-3a			80.00	110.00	45.00	120.00
BP-3b			80.00	110.00	45.00	120.00
BP-3c			80.00	110.00	45.00	120.00
BP-4			80.00	110.00	45.00	120.00
BP-5			325.00	425.00	175.00	450.00
BP-6a			60.00	85.00	35.00	90.00
BP-10a			60.00	85.00	35.00	90.00

Small size, yellow scarf clip

FIRST VERSION: SMALL SIZE
SECOND VARIATION: GLOSS FINISH, GOLD SCARF CLIP

Colour: Mauve or pink shawl, light blue bonnet, gold scarf clip
Issued: 1997 - 1997

Back	Beswick	Doulton	Price			
Stamp	Number	Number	U.S. $	Can. $	U.K. £	Aust. $
BP-9b	1092/2	PG1092	80.00	110.00	45.00	120.00

FIRST VERSION: SMALL SIZE
THIRD VARIATION: SATIN FINISH

Colour: Pink shawl with blue design, light blue bonnet, yellow scarf clip
Issued: 2001 - 2002

Back	Beswick	Doulton	Price			
Stamp	Number	Number	U.S. $	Can. $	U.K. £	Aust. $
BP-11a	1092/3	PS1092	450.00	600.00	250.00	650.00

Small size, gold scarf clip

Large size, yellow scarf clip

JEMIMA PUDDLE-DUCK™

Modeller:	Martyn Alcock
Height:	6", 15.0 cm
Size:	Large

SECOND VERSION: LARGE SIZE
FIRST VARIATION: YELLOW SCARF CLIP

Colour:	White duck, mauve shawl, light blue bonnet, yellow scarf clip
Issued:	1993 - 1997

Back Stamp	Beswick Number	Doulton Number	Price U.S. $	Can. $	U.K. £	Aust. $
BP-6b	3373/1	P3373	80.00	110.00	45.00	120.00
BP-9a	Beswick Centenary		110.00	150.00	60.00	160.00

Large size, gold scarf clip

SECOND VERSION: LARGE SIZE
SECOND VARIATION: GOLD SCARF CLIP

Colour:	White duck, mauve shawl, light blue bonnet, gold scarf clip
Issued:	1998 in a limited edition of 1,947
Series:	Gold edition

Back Stamp	Beswick Number	Doulton Number	Price U.S. $	Can. $	U.K. £	Aust. $
BP-9c	3373/2	PG3373	110.00	150.00	60.00	160.00

Note: The second variation was issued, numbered and sold as a pair with Mrs. Tiggy-Winkle, second version, second variation.

JEMIMA PUDDLE-DUCK MADE A FEATHER NEST™

Modeller:	David Lyttleton
Height:	2 ¼", 5.7 cm
Colour:	White duck, mauve or pink shawl, blue hat
Issued:	1983 - 1997

Back Stamp	Beswick Number	Doulton Number	Price U.S. $	Can. $	U.K. £	Aust. $
BP-3b	2823	P2823	90.00	120.00	50.00	130.00
BP-3c			100.00	135.00	55.00	150.00
BP-4			110.00	150.00	60.00	160.00
BP-6a			100.00	135.00	35.00	150.00

Note: This model was issued with either a mauve or pink shawl.

JEMIMA PUDDLE-DUCK WITH FOXY WHISKERED GENTLEMAN™

Modeller: Ted Chawner
Height: 4 ¾", 12.1 cm
Colour: Brown, green, white and blue
Issued: 1990 - 1999

Back Stamp	Beswick Number	Doulton Number	Price			
			U.S. $	Can. $	U.K. £	Aust. $
BP-6a	3193	P3193	60.00	85.00	35.00	90.00
BP-10a			80.00	110.00	45.00	120.00

JEREMY FISHER CATCHES A FISH™

Modeller: Martyn Alcock
Height: 3", 7.6 cm
Colour: Green frog with brown spots,
            lilac coat, green, yellow and red fish
Issued: 1999 - 2002

Back Stamp	Beswick Number	Doulton Number	Price			
			U.S. $	Can. $	U.K. £	Aust. $
BP-10a	3919	P3919	110.00	150.00	60.00	160.00

Note: There are two variations of P3919: the base can be found with a cut-out "v" through both the lilypad and the water, and with a half-way "v" through the lilypad but not through the water (as illustrated).

JOHN JOINER™

Modeller: Graham Tongue
Height: 2 ½", 6.4 cm
Colour: Brown dog wearing
            green jacket
Issued: 1990 - 1997

Back Stamp	Beswick Number	Doulton Number	Price			
			U.S. $	Can. $	U.K. £	Aust. $
BP-6a	2965	P2965	80.00	110.00	45.00	120.00

Note: John Joiner will vary in shade from black to blue-black.

JOHNNY TOWN-MOUSE™

Modeller:	Arthur Gredington
Height:	3 ½", 8.9 cm
Colour:	Pale blue jacket, white and brown waistcoat
Issued:	1954 - 1993

Back Stamp	Beswick Number	Doulton Number	Price			
			U.S. $	Can. $	U.K. £	Aust. $
BP-1a	1276	P1276	Very rare			
BP-2			200.00	265.00	110.00	285.00
BP-3a			110.00	150.00	60.00	160.00
BP-3b			125.00	170.00	70.00	180.00
BP-3c			110.00	150.00	60.00	160.00
BP-6a			110.00	150.00	60.00	160.00

Note: 1. Jacket colouring varies from pale to deep blue.
2. Because of it's small base very few figures have the BP-1a backstamp.

JOHNNY TOWN-MOUSE EATING CORN™

Modeller:	Martyn Alcock
Height:	3 ¾", 9.5 cm
Colour:	Blue jacket, green and white waistcoat, pink trousers
Issued:	2000 - 2002

Back Stamp	Beswick Number	Doulton Number	Price			
			U.S. $	Can. $	U.K. £	Aust. $
BP-10a	3931	P3931	125.00	170.00	70.00	180.00

JOHNNY TOWN-MOUSE WITH BAG™

Modeller:	Ted Chawner
Height:	3 ½", 8.9 cm
Colour:	Light brown coat and hat, yellow-cream waistcoat
Issued:	1988 - 1994

Back Stamp	Beswick Number	Doulton Number	Price			
			U.S. $	Can. $	U.K. £	Aust. $
BP-4	3094	P3094	350.00	475.00	200.00	500.00
BP-6a			325.00	425.00	175.00	450.00

For **Kep and Jemima** see the Tableaux Section, page 85.

LADY MOUSE™

Modeller:	Arthur Gredington
Height:	4", 10.1 cm
Colour:	White dress with yellow trim and blue polka-dot sleeves, white hat with purple and blue highlights
Issued:	1950 - 2000

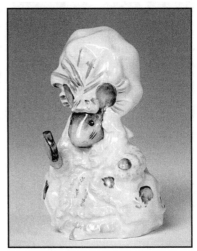

Back Stamp	Beswick Number	Doulton Number	Price			
			U.S. $	Can. $	U.K. £	Aust. $
BP-1a	1183	P1183	325.00	425.00	175.00	450.00
BP-2			150.00	200.00	85.00	225.00
BP-3a			90.00	120.00	50.00	130.00
BP-3b			90.00	120.00	50.00	130.00
BP-3c			90.00	120.00	50.00	130.00
BP-6a			55.00	70.00	30.00	75.00
BP-10a			85.00	110.00	45.00	120.00

LADY MOUSE MADE A CURTSY™

Modeller:	Amanda Hughes-Lubeck
Height:	3 ¼", 8.3 cm
Colour:	Purple-pink and white
Issued:	1990 - 1997

Back Stamp	Beswick Number	Doulton Number	Price			
			U.S. $	Can. $	U.K. £	Aust. $
BP-6a	3220	P3220	110.00	150.00	60.00	160.00

LITTLE BLACK RABBIT™

Modeller:	David Lyttleton
Height:	4 ½", 11.4 cm
Colour:	Black rabbit wearing green waistcoat
Issued:	1977 - 1997

Back Stamp	Beswick Number	Doulton Number	Price			
			U.S. $	Can. $	U.K. £	Aust. $
BP-3b	2585	P2585	115.00	155.00	65.00	165.00
BP-3c			115.00	155.00	65.00	165.00
BP-4				Very Rare		
BP-6a			110.00	150.00	60.00	160.00

Note: 1. The jacket colouring varies from light to dark green.
2. The BP-4 version is very rare.

First version: Blue striped outfit

LITTLE PIG ROBINSON™

Modeller: Arthur Gredington

FIRST VARIATION: BLUE STRIPED DRESS

Height: 4", 10.2 cm
Colour: White and blue striped dress,
           brown basket with yellow
           cauliflowers
Issued: 1948 - 1974

Back Stamp	Beswick Number	Doulton Number	Price			
			U.S. $	Can. $	U.K. £	Aust. $
BP-1a	1104/1	P1104/1	450.00	600.00	250.00	625.00
BP-1b					Rare	
BP-2			275.00	350.00	150.00	375.00
BP-3a			225.00	300.00	125.00	325.00
BP-3b			225.00	300.00	125.00	325.00

Second version: Blue checked outfit

SECOND VARIATION: BLUE CHECKED DRESS

Height: 3 ½", 8.9 cm
Colour: Blue checked dress, brown basket
           with cream cauliflowers
Issued: c.1974 - 1999
Re-issued: 2002

Back Stamp	Beswick Number	Doulton Number	Price			
			U.S. $	Can. $	U.K. £	Aust. $
BP-3b	1104/2	P1104/2	80.00	110.00	45.00	120.00
BP-3c			80.00	110.00	45.00	120.00
BP-6a			55.00	70.00	30.00	75.00
BP-10c			55.00	70.00	30.00	75.00
BP-11a			55.00	70.00	30.00	75.00

LITTLE PIG ROBINSON SPYING™

Modeller: Ted Chawner
Height: 3 ½", 8.9 cm
Colour: Blue and white striped
           outfit, rose-pink chair
Issued: 1987 - 1993

Back Stamp	Beswick Number	Doulton Number	Price			
			U.S. $	Can. $	U.K. £	Aust. $
BP-3c	3031	P3031	225.00	300.00	125.00	325.00
BP-6a			225.00	300.00	125.00	325.00

MISS DORMOUSE™

Modeller:	Martyn Alcock
Height:	4", 10.1 cm
Colour:	Blue, white and pink
Issued:	1991 - 1995

Back Stamp	Beswick Number	Doulton Number	Price			
			U.S. $	Can. $	U.K. £	Aust. $
BP-6a	3251	P3251	125.00	170.00	70.00	180.00

MISS MOPPET™

The BP-1a, BP-2 and BP-3a striped variations are subtle and appear to be more a matter of decorator discretion than the deliberate bold stripes that began with the BP-3b's.

Modeller:	Arthur Gredington
Height:	3", 7.6 cm

FIRST VARIATION: MOTTLED BROWN CAT

Colour:	Mottled brown cat, blue checkered kerchief
Issued:	1954 - c.1978

Back Stamp	Beswick Number	Doulton Number	Price			
			U.S. $	Can. $	U.K. £	Aust. $
BP-1a	1275/1	P1275/1	900.00	1,200.00	500.00	1,300.00
BP-2			175.00	250.00	100.00	275.00
BP-3a			115.00	155.00	65.00	165.00
BP-3b			90.00	120.00	50.00	130.00

First version: Mottled brown cat

SECOND VARIATION: BROWN STRIPED CAT

Colour:	Striped brown cat, blue checkered kerchief
Issued:	1978 - 2002

Back Stamp	Beswick Number	Doulton Number	Price			
			U.S. $	Can. $	U.K. £	Aust. $
BP-1a	1275/2	P1275/2	725.00	950.00	400.00	1,000.00
BP-2			175.00	250.00	100.00	275.00
BP-3a			170.00	230.00	95.00	250.00
BP-3b			80.00	110.00	45.00	120.00
BP-3c			80.00	110.00	45.00	120.00
BP-6a			80.00	110.00	45.00	120.00
BP-10b			80.00	110.00	45.00	120.00

Second version: Brown striped cat

MITTENS AND MOPPET™

Modeller:	Ted Chawner
Height:	3 ¾", 9.5 cm
Colour:	Blue, brown and grey
Issued:	1990 - 1994

Back Stamp	Beswick Number	Doulton Number	Price			
			U.S. $	Can. $	U.K. £	Aust. $
BP-6a	3197	P3197	225.00	300.00	125.00	325.00

For **Mittens, Tom Kitten and Moppet** see the Tableaux Section, page 86.

MOTHER LADYBIRD™

Modeller:	Warren Platt
Height:	2 ½", 6.4 cm
Colour:	Red and black
Issued:	1989 - 1996

Back Stamp	Beswick Number	Doulton Number	Price			
			U.S. $	Can. $	U.K. £	Aust. $
BP-6a	2966	P2966	175.00	200.00	100.00	225.00

MR. ALDERMAN PTOLEMY™

Modeller:	Graham Tongue
Height:	3 ½", 8.9 cm
Colour:	Brown, grey and green
Issued:	1973 - 1997

Back Stamp	Beswick Number	Doulton Number	Price			
			U.S. $	Can. $	U.K. £	Aust. $
BP-3a	2424	P2424	175.00	250.00	100.00	275.00
BP-3b			145.00	190.00	80.00	200.00
BP-3c			175.00	250.00	100.00	275.00
BP-6a			60.00	85.00	35.00	90.00

Note: Mr. Alderman Ptolemy and Sir Isaac Newton are the only figures with backstamps using the words "Made in England" vice "England."

MR. BENJAMIN BUNNY™

Modeller: Arthur Gredington
Height: 4 ¼", 10.8 cm

FIRST VERSION: PIPE OUT

Colour: Variation No. 1 Dark maroon jacket
           Variation No. 2 Lilac jacket
Issued: 1965 - 1974

Back Stamp	Beswick Number	Colour Variation	Price			
			U.S. $	Can. $	U.K. £	Aust. $
BP-2a	1940/1	Dark maroon	450.00	600.00	250.00	650.00
BP-3a		Dark maroon	400.00	550.00	225.00	575.00
BP-3a		Lilac		Very Rare		

First version: Pipe out

SECOND VERSION: PIPE IN

Colour: Variation No. 1 Dark maroon jacket
             Variation No. 2 Lilac jacket
Issued: 1. c.1970 - c.1974
             2. 1975 - 2000
Re-issued: 2. 2002

Back Stamp	Beswick Number	Colour Variation	Price			
			U.S. $	Can. $	U.K. £	Aust. $
BP-2b	1940/2	Lilac		Rare		
BP-3a		Dark maroon	400.00	550.00	225.00	600.00
BP-3a		Lilac	500.00	650.00	275.00	700.00
BP-3b		Dark maroon	400.00	550.00	225.00	600.00
BP-3b		Lilac	90.00	120.00	50.00	130.00
BP-3c		Lilac	90.00	120.00	50.00	130.00
BP-4		Lilac	80.00	110.00	45.00	120.00
BP-6a		Lilac	70.00	95.00	40.00	100.00
BP-10b		Lilac	70.00	95.00	40.00	100.00
BP-11a		Lilac	70.00	95.00	40.00	100.00

Second version: Pipe in

MR. BENJAMIN BUNNY AND PETER RABBIT™

Modeller: Alan Maslankowski
Height: 4", 10.1 cm
Colour: Benjamin Bunny: lilac jacket,
             yellow waistcoat
             Peter Rabbit: blue jacket
Issued: 1975 - 1995

Back Stamp	Beswick Number	Doulton Number	Price			
			U.S. $	Can. $	U.K. £	Aust. $
BP-3b	2509	P2509	200.00	265.00	110.00	290.00
BP-3c			160.00	215.00	90.00	235.00
BP-6a			135.00	175.00	75.00	185.00

MR. DRAKE PUDDLE-DUCK™

Modeller: David Lyttleton
Height: 4", 10.1 cm
Colour: White duck, blue
waistcoat and trousers
Issued: 1979 - 2000

BEATRIX POTTER
"Mr. Drake Puddle-Duck"
© Frederick Warne & Co. 1979
Licensed by Copyrights
BESWICK ENGLAND

Back Stamp	Beswick Number	Doulton Number	Price			
			U.S. $	Can. $	U.K. £	Aust. $
BP-3b	2628	P2628	70.00	95.00	40.00	100.00
BP-3c			90.00	120.00	50.00	130.00
BP-4			90.00	120.00	50.00	130.00
BP-6a			55.00	70.00	30.00	75.00
BP-10b			60.00	85.00	35.00	90.00

First version: Green toad

MR. JACKSON™

Modeller: Albert Hallam
Height: 2 ¾", 7.0 cm

FIRST VARIATION: GREEN TOAD

Colour: Green toad wearing
mauve jacket
Issued: 1974 - c.1974

BEATRIX POTTER'S
"Mr Jackson"
F. Warne & Co. Ltd.
Copyright
BESWICK ENGLAND

Back Stamp	Beswick Number	Doulton Number	Price			
			U.S. $	Can. $	U.K. £	Aust. $
BP-3a	2453/1	P2453/1	550.00	725.00	300.00	750.00

Second version: Brown toad

SECOND VARIATION: BROWN TOAD

Colour: Brown toad wearing mauve jacket
Issued: 1975 - 1997

BEATRIX POTTER'S
"Mr Jackson"
F. Warne & Co. Ltd.
© Copyright 1974
BESWICK ENGLAND

Back Stamp	Beswick Number	Doulton Number	Price			
			U.S. $	Can. $	U.K. £	Aust. $
BP-3b	2453/2	P2453/2	115.00	155.00	65.00	165.00
BP-3c			110.00	150.00	60.00	160.00
BP-6a			70.00	95.00	40.00	100.00

MR. JEREMY FISHER™

Modeller:	Arthur Gredington
Height:	3", 7.6 cm
Size:	Small

FIRST VERSION: SMALL SIZE
FIRST VARIATION: SPOTTED LEGS

Colour: Lilac coat, green frog with small
           brown spots on head and legs
Issued: 1950 - c.1974

Back Stamp	Beswick Number	Doulton Number	Price			
			U.S. $	Can. $	U.K. £	Aust. $
BP-1a	1157/1	P1157/1	550.00	700.00	300.00	750.00
BP-2			225.00	300.00	125.00	325.00
BP-3a			135.00	175.00	75.00	190.00
BP-3b			100.00	135.00	55.00	145.00

FIRST VERSION: SMALL SIZE
SECOND VARIATION: STRIPED LEGS

Colour: Lilac coat, green frog with large
           spots on head and stripes on legs
Issued: c.1950 - 2002

Back Stamp	Beswick Number	Doulton Number	Price			
			U.S. $	Can. $	U.K. £	Aust. $
BP-1a	1157/2	P1157/2	450.00	600.00	250.00	650.00
BP-3b			80.00	110.00	45.00	120.00
BP-3c			90.00	120.00	50.00	130.00
BP-6a			70.00	95.00	40.00	100.00
BP-10a			70.00	95.00	40.00	100.00

Note: BP-3c backstamp name exists with and without "Mr."

Small size, spotted legs

FIRST VERSION: SMALL SIZE
THIRD VARIATION: SATIN FINISH

Colour: Lilac coat, beige frog with large
           spots on head and stripes on legs
Issued: 2001 - 2002

Back Stamp	Beswick Number	Doulton Number	Price			
			U.S. $	Can. $	U.K. £	Aust. $
BP-11a	1157/3	PS1157	450.00	600.00	250.00	650.00

SECOND VERSION: LARGE SIZE
FIRST VARIATION: LILAC BUTTONS

Modeller:	Martyn Alcock
Height:	5", 12.7 cm
Size:	Large
Colour:	Lilac coat, green frog with stripes on legs
Issued:	1994 - 1997

Back Stamp	Beswick Number	Doulton Number	Price			
			U.S. $	Can. $	U.K. £	Aust. $
BP-6b	3372/1	P3372	80.00	110.00	45.00	120.00

Small size, striped legs

SECOND VERSION: LARGE SIZE
SECOND VARIATION: GOLD BUTTONS

Colour: Green frog with stripes on legs, lilac coat with gold buttons
Issued: 1998 in a limited edition of 1,947
Series: Gold edition

Back Stamp	Beswick Number	Doulton Number	Price			
			U.S. $	Can. $	U.K. £	Aust. $
BP-9c	3372/2	PG3372	110.00	150.00	60.00	160.00

Note: Issued, numbered and sold as a pair with Tom Kitten, second version, second variation.

Large size, striped legs

MR. JEREMY FISHER DIGGING™

Modeller:	Ted Chawner
Height:	3 ¾", 9.5 cm
Colour:	Mauve coat, pink waistcoat, white cravat, green frog with brown highlights
Issued:	1988 - 1994

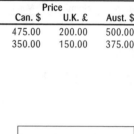

BEATRIX POTTER
"Mr. Jeremy Fisher Digging"
© F. Warne & Co. 1988
Licensed by Copyrights
John Beswick
Studio of Royal Doulton
England

Back Stamp	Beswick Number	Doulton Number	Price			
			U.S. $	Can. $	U.K. £	Aust. $
BP-4	3090	P3090	350.00	475.00	200.00	500.00
BP-6a			275.00	350.00	150.00	375.00

Note: Jeremy Fisher's skin may have dark or light spots.

MR. McGREGOR™

Modeller:	Martyn Alcock
Height:	5 ¼", 13.5 cm
Colour:	Brown hat and trousers, tan vest and pale blue shirt
Issued:	1995 - 2002

ROYAL ALBERT ®
ENGLAND
Mr McGregor
Beatrix Potter
© F. WARNE & CO. 1995
© 1995 ROYAL ALBERT LTD

Back Stamp	Beswick Number	Doulton Number	Price			
			U.S. $	Can. $	U.K. £	Aust. $
BP-6a	3506/1	P3506/1	70.00	95.00	40.00	100.00
BP-10b			80.00	110.00	45.00	120.00

Note: A variation of this figure exists with the right arm at chest height.

MR. TOD™

Modeller:	Ted Chawner
Height:	4 ¾", 12.1 cm
Colour:	Green suit, red waistcoat, dark brown walking stick
Issued:	1988 - 1993

BEATRIX POTTER
"Mr. Tod"
© F. Warne & Co. 1988
Licensed by Copyrights
John Beswick
Studio of Royal Doulton
England

Back Stamp	Beswick Number	Doulton Number	Price			
			U.S. $	Can. $	U.K. £	Aust. $
BP-4	3091/1	P3091/1	450.00	600.00	250.00	650.00
BP-6a			225.00	300.00	125.00	325.00

Note: Variations occur with the head facing right or left, and the base in either green or brown.

MRS. FLOPSY BUNNY™

Modeller:	Arthur Gredington
Height:	4", 10.1 cm
Colour:	1. Dark blue dress, pink bag
	2. Light blue dress, pink bag
Issued:	1965 - 1998

Back Stamp	Beswick Number	Colour Variation	U.S. $	Can. $	U.K. £	Aust. $
				Price		
BP-2	1942	Dark blue	225.00	300.00	125.00	325.00
BP-3a		Dark blue	90.00	120.00	50.00	130.00
BP-3b		Dark blue	70.00	95.00	40.00	100.00
BP-3b		Light blue	70.00	95.00	40.00	100.00
BP-3c		Light blue	110.00	150.00	60.00	165.00
BP-4		Light blue	110.00	150.00	60.00	165.00
BP-6a		Light blue	55.00	70.00	30.00	75.00
BP-10b		Light blue	55.00	70.00	30.00	75.00

MRS. RABBIT™

Modeller:	Arthur Gredington
Height:	4 ¼", 10.8 cm
Size:	Small

FIRST VERSION: SMALL SIZE, UMBRELLA OUT

Colour:	1. Pink and yellow striped dress
	2. Lilac and yellow striped dress
Issued:	1951 - c.1974

Back Stamp	Beswick Number	Colour Variation	U.S. $	Can. $	U.K. £	Aust. $
				Price		
BP-1a	1200/1	Pink		Very Rare		
BP-2		Pink	275.00	350.00	150.00	375.00
BP-2		Lilac	275.00	350.00	150.00	375.00
BP-3a		Lilac	225.00	300.00	125.00	325.00
BP-3b		Lilac	225.00	300.00	125.00	325.00

Note: 1. Due to its small base a gold oval backstamp was used for the bulk of pre-1955 production; the gold circle backstamp is very rare.
2. The BP-1a umbrella colour was pale green but became darker green with the BP-2 and BP-3a.

First version: Umbrella out

**SECOND VERSION: SMALL SIZE
UMBRELLA MOULDED TO DRESS**

Colour:	Lilac and yellow striped dress, red collar and cap, light straw coloured basket
Issued:	c.1975 - 2002

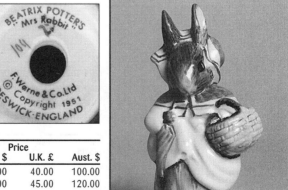

Back Stamp	Beswick Number	Doulton Number	U.S. $	Can. $	U.K. £	Aust. $
				Price		
BP-3b	1200/2	P1200/2	70.00	95.00	40.00	100.00
BP-3c			80.00	110.00	45.00	120.00
BP-4			110.00	150.00	60.00	160.00
BP-6a			70.00	95.00	40.00	100.00
BP-10c			70.00	95.00	40.00	100.00

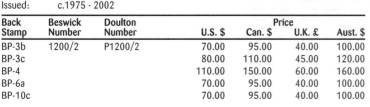

Second version: Umbrella moulded to dress

Brown umbrella point and handle

MRS. RABBIT™

Modeller:	Martyn Alcock
Height:	6 ¼", 15.9 cm
Size:	Large

THIRD VERSION: LARGE SIZE
FIRST VARIATION: BROWN UMBRELLA POINT AND HANDLE

Colour:	White, pink, yellow and green
Issued:	1994 - 1997

ROYAL ALBERT ®
ENGLAND
Mrs Rabbit
Beatrix Potter
© F.WARNE & CO.1993
© 1993 ROYAL ALBERT LTD.

Back Stamp	Beswick Number	Doulton Number	Price			
			U.S. $	Can. $	U.K. £	Aust. $
BP-6b	3398/1	P3398	60.00	85.00	35.00	90.00

Gold umbrella point and handle

THIRD VERSION: LARGE SIZE
SECOND VARIATION: GOLD UMBRELLA POINT AND HANDLE

Colour:	White, pink, yellow and green, gold umbrella point and handle
Issued:	1998 in a limited edition of 1,947
Series:	Gold edition

Back Stamp	Beswick Number	Doulton Number	Price			
			U.S. $	Can. $	U.K. £	Aust. $
BP-9c	3398/2	PG3398	90.00	120.00	50.00	130.00

Note: Issued, numbered and sold as a pair with Foxy Whiskered Gentleman, second version, second variation.

MRS. RABBIT AND BUNNIES™

Modeller:	David Lyttleton
Height:	3 ¾", 9.5 cm
Colour:	Blue dress with white apron, dark blue chair
Issued:	1976 - 1997

BEATRIX POTTER'S
Mrs. Rabbit and Bunnies
F. Warne & Co.Ltd.
© Copyright 1976
BESWICK ENGLAND

Back Stamp	Beswick Number	Doulton Number	Price			
			U.S. $	Can. $	U.K. £	Aust. $
BP-3b	2543	P2543	80.00	110.00	45.00	120.00
BP-3c			110.00	150.00	60.00	160.00
BP-4			110.00	150.00	60.00	160.00
BP-5			175.00	250.00	100.00	275.00
BP-6a			60.00	85.00	35.00	90.00

MRS. RABBIT AND PETER™
FIRST VERSION: SMALL SIZE

Modeller:	Warren Platt
Height:	3 ½", 8.9 cm
Size:	Small
Colour:	Mrs. Rabbit: Pale blue dress, white apron
	Peter: Pale blue coat, yellow buttons
Issued:	1997 - 2002

Back Stamp	Beswick Number	Doulton Number	Price			
			U.S. $	Can. $	U.K. £	Aust. $
BP-6a	3646	P3646	90.00	120.00	50.00	130.00
BP-10b			70.00	95.00	40.00	100.00

First version: Small size

SECOND VERSION: LARGE SIZE

Modeller:	Amanda Hughes-Lubeck
Height:	5 ¼", 13.3 cm
Size:	Large
Colour:	Mrs. Rabbit: Pale blue dress; white apron
	Peter: Pale blue coat with gold buttons
Issued:	1999 in a limited edition of 2,500

Back Stamp	Beswick Number	Doulton Number	Price			
			U.S. $	Can. $	U.K. £	Aust. $
BP-9c	3978	PG3978	170.00	230.00	95.00	250.00

Second version: Large size, gold buttons

MRS. RABBIT COOKING™

Modeller:	Martyn Alcock
Height:	4", 10.1 cm
Colour:	Blue dress, white apron
Issued:	1992 - 1999

Back Stamp	Beswick Number	Doulton Number	Price			
			U.S. $	Can. $	U.K. £	Aust. $
BP-6a	3278	P3278	60.00	85.00	35.00	90.00
BP-10b			70.00	95.00	40.00	100.00

For **Mrs. Rabbit and the Four Bunnies** see the Tableaux Section, page 86.

Small size, diagonal stripes

Small size, plaid

Small size, platinum iron

MRS. TIGGY-WINKLE™

Modeller:	Arthur Gredington
Height:	3 ¼", 8.3 cm
Size:	Small

FIRST VERSION: SMALL SIZE
FIRST VARIATION: GLOSS FINISH, DIAGONAL STRIPES

Colour:	Diagonal striped red-brown and white dress, green and blue striped skirt, white apron
Issued:	1948 - 1974

Back Stamp	Beswick Number	Doulton Number	Price			
			U.S. $	Can. $	U.K. £	Aust. $
BP-1a	1107/1	P1107/1	325.00	425.00	175.00	450.00
BP-2			225.00	300.00	125.00	325.00
BP-3a			115.00	155.00	65.00	165.00

Note: This figurine is also recognizable by the heavily patterned bustle.

FIRST VERSION: SMALL SIZE
SECOND VARIATION: GLOSS FINISH, PLAID

Colour:	Red-brown and white plaid dress, green and blue striped skirt, white apron
Issued:	1972 - 2000

Back Stamp	Beswick Number	Doulton Number	Price			
			U.S. $	Can. $	U.K. £	Aust. $
BP-2	1107/2	P1107/2	175.00	250.00	100.00	275.00
BP-3a			70.00	95.00	40.00	100.00
BP-3b			70.00	95.00	40.00	100.00
BP-3c			70.00	95.00	40.00	100.00
BP-4			80.00	110.00	45.00	120.00
BP-6a			70.00	95.00	40.00	100.00
BP-10c			70.00	95.00	40.00	100.00

FIRST VERSION: SMALL SIZE
THIRD VARIATION: GLOSS FINISH, PLATINUM IRON

Colour:	Red-brown and white dress, green and blue striped skirt, white apron, platinum iron
Issued:	1998 - 1998

Back Stamp	Beswick Number	Doulton Number	Price			
			U.S. $	Can. $	U.K. £	Aust. $
BP-9b	1107/3	PG1107	110.00	150.00	60.00	160.00

FIRST VERSION: SMALL SIZE
FOURTH VARIATION: SATIN FINISH

Colour:	Red-brown and white dress, tan and blue striped skirt, white apron; satin glaze
Issued:	2001 - 2002

Back Stamp	Beswick Number	Doulton Number	Price			
			U.S. $	Can. $	U.K. £	Aust. $
BP-11a	1107/4	PS1107	450.00	600.00	250.00	650.00

MRS. TIGGY-WINKLE™

Modeller:	Amanda Hughes-Lubeck
Height:	4 ½", 11.9 cm
Size:	Large

SECOND VERSION: LARGE SIZE
FIRST VARIATION: CREAMY-BROWN IRON

Colour:	Brown and white striped dress, white apron, creamy-brown iron
Issued:	1996 - 1997

Back Stamp	Beswick Number	Doulton Number	Price			
			U.S. $	Can. $	U.K. £	Aust. $
BP-6b	3437/1	P3437	80.00	110.00	45.00	120.00

Large size, creamy-brown iron

SECOND VERSION: LARGE SIZE
SECOND VARIATION: PLATINUM IRON

Colour:	Brown and white striped dress, white apron, platinum iron
Issued:	1998 in a limited edition of 1,947
Series	Gold edition

Back Stamp	Beswick Number	Doulton Number	Price			
			U.S. $	Can. $	U.K. £	Aust. $
BP-9c	3437/2	PG3437	110.00	150.00	60.00	165.00

Note: Issued, numbered and sold as a pair with Jemima Puddle-Duck, second version, second variation.

For **Mrs. Tiggy-Winkle and Lucie** see the Tableaux Section, page 86.

Large size, platinum iron

MRS. TIGGY-WINKLE BUYS PROVISIONS™

Modeller:	Martin Alcock
Height:	3 ¼", 8.3 cm
Colour:	Pink and white dress, white and brown mob cap
Issued:	2002 - 2002

Back Stamp	Beswick Number	Doulton Number	Price			
			U.S. $	Can. $	U.K. £	Aust. $
BP-11a	4234	P4234	225.00	300.00	125.00	325.00

MRS. TIGGY WINKLE TAKES TEA™

Modeller:	David Lyttleton
Height:	3 ¼", 8.3 cm
Colour:	Pink and white dress, white and brown mob cap
Issued:	1985 - 2002

Back Stamp	Beswick Number	Doulton Number	Price			
			U.S. $	Can. $	U.K. £	Aust. $
BP-3b	2877	P2877	110.00	150.00	60.00	160.00
BP-3c			110.00	150.00	60.00	160.00
BP-4			145.00	190.00	80.00	210.00
BP-6a			60.00	85.00	35.00	90.00
BP-10a			60.00	85.00	35.00	90.00

MRS. TIGGY-WINKLE WASHING™

Modeller:	David Lyttleton
Height:	2 ½", 6.4 cm
Colour:	Brown and white
Issued:	1998 - 2000

Back Stamp	Beswick Number	Doulton Number	Price			
			U.S. $	Can. $	U.K. £	Aust. $
BP-8a	3789	P3789	225.00	300.00	125.00	325.00
BP-10a			70.00	95.00	45.00	100.00

Note: Approximately 1,800 pieces were issued with the BP-8a backstamp.

MRS. TITTLEMOUSE™
STYLE ONE

Modeller:	Arthur Gredington
Height:	3 ½", 8.9 cm
Colour:	White and red striped blouse, blue and white striped skirt
Issued:	1948 - 1993

Back Stamp	Beswick Number	Doulton Number	Price U.S. $	Can. $	U.K. £	Aust. $
BP-1a	1103	P1103	225.00	300.00	125.00	325.00
BP-2			160.00	215.00	90.00	230.00
BP-3a			90.00	120.00	50.00	130.00
BP-3b			90.00	120.00	50.00	130.00
BP-3c			90.00	120.00	50.00	130.00
BP-6a			90.00	120.00	50.00	130.00

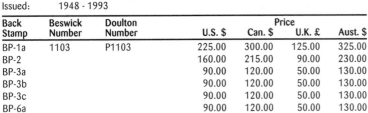

MRS. TITTLEMOUSE™
STYLE TWO

Modeller:	Shane Ridge
Height:	3 ½", 8.9 cm
Colour:	White and red striped blouse, blue and white striped skirt, white apron
Issued:	2000 - 2002

Back Stamp	Beswick Number	Doulton Number	Price U.S. $	Can. $	U.K. £	Aust. $
BP-10a	4015	P4015	70.00	95.00	40.00	100.00

For **My Dear Son Thomas** see the Tableaux Section, page 87.

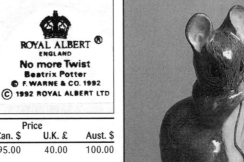

NO MORE TWIST™

Modeller:	Martyn Alcock
Height:	3 ½", 9.2 cm
Colour:	Brown and white mouse
Issued:	1992 - 1997

Back Stamp	Beswick Number	Doulton Number	Price U.S. $	Can. $	U.K. £	Aust. $
BP-6a	3325	P3325	70.00	95.00	40.00	100.00

OLD MR. BOUNCER™

Modeller:	David Lyttleton
Height:	3", 7.6 cm
Colour:	Brown jacket and trousers, blue scarf
Issued:	1986 - 1995

BEATRIX POTTER
"Old Mr. Bouncer"
© Frederick Warne & Co. 1986
Licensed by Copyrights
BESWICK ENGLAND

Back Stamp	Beswick Number	Doulton Number	Price			
			U.S. $	Can. $	U.K. £	Aust. $
BP-3c	2956	P2956	110.00	150.00	60.00	160.00
BP-6a			110.00	150.00	60.00	160.00

OLD MR. BROWN™

Modeller:	Albert Hallam
Height:	3 ¼", 8.3 cm
Colour:	1. Brown owl, red squirrel
	2. Orange owl, red squirrel
Issued:	1963 - 1999

BEATRIX POTTER'S
Old. Mr. Brown
F. WARNE & CO. LTD
COPYRIGHT
BESWICK
ENGLAND

Back Stamp	Beswick Number	Colour Variation	Price			
			U.S. $	Can. $	U.K. £	Aust. $
BP-2	1796	Brown	175.00	250.00	100.00	275.00
BP-3a		Brown	90.00	120.00	50.00	135.00
BP-3b		Brown	90.00	120.00	50.00	135.00
BP-3b		Orange	80.00	110.00	45.00	120.00
BP-3c		Orange	80.00	110.00	45.00	120.00
BP-6a		Orange	60.00	85.00	35.00	90.00
BP-10a		Orange	60.00	85.00	35.00	90.00

OLD MR. PRICKLEPIN™

Modeller:	David Lyttleton
Height:	2 ½", 6.4 cm
Colour:	Brown
Issued:	1983 - 1989

BEATRIX POTTER'S
"Old Mr Pricklepin"
© Frederick Warne P.L.C. 1983
BESWICK ENGLAND

Back Stamp	Beswick Number	Doulton Number	Price			
			U.S. $	Can. $	U.K. £	Aust. $
BP-3b	2767	P2767	175.00	250.00	100.00	275.00
BP-3c			225.00	300.00	125.00	325.00
BP-6a			1,250.00	1,650.00	700.00	1,750.00

For **Peter and Benjamin Picking Apples and Peter and Benjamin Picking Up Onions** see the Tableaux Section, page 87.

PETER AND THE RED POCKET HANDKERCHIEF™

Modeller: Martyn Alcock
Height: 4 ¾", 12.3 cm
Size: Small

FIRST VERSION: SMALL SIZE
FIRST VARIATION: YELLOW BUTTONS

Colour: Light blue jacket with yellow
       buttons, red handkerchief
Issued: 1991 - 1999

Back Stamp	Beswick Number	Doulton Number	Price			
			U.S. $	Can. $	U.K. £	Aust. $
BP-6a	3242	P3242	60.00	85.00	35.00	90.00
BP-10a			60.00	85.00	35.00	90.00

First version: Small size

FIRST VERSION: SMALL SIZE
SECOND VARIATION: GOLD BUTTONS

Colour: Dark blue jacket with gold buttons,
       red handkerchief
Issued: 1997 - 1997

Back Stamp	Beswick Number	Doulton Number	Price			
			U.S. $	Can. $	U.K. £	Aust. $
BP-9d	5190	PG5190	90.00	120.00	50.00	130.00

Note: Peter Rabbit, first version, second variation was commissioned by Petter Rabbit and Friends.

Second version: Small size, gold buttons

Second version: Large size

PETER AND THE RED POCKET HANDKERCHIEF™

Modeller:	Amanda Hughes-Lubeck
Height:	7 ¼", 18.4 cm
Size:	Large

SECOND VERSION: LARGE SIZE
FIRST VARIATION: YELLOW BUTTONS

Colour:	Light blue coat with yellow buttons, red handkerchief
Issued:	1996 - 1997

Back Stamp	Beswick Number	Doulton Number	Price			
			U.S. $	Can. $	U.K. £	Aust. $
BP-6b	3592/1	P3592	80.00	110.00	45.00	120.00

Note: The backstamp on this version reads Peter "with" the Red Pocket Handkerchief.

Second version: Large size, gold buttons

SECOND VERSION: LARGE SIZE
SECOND VARIATION: GOLD BUTTONS

Colour:	Light blue coat with gold buttons, red handkerchief
Issued:	1998 in a limited edition of 1,947
Series:	Gold edition

Back Stamp	Beswick Number	Doulton Number	Price			
			U.S. $	Can. $	U.K. £	Aust. $
BP-9c	3592/2	PG3592	115.00	155.00	65.00	165.00

Note: Issued, numbered and sold as a pair with The Tailor of Gloucester, second version, second variation.

PETER ATE A RADISH™

Modeller:	Warren Platt
Height:	4", 10.1 cm
Colour:	Blue jacket, brown and white rabbit, red radishes
Issued:	1995 - 1998

Back Stamp	Beswick Number	Doulton Number	Price			
			U.S. $	Can. $	U.K. £	Aust. $
BP-6a	3533	P3533	60.00	85.00	35.00	90.00

Note: BP-10b backstamp was reported by Royal Doulton in the backstamp changeover in 1998. We need confirmation that this backstamp was used on an actual issued figure. If it does exist, it is very rare.

PETER IN BED™

Modeller: Martyn Alcock
Height: 2 ¾", 7.0 cm
Colour: Blue, white, pink and green
Issued: 1995 - 2002

Back Stamp	Beswick Number	Doulton Number	Price			
			U.S. $	Can. $	U.K. £	Aust. $
BP-6a	3473	P3473	60.00	85.00	35.00	90.00
BP-10a			60.00	85.00	35.00	90.00

PETER IN THE GOOSEBERRY NET™

Modeller: David Lyttleton
Height: 2", 4.6 cm
Colour: Brown and white rabbit wearing blue jacket, green netting
Issued: 1989 - 1995

Back Stamp	Beswick Number	Doulton Number	Price			
			U.S. $	Can. $	U.K. £	Aust. $
BP-6a	3157	P3157	135.00	175.00	75.00	185.00

PETER IN THE WATERING CAN™

Modeller: Warren Platt
Height: 5", 12.7 cm
Colour: Brown rabbit in a green watering can
Issued: 1999 - 2002

Back Stamp	Beswick Number	Doulton Number	Price			
			U.S. $	Can. $	U.K. £	Aust. $
BP-10a	3940	P3940	70.00	95.00	40.00	100.00

PETER ON HIS BOOK™

Modeller:	Martyn Alcock
Height:	5", 12.7 cm
Colour:	Pale blue jacket, gold buttons, white book
Issued:	2002 - 2002

Back Stamp	Beswick Number	Doulton Number	Price			
			U.S. $	Can. $	U.K. £	Aust. $
BP-11b	P4217	P4217	115.00	155.00	65.00	165.00

Note: Issued to commemorate the 100th anniversary of the book The Tales of Peter Rabbit.

PETER RABBIT™

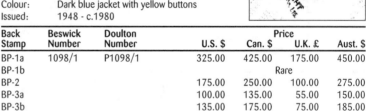

Modeller:	Arthur Gredington
Height:	4 ½", 11.4 cm
Size:	Small

FIRST VERSION: SMALL SIZE
FIRST VARIATION: DEEP BLUE JACKET

Colour:	Dark blue jacket with yellow buttons
Issued:	1948 - c.1980

Back Stamp	Beswick Number	Doulton Number	Price			
			U.S. $	Can. $	U.K. £	Aust. $
BP-1a	1098/1	P1098/1	325.00	425.00	175.00	450.00
BP-1b					Rare	
BP-2			175.00	250.00	100.00	275.00
BP-3a			100.00	135.00	55.00	150.00
BP-3b			135.00	175.00	75.00	185.00

FIRST VERSION: SMALL SIZE; SECOND VARIATION: LIGHT BLUE JACKET

Colour:	Light blue jacket with yellow buttons
Issued:	c.1980 - 2002

Back Stamp	Beswick Number	Base Variation	Price			
			U.S. $	Can. $	U.K. £	Aust. $
BP-3b	1098/2	Short base	70.00	95.00	40.00	100.00
BP-3b		Long base	70.00	95.00	40.00	100.00
BP-3c		Long base	85.00	110.00	45.00	120.00
BP-4		Long base	90.00	120.00	50.00	130.00
BP-5		Long base	110.00	150.00	60.00	160.00
BP-6a		Long base	55.00	70.00	30.00	75.00
BP-10b		Long base	55.00	70.00	30.00	75.00

FIRST VERSION: SMALL SIZE; THIRD VARIATION: LIGHT BLUE JACKET, GOLD BUTTONS

Colour:	Light blue jacket with gold buttons
Issued:	1997 - 1997

Back Stamp	Beswick Number	Doulton Number	Price			
			U.S. $	Can. $	U.K. £	Aust. $
BP-9b	1098/3	PG1098	70.00	95.00	40.00	100.00

FIRST VERSION: SMALL SIZE; FOURTH VARIATION: SATIN FINISH

Colour:	Blue jacket with yellow buttons
Issued:	2001 - 2002

Back Stamp	Beswick Number	Doulton Number	Price			
			U.S. $	Can. $	U.K. £	Aust. $
BP-11a	1098/4	PS1098	450.00	600.00	250.00	650.00

Small size, deep blue jacket

Small size, gold buttons

PETER RABBIT™

Modeller: Martyn Alcock
Height: 6 ¾", 17.1 cm
Size: Large

SECOND VERSION: LARGE SIZE
FIRST VARIATION: YELLOW BUTTONS

Colour: Light blue jacket, yellow buttons
Issued: 1993 - 1997

Back Stamp	Beswick Number	Doulton Number	Price			
			U.S. $	Can. $	U.K. £	Aust. $
BP-6b	3356/1	P3356	70.00	95.00	40.00	100.00
BP-7	100th Anniversary		115.00	155.00	65.00	165.00

Note: The BP-7 backstamp was used only in 1993.

Large size, yellow buttons

SECOND VERSION: LARGE SIZE
SECOND VARIATION: GOLD BUTTONS

Colour: Blue jacket with gold buttons
Issued: 1997 in a limited edtion of 1,947
Series: Gold edition

Back Stamp	Beswick Number	Doulton Number	Price			
			U.S. $	Can. $	U.K. £	Aust. $
BP-9c	3356/2	PG3356	115.00	155.00	65.00	165.00

Note: The second variation of this model was issued, numbered and sold as a pair with Benjamin Bunny, fourth version, fourth variation.

Large size, gold buttons

PETER RABBIT DIGGING™

Modeller: Martyn Alcock
Height: 5", 12.7 cm
Colour: Pale blue jacket
Issued: 2001 - 2002

Back Stamp	Beswick Number	Doulton Number	Price			
			U.S. $	Can. $	U.K. £	Aust. $
BP-11a	P4075	P4075	90.00	120.00	50.00	130.00

PETER RABBIT GARDENING™

Modeller:	Warren Platt
Height:	5", 12.7 cm
Colour:	Blue jacket, brown shovel, basket of carrots
Issued:	1998 - 1999

Back Stamp	Beswick Number	Doulton Number	Price			
			U.S. $	Can. $	U.K. £	Aust. $
BP-10a	3739	P3739	80.00	110.00	45.00	120.00

PETER WITH DAFFODILS™

Modeller:	Warren Platt
Height:	4 ¾", 12.1 cm
Colour:	Light blue coat, yellow daffodils
Issued:	1996 - 1999

Back Stamp	Beswick Number	Doulton Number	Price			
			U.S. $	Can. $	U.K. £	Aust. $
BP-6a	3597	P3597	70.00	95.00	40.00	100.00
BP-10b			70.00	95.00	40.00	100.00

PETER WITH POSTBAG™

Modeller:	Amanda Hughes-Lubeck
Height:	4 ¾", 12.1 cm
Colour:	Light brown rabbit and postbag, lilac jacket trimmed in red
Issued:	1996 - 2002

Back Stamp	Beswick Number	Doulton Number	Price			
			U.S. $	Can. $	U.K. £	Aust. $
BP-6a	3591	P3591	60.00	85.00	35.00	90.00
BP-10b			55.00	70.00	30.00	75.00

PICKLES™

Modeller:	Albert Hallam
Height:	4 ½", 11.4 cm
Colour:	Black face dog with brown jacket and white apron, pink book
Issued:	1971 - 1982

Back Stamp	Beswick Number	Doulton Number	Price			
			U.S. $	Can. $	U.K. £	Aust. $
BP-2	2334	P2334	550.00	725.00	300.00	775.00
BP-3a			400.00	550.00	225.00	575.00
BP-3b			350.00	475.00	200.00	500.00

PIGLING BLAND™

Modeller:	Graham Orwell
Height:	4 ¼", 10.8 cm

FIRST VARIATION: DEEP MAROON JACKET

Colour:	Purple jacket, blue waistcoat, yellow trousers
Issued:	1955 - 1974

Back Stamp	Beswick Number	Doulton Number	Price			
			U.S. $	Can. $	U.K. £	Aust. $
BP-1a	1365/1	P1365/1		Very rare		
BP-2			350.00	475.00	200.00	500.00
BP-3a			275.00	350.00	150.00	375.00
BP-3b			275.00	350.00	150.00	375.00

First variation: Purple jacket

SECOND VARIATION: LILAC JACKET

Colour:	Lilac jacket, blue waistcoat, yellow trousers
Issued:	c.1975 - 1998

Back Stamp	Beswick Number	Doulton Number	Price			
			U.S. $	Can. $	U.K. £	Aust. $
BP-3b	1365/2	P1365/2	80.00	110.00	45.00	120.00
BP-3c			90.00	120.00	50.00	130.00
BP-6a			60.00	85.00	35.00	90.00
BP-10c			60.00	85.00	35.00	90.00

Note: An example is known to exist with a grey jacket, light blue waistcoat, white trousers and tie. (BP-6a).

Second variation: Lilac jacket

PIGLING EATS HIS PORRIDGE™

Modeller:	Martyn Alcock
Height:	4", 10.1 cm
Colour:	Brown coat, blue waistcoat and yellow trousers
Issued:	1991 - 1994

Back Stamp	Beswick Number	Doulton Number	U.S. $	Can. $	U.K. £	Aust. $
BP-6a	3252	P3252	275.00	350.00	150.00	375.00

PIG-WIG™

Modeller:	Albert Hallam
Height:	4", 10.1 cm
Colour:	1. Grey pig, pale blue dress
	2. Black pig, deep blue dress
Issued:	1972 - 1982

Back Stamp	Beswick Number	Colour Variation	U.S. $	Can. $	U.K. £	Aust. $
BP-2	2381	Grey pig	5,750.00	7,800.00	3,250.00	8,000.00
BP-3a		Black pig	450.00	600.00	250.00	625.00
BP-3b		Black pig	450.00	600.00	250.00	625.00

POORLY PETER RABBIT™

Modeller:	David Lyttleton
Height:	3 ¾", 9.5 cm
Colour:	Brown-red and white blanket
Issued:	1976 - 1997

Back Stamp	Beswick Number	Doulton Number	U.S. $	Can. $	U.K. £	Aust. $
BP-3b	2560	P2560	115.00	155.00	65.00	165.00
BP-3c			125.00	170.00	70.00	180.00
BP-4			115.00	155.00	65.00	165.00
BP-6a			80.00	110.00	45.00	120.00

Note: Later models have a lighter brown blanket.

REBECCAH PUDDLE-DUCK™

Modeller:	David Lyttleton
Height:	3 ¼", 8.3 cm
Colour:	White goose, pale blue coat and hat
Issued:	1981 - 2000
Re-Issued:	2002

Back Stamp	Beswick Number	Doulton Number	Price			
			U.S. $	Can. $	U.K. £	Aust. $
BP-3b	2647	P2647	70.00	95.00	40.00	100.00
BP-3c			90.00	120.00	50.00	130.00
BP-4			135.00	175.00	75.00	185.00
BP-6a			70.00	95.00	40.00	100.00
BP-10b			70.00	95.00	40.00	100.00
BP-11a			70.00	95.00	40.00	100.00

RIBBY™

Modeller:	Arthur Gredington
Height:	3 ¼", 8.3 cm
Colour:	White dress with blue rings, white apron, pink and white striped shawl
Issued:	1951 - 2000

Back Stamp	Beswick Number	Doulton Number	Price			
			U.S. $	Can. $	U.K. £	Aust. $
BP-1a	1199	P1199	350.00	475.00	200.00	500.00
BP-2			175.00	250.00	100.00	275.00
BP-3a			90.00	120.00	50.00	130.00
BP-3b			90.00	120.00	50.00	130.00
BP-3c			80.00	110.00	45.00	120.00
BP-6a			60.00	85.00	35.00	90.00
BP-10c			60.00	85.00	35.00	90.00

Note: The name shown on BP-6a and BP-10c is Mrs Ribby.

RIBBY AND THE PATTY PAN™

Modeller:	Martyn Alcock
Height:	3 ½", 8.9 cm
Colour:	Blue dress, white apron
Issued:	1992 - 1998

Back Stamp	Beswick Number	Doulton Number	Price			
			U.S. $	Can. $	U.K. £	Aust. $
BP-6a	3280	P3280	60.00	85.00	30.00	90.00

SALLY HENNY PENNY™

Modeller: Albert Hallam
Height: 4", 10.1 cm
Colour: Brown and gold chicken, black
             hat and cloak, two yellow chicks
Issued: 1974 - 1993

BEATRIX POTTER'S
"Sally Henny Penny"
F. Warne & Co.Ltd.
© Copyright 1974
BESWICK ENGLAND

Back Stamp	Beswick Number	Doulton Number	Price			
			U.S. $	Can. $	U.K. £	Aust. $
BP-3a	2452	P2452	175.00	250.00	100.00	275.00
BP-3b			175.00	250.00	100.00	275.00
BP-3c			160.00	215.00	90.00	230.00
BP-6a			175.00	250.00	100.00	275.00

SAMUEL WHISKERS™

Modeller: Arthur Gredington
Height: 3 ¼", 8.3 cm
Colour: Light green coat, yellow
             waistcoat and trousers
Issued: 1948 - 1995

BEATRIX POTTER'S
Samuel Whiskers
COPYRIGHT
F. WARNE & Co. Ltd.

ROYAL ALBERT ®
ENGLAND
Samual Whiskers
Beatrix Potter
© F. WARNE & CO. 1948
1989 ROYAL ALBERT LTD

Correct   Error

Backstamp Variations

Back Stamp	Beswick Number	Doulton Number	Price			
			U.S. $	Can. $	U.K. £	Aust. $
BP-1a	1106	P1106	400.00	550.00	225.00	575.00
BP-1b					Rare	
BP-2			225.00	300.00	125.00	325.00
BP-3a			115.00	155.00	65.00	165.00
BP-3b			90.00	120.00	50.00	130.00
BP-3c			80.00	110.00	45.00	120.00
BP-4			625.00	850.00	350.00	900.00
BP-6a			90.00	120.00	50.00	130.00

Note: "Samuel" is spelled "Samual" on the BP-4 and BP-6a backstamps.

SIMPKIN™

Modeller: Alan Maslankowski
Height: 4", 10.1 cm
Colour: Green coat
Issued: 1975 - 1983

BEATRIX POTTER'S
"Simpkin"
F. Warne & Co.Ltd.
© Copyright 1975
BESWICK ENGLAND

Back Stamp	Beswick Number	Doulton Number	Price			
			U.S. $	Can. $	U.K. £	Aust. $
BP-3b	2508	P2508	450.00	600.00	250.00	650.00

SIR ISAAC NEWTON™

Modeller: Graham Tongue
Height: 3 ¾", 9.5 cm
Colour: Pale green jacket, yellow
waistcoat with tan markings
Issued: 1973 - 1984

BEATRIX POTTER'S
"Sir Isaac Newton"
F. Warne & Co. Ltd.
© Copyright 1973
BESWICK
MADE IN ENGLAND

Back Stamp	Beswick Number	Doulton Number	Price			
			U.S. $	Can. $	U.K. £	Aust. $
BP-3a	2425	P2425	450.00	600.00	250.00	650.00
BP-3b			550.00	725.00	300.00	775.00

Note: 1. The colour and size of Sir Isaac Newton may vary.
2. Sir Isaac Newton and Mr. Alderman Ptolemy are the only figures with backstamps using the words "Made in England" vice "England."

SQUIRREL NUTKIN™

Modeller: Arthur Gredington
Height: 3 ¾", 9.5 cm
Size: Small

FIRST VERSION: SMALL SIZE
FIRST VARIATION: RED-BROWN SQUIRREL

Colour: Red-brown squirrel, green-brown apple
Issued: 1948 - c.1980

BEATRIX POTTER'S
Squirrel Nutkin
copyright
BESWICK · ENGLAND

Back Stamp	Beswick Number	Doulton Number	Price			
			U.S. $	Can. $	U.K. £	Aust. $
BP-1a	1102/1	P1102/1	350.00	475.00	200.00	500.00
BP-2			225.00	300.00	125.00	325.00
BP-3a			125.00	170.00	70.00	180.00
BP-3b			110.00	150.00	60.00	160.00

Small size, red-brown squirrel

FIRST VERSION: SMALL SIZE
SECOND VARIATION: GOLDEN BROWN SQUIRREL

Colour: Golden brown squirrel, green apple
Issued: c.1980 - 2000

Back Stamp	Beswick Number	Doulton Number	Price			
			U.S. $	Can. $	U.K. £	Aust. $
BP-3b	1102/2	P1102/2	80.00	110.00	45.00	120.00
BP-3c			90.00	120.00	50.00	130.00
BP-6a			55.00	70.00	30.00	75.00
BP-10a			55.00	70.00	30.00	75.00

SECOND VERSION: LARGE SIZE
RED CRAB APPLE, GOLD CORE

Modeller: Amanda Hughes-Lubeck
Height: 5 ¼", 13.3 cm
Size: Large
Colour: Golden brown squirrel, red crab-apple, gold core
Issued: 1999 in a limited edition of 1,947
Series: Gold edition

Back Stamp	Beswick Number	Doulton Number	Price			
			U.S. $	Can. $	U.K. £	Aust. $
BP-9c	3893	PG3893	110.00	150.00	60.00	160.00

Note: The second version of Squirrel Nutkin was issued, numbered and sold as a pair with Hunca Munca Sweeping, second version.

Large size, gold core

SUSAN™

Modeller:	David Lyttleton
Height:	4", 10.1 cm
Colour:	Blue dress, green, pink and black shawl and hat
Issued:	1983 - 1989

BEATRIX POTTER
"Susan"
© F. Warne & Co. 1983
Licensed by Copyrights
BES WICK ENGLAND

Back Stamp	Beswick Number	Doulton Number	Price			
			U.S. $	Can. $	U.K. £	Aust. $
BP-3b	2716	P2716	350.00	475.00	200.00	500.00
BP-3c			350.00	475.00	200.00	500.00
BP-6a			2,700.00	3,600.00	1,500.00	3,700.00

Note: The colour and size of Susan may vary.

SWEET PETER RABBIT™

Modeller:	Shane Ridge
Height:	4 ¾", 12.1 cm
Colour:	Beige and cream rabbit, blue jacket, green and beige base
Issued:	1999 in a special edition of 2,950

BESWICK
Ⓑ
ENGLAND
MADE IN ENGLAND   ™
Sweet Peter Rabbit
Beatrix Potter
© F. WARNE & CO. 1999
© 1999 ROYAL DOULTON
SPECIAL GOLD EDITION OF 2,950
FOR
PETER RABBIT AND FRIENDS
© F.W. and Co. 1999

Back Stamp	Beswick Number	Doulton Number	Price			
			U.S. $	Can. $	U.K. £	Aust. $
BP-10d	3888	P3888	350.00	475.00	200.00	500.00

Note: This figure was commissioned by Peter Rabbit and Friends to commemorate the Year of the Rabbit, 1999.

First variation: Blue striped top

TABITHA TWITCHIT™

Modeller: Arthur Gredington
Height: 3 ½", 8.9 cm

FIRST VARIATION: BLUE STRIPED TOP

Colour: Blue and white striped dress, white apron
Issued: 1961 - 1974

Back Stamp	Beswick Number	Doulton Number	Price			
			U.S. $	Can. $	U.K. £	Aust. $
BP-2	1676/1	P1676/1	325.00	425.00	175.00	450.00
BP-3a			175.00	250.00	100.00	275.00
BP-3b			175.00	250.00	100.00	275.00

Note: Tabitha "Twitchit" is spelled "Twichett" on the BP-3a and BP-3b backstamps.

Second variation: White top

SECOND VARIATION: WHITE TOP

Colour: Blue and white striped dress, white apron
Issued: c.1975 - 1995

Back Stamp	Beswick Number	Doulton Number	Price			
			U.S. $	Can. $	U.K. £	Aust. $
BP-3b	1676/2	P1676/2	125.00	170.00	70.00	185.00
BP-3c			110.00	150.00	60.00	160.00
BP-6a			110.00	150.00	60.00	160.00

Note: 1. BP-3b has Twitchit spelled "Twitchett."
2. The white face became very dark/mottled shortly after the second variation was introduced.

First version: Small size

TABITHA TWITCHIT AND MISS MOPPET™
FIRST VERSION: SMALL SIZE

Modeller:	David Lyttleton
Height:	3 ½", 8.9 cm
Size:	Small
Colour:	Lilac dress, white apron, yellow sponge and hassock
Issued:	1976 - 1993

BEATRIX POTTER'S
Tabitha Twitchit and Miss Moppet
F. Warne & Co.Ltd.
© Copyright 1976
BESWICK ENGLAND

Back Stamp	Beswick Number	Doulton Number	Price			
			U.S. $	Can. $	U.K. £	Aust. $
BP-3b	2544	P2544	175.00	250.00	100.00	275.00
BP-3c			225.00	300.00	125.00	325.00
BP-4			275.00	350.00	150.00	375.00
BP-6a			225.00	300.00	125.00	325.00

Second version: Large size

TABITHA TWITCHIT AND MOPPET™
SECOND VERSION: LARGE SIZE

Modeller:	Martyn Alcock
Height:	5 ½", 14.0 cm
Size:	Large
Colour:	Tabitha Twitchit: Dark purple dress and white apron
	Moppet: Grey striped kitten
	Stool: Yellow with gold legs
Issued:	2000 in a limited edition of 2,000
Series:	Gold edition

Back Stamp	Beswick Number	Doulton Number	Price			
			U.S. $	Can. $	U.K. £	Aust. $
BP-9c	4020	PG4020	145.00	190.00	80.00	200.00

First version, Small size

TAILOR OF GLOUCESTER™
FIRST VERSION: SMALL SIZE

Modeller:	Arthur Gredington
Height:	3 ½", 8.9 cm
Size:	Small
Colour:	Brown mouse, yellow bobbin of red thread
Issued:	1949 - 2002

Back Stamp	Beswick Number	Doulton Number	U.S. $	Price Can. $	U.K. £	Aust. $
BP-1a	1108	P1108	675.00	900.00	375.00	1,000.00
BP-1b				Very rare		
BP-2			145.00	190.00	80.00	200.00
BP-3a			70.00	95.00	40.00	100.00
BP-3b			70.00	95.00	40.00	100.00
BP-3c			70.00	95.00	40.00	100.00
BP-4			90.00	120.00	50.00	130.00
BP-6a			70.00	95.00	40.00	100.00
BP-10c			55.00	70.00	30.00	75.00

Note: Only a very small quantity with the BP-1a backstamp are known to exist.

Second version: Large size

SECOND VERSION: LARGE SIZE
FIRST VARIATION: STANDARD COLOURS

Modeller:	Arthur Gredington
Height:	6", 15.0 cm
Size:	Large
Colour:	Brown mouse, yellow bobbin of red thread
Issued:	1995 - 1997

Back Stamp	Beswick Number	Doulton Number	U.S. $	Price Can. $	U.K. £	Aust. $
BP-6b	3449/1	P3449	80.00	110.00	45.00	120.00

Second version: Large size, gold accents

SECOND VERSION: LARGE SIZE
SECOND VARIATION: GOLD ACCENTS

Colour:	Brown mouse, yellow bobbin of red thread, gold accents
Issued:	1998 in a limited edition of 1,947
Series:	Gold edition

Back Stamp	Beswick Number	Doulton Number	U.S. $	Price Can. $	U.K. £	Aust. $
BP-9c	3449/2	PG3449	110.00	150.00	60.00	160.00

Note: The second version, second variation of this model was issued, numbered and sold as a pair with Peter Rabbit and the Red Pocket Handkerchief, second version, second variation.

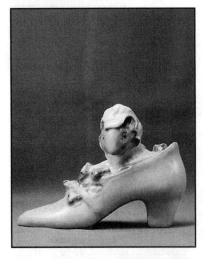

THE OLD WOMAN WHO LIVED IN A SHOE™

Modeller:	Colin Melbourne
Size:	2 ¾" x 3 ¾", 7.0 cm x 9.5 cm
Colour:	Blue shoe
Issued:	1959 - 1998

Back Stamp	Beswick Number	Doulton Number	Price			
			U.S. $	Can. $	U.K. £	Aust. $
BP-2	1545	P1545	200.00	265.00	110.00	280.00
BP-3a			80.00	110.00	45.00	120.00
BP-3b			90.00	120.00	50.00	130.00
BP-3c			90.00	120.00	50.00	130.00
BP-6a			60.00	85.00	35.00	90.00

Note: The lettering of the BP-2 backstanp, which is gold, is frequently not very bright.

THE OLD WOMAN WHO LIVED IN A SHOE KNITTING™

Modeller:	David Lyttleton
Height:	3", 7.5 cm
Colour:	Purple dress, white apron, pale blue shawl and mob cap, yellow chair
Issued:	1983 - 2002

Back Stamp	Beswick Number	Doulton Number	Price			
			U.S. $	Can. $	U.K. £	Aust. $
BP-3b	2804	P2804	175.00	250.00	100.00	275.00
BP-3c			175.00	250.00	100.00	275.00
BP-6a			60.00	85.00	35.00	90.00
BP-10a			60.00	85.00	35.00	90.00

THIS PIG HAD A BIT OF MEAT™

Modeller:	Martyn Alcock
Height:	4", 10.1 cm
Colour:	Lilac dress, grey shawl, white apron and cap, gold-framed spectacles
Issued:	2000 in a special edition of 1,500

Back Stamp	Beswick Number	Doulton Number	Price			
			U.S. $	Can. $	U.K. £	Aust. $
BP-9d	4030	P4030	900.00	1,200.00	500.00	1,300.00

Note: Commissioned by Peter Rabbit and Friends.

THOMASINA TITTLEMOUSE™

Modeller:	David Lyttleton
Height:	3 ¼", 8.3 cm
Colour:	Brown and pink highlights
Issued:	1981 - 1989

Back Stamp	Beswick Number	Doulton Number	Price			
			U.S. $	Can. $	U.K. £	Aust. $
BP-3b	2668	P2668	150.00	200.00	85.00	225.00
BP-3c			175.00	250.00	100.00	275.00
BP-6a			1,075.00	1,450.00	600.00	1,500.00

Note: "Thomasina" is spelled "Tomasina" on the BP-3c backstamp.

Correct   Incorrect

Backstamp Variations

TIMMY TIPTOES™

Modeller:	Arthur Gredington
Height:	3 ¾", 9.5 cm

FIRST VARIATION: RED JACKET

Colour:	1. Brown-grey squirrel, red jacket
	2. Grey squirrel, red jacket
Issued:	1948 - c.1980

Back Stamp	Beswick Number	Colour Variation	Price			
			U.S. $	Can. $	U.K. £	Aust. $
BP-1a	1101/1	Brown-grey	275.00	350.00	150.00	375.00
BP-1a		Grey	275.00	350.00	150.00	375.00
BP-1b			Rare			
BP-2a		Brown-grey	175.00	250.00	100.00	275.00
BP-2a		Grey	175.00	250.00	100.00	275.00
BP-3a		Brown-grey	125.00	170.00	70.00	185.00
BP-3a		Grey	125.00	170.00	70.00	185.00
BP-3b		Brown-grey	110.00	150.00	60.00	165.00
BP-3b		Grey	110.00	150.00	60.00	165.00

First variation: Red jacket

SECOND VARIATION: LIGHT PINK JACKET

Colour:	Grey squirrel, pink jacket
Issued:	c.1970 - 1997

Back Stamp	Beswick Number	Doulton Number	Price			
			U.S. $	Can. $	U.K. £	Aust. $
BP-2a	1101/2	P1101/2	175.00	250.00	100.00	275.00
BP-3b			110.00	150.00	60.00	165.00
BP-3c			110.00	150.00	60.00	165.00
BP-6a			60.00	85.00	35.00	90.00

Note: Second variations will vary in colour in a similar manner as the first.

Second variation: Pink jacket

TIMMY WILLIE FETCHING MILK™

Modeller:	Warren Platt
Height:	3 ¼", 8.3 cm
Colour:	Brown and white mouse, blue milk jug
Issued:	2000 - 2002

Back Stamp	Beswick Number	Doulton Number	Price U.S. $	Can. $	U.K. £	Aust. $
BP-10a	3976	P3976	90.00	120.00	50.00	130.00

TIMMY WILLIE FROM JOHNNY TOWN-MOUSE™

Modeller:	Arthur Gredington
Height:	2 ½", 6.4 cm
Colour:	Brown and white mouse, green or multicoloured base
Issued:	1949 - 1993

Back Stamp	Beswick Number	Doulton Number	Price U.S. $	Can. $	U.K. £	Aust. $
BP-1a	1109	P1109	215.00	285.00	120.00	300.00
BP-2			175.00	250.00	100.00	225.00
BP-3a			90.00	120.00	50.00	130.00
BP-3b			110.00	150.00	60.00	160.00
BP-3c			110.00	150.00	60.00	160.00
BP-4			110.00	150.00	60.00	160.00
BP-6a			80.00	110.00	45.00	120.00

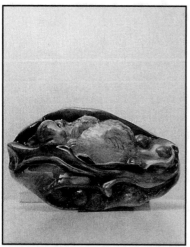

TIMMY WILLIE SLEEPING™

Modeller:	Graham Tongue
Size:	1 ¼" x 3 ¾", 3.2 cm x 9.5 cm
Colour:	Green, white and brown
Issued:	1986 - 1996

Back Stamp	Beswick Number	Doulton Number	Price U.S. $	Can. $	U.K. £	Aust. $
BP-3c	2996	P2996	175.00	250.00	100.00	275.00
BP-6a			90.00	120.00	50.00	135.00

TOM KITTEN™

Modeller: Arthur Gredington
Height: 3 ½", 8.9 cm
Size: Small

FIRST VERSION: SMALL SIZE
FIRST VARIATION: DEEP BLUE OUTFIT

Colour: Tabby kitten wearing deep blue jacket and trousers, dark green base
Issued: 1948 - c.1980

Back Stamp	Beswick Number	Doulton Number	Price			
			U.S. $	Can. $	U.K. £	Aust. $
BP-1a	1100/1	P1100/1	225.00	300.00	125.00	325.00
BP-2			150.00	200.00	85.00	225.00
BP-3a			80.00	110.00	45.00	120.00
BP-3b			80.00	110.00	45.00	120.00

Small size, deep blue colourway

FIRST VERSION: SMALL SIZE
SECOND VARIATION: LIGHT BLUE OUTFIT

Colour: Tabby kitten wearing light blue jacket and trousers, light green base
Issued: c.1980 - 1999

Back Stamp	Beswick Number	Doulton Number	Price			
			U.S. $	Can. $	U.K. £	Aust. $
BP-3b	1100/2	P1100/2	90.00	120.00	50.00	130.00
BP-3c			80.00	110.00	45.00	120.00
BP-4			90.00	120.00	50.00	130.00
BP-6a			45.00	60.00	25.00	65.00
BP-10c			55.00	70.00	30.00	75.00

Small size, light blue colourway

FIRST VERSION: SMALL SIZE
THIRD VARIATION: GOLD BUTTONS

Colour: Tabby kitten wearing light blue jacket and trousers; gold buttons
Issued: 1997 - 1997

Back Stamp	Beswick Number	Doulton Number	Price			
			U.S. $	Can. $	U.K. £	Aust. $
BP-9b	1100/3	PG1100	70.00	95.00	40.00	100.00

Note: The small version of Tom Kitten was issued with two different style bases.

Small size, gold buttons

Large size, yellow buttons

TOM KITTEN™
SECOND VERSION: LARGE SIZE
FIRST VARIATION: YELLOW BUTTONS

Modeller:	Martyn Alcock
Height:	5 ¼", 13.3 cm
Size:	Large
Colour:	Tabby kitten wearing light blue jacket and trousers; light green base
Issued:	1994 - 1997

Back Stamp	Beswick Number	Doulton Number	U.S. $	Can. $	U.K. £	Aust. $
				Price		
BP-8	3405/1	P3405	80.00	110.00	45.00	120.00

SECOND VERSION: LARGE SIZE
SECOND VARIATION: GOLD BUTTONS

Colour:	Light blue jacket and trousers; gold buttons
Issued:	1994 - 1997
Series:	Gold edition

Back Stamp	Beswick Number	Doulton Number	U.S. $	Can. $	U.K. £	Aust. $
				Price		
BP-9c	3405/2	PG3405	110.00	150.00	60.00	165.00

Note: The second variation was issued, numbered and sold as a pair with Mr. Jeremy Fisher, second version, second variation.

TOM KITTEN AND BUTTERFLY™

Modeller:	Ted Chawner
Height:	3 ½", 8.9 cm
Colour:	Blue outfit, yellow hat
Issued:	1987 - 1994

Back Stamp	Beswick Number	Doulton Number	U.S. $	Can. $	U.K. £	Aust. $
				Price		
BP-3c	3030	P3030	325.00	425.00	175.00	450.00
BP-6a			275.00	350.00	150.00	375.00

TOM KITTEN IN THE ROCKERY™

Modeller: Warren Platt
Height: 3 ½", 8.9 cm
Colour: Pale blue jacket and trousers, yellow hat
Issued: 1998 - 2002

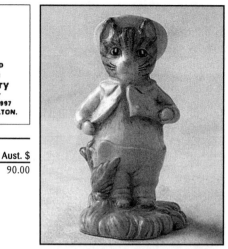

Back Stamp	Beswick Number	Doulton Number	Price			
			U.S. $	Can. $	U.K. £	Aust. $
BP-10a	3719	P3719	60.00	85.00	35.00	90.00

TOM THUMB™

Modeller: Warren Platt
Height: 3 ¼", 8.3 cm
Colour: Rose-pink and yellow chimney
Issued: 1987 - 1997

Back Stamp	Beswick Number	Doulton Number	Price			
			U.S. $	Can. $	U.K. £	Aust. $
BP-3c	2989	P2989	150.00	200.00	85.00	225.00
BP-6a			70.00	95.00	40.00	100.00

TOMMY BROCK™

Modeller: Graham Orwell
Height: 3 ½", 8.9 cm

FIRST VERSION: SPADE HANDLE OUT
FIRST VARIATION: SMALL EYE PATCH

Colour: Blue jacket, pink waistcoat,
             yellow-green trousers
Issued: 1955 - 1974

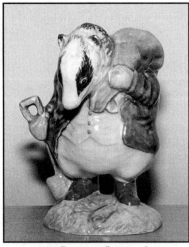

Back Stamp	Beswick Number	Doulton Number	Price			
			U.S. $	Can. $	U.K. £	Aust. $
BP-1a	1348/1	P1348/1	Extremely rare			
BP-2			400.00	550.00	225.00	575.00
BP-3a			325.00	425.00	175.00	450.00

Note: Until the 1972-1974 time period the eye patches curved inward towards the centre of the forehead; they also tended to have a feathery appearance.

Handle out, small eye patch

FIRST VERSION: SPADE HANDLE OUT
SECOND VARIATION: LARGE EYE PATCH

Colour: Blue jacket, pink waistcoat,
             yellow trousers
Issued: c.1970 - c.1974

Back Stamp	Beswick Number	Doulton Number	Price			
			U.S. $	Can. $	U.K. £	Aust. $
BP-2	1348/2	P1348/2	Rare			
BP-3a			350.00	475.00	200.00	500.00

Note: Beginning in 1972-1974 the eye patches, large and small, tended to run straight up towards the ears; also, they were a solid black.

Handle out, large eye patch

Handle in, small eye patch

TOMMY BROCK™

Modeller:	Graham Orwell
Height:	3 ½", 8.9 cm
Colour:	Blue-grey jacket, pink waistcoat, yellow trousers
Issued:	c.1974 - 1976

SECOND VERSION: HANDLE IN
FIRST VARIATION: SMALL EYE PATCH

Back Stamp	Beswick Number	Doulton Number	Price			
			U.S. $	Can. $	U.K. £	Aust. $
BP-3a	1348/3	P1348/3	125.00	170.00	70.00	185.00
BP-3b			110.00	150.00	60.00	165.00

Handle in, large eye patch

SECOND VERSION: HANDLE IN
SECOND VARIATION: LARGE EYE PATCH

Colour:	Blue-grey jacket, red waistcoat, yellow trousers
Issued:	c.1975 - 2002

Back Stamp	Beswick Number	Doulton Number	Price			
			U.S. $	Can. $	U.K. £	Aust. $
BP-3b	1348/4	P1348/4	70.00	95.00	40.00	100.00
BP-3c			90.00	120.00	50.00	130.00
BP-4			90.00	120.00	50.00	130.00
BP-6a			55.00	70.00	30.00	75.00
BP-10a			55.00	70.00	30.00	75.00

Note: The jacket colour varies from pale to dark blue in BP-3b.

TWO GENTLEMEN RABBITS™

Modeller:	Shane Ridge
Height:	5", 12.5 cm
Colour:	Brown, green and red
Issued:	2002 - 2002

Back Stamp	Beswick Number	Doulton Number	U.S. $	Price Can. $	U.K. £	Aust. $
BP-11a	P4210	P4210	325.00	425.00	175.00	450.00

YOCK-YOCK IN THE TUB™

Modeller:	Warren Platt
Height:	3", 7.6 cm
Colour:	Pink pig, brown tub
Issued:	2000 to the present

Back Stamp	Beswick Number	Doulton Number	U.S. $	Price Can. $	U.K. £	Aust. $
BP-10a	3946	P3946	90.00	120.00	50.00	130.00

BEATRIX POTTER

TABLEAUX

TABLEAUX

DUCHESS AND RIBBY™

Modeller:	Martyn Alcock
Length:	7 ¾", 19.7 cm
Colour:	Black, lilac, grey and gold
Issued:	2000 in a limited edition of 1,500
Series:	Tableau

Back Stamp	Beswick Number	Doulton Number	Price			
			U.S. $	Can. $	U.K. £	Aust. $
BP-9d	3983	P3983	350.00	475.00	200.00	500.00

Note: This figure was commissioned by Peter Rabbit and Friends.

FLOPSY AND BENJAMIN BUNNY™

Modeller:	Shane Ridge
Height:	5", 12.7 cm
Colour:	Benjamin: Pink jacket
	Flopsy: Blue dress
Issued:	2001 - 2002

Back Stamp	Beswick Number	Doulton Number	Price			
			U.S. $	Can. $	U.K. £	Aust. $
BP-11b	P4155	P4155	135.00	175.00	75.00	190.00

FLOPSY, MOPSY AND COTTONTAIL™
Style Two

Modeller:	Shane Ridge
Height:	3 ¾", 9.5 cm
Colour:	Brown, pink and white
Issued:	2002 in a limited edition of 1,500 (C of A)
Comm. by:	Doulton-Direct

Back Stamp	Beswick Number	Doulton Number	Price			
			U.S. $	Can. $	U.K. £	Aust. $
BP-11b	–	P4161	225.00	300.00	125.00	325.00

Note: Final piece in the series.

GINGER AND PICKLES™

Modeller:	David Lyttleton
Height:	3 ¾", 9.5 cm
Colour:	Green, white and brown
Issued:	1998 in a limited edition of 2,750
Series:	Tableau

Back Stamp	Beswick Number	Doulton Number	Price			
			U.S. $	Can. $	U.K. £	Aust. $
BP-9d	3790	P3790	350.00	475.00	200.00	500.00

Note: This figure was commissioned by Peter Rabbit and Friends.

HIDING FROM THE CAT™

Modeller:	Graham Tongue
Height:	5", 12.7 cm
Colour:	Brown, blue and grey
Issued:	1998 in a limited edition of 3,500
Series:	Tableau of the Year

Back Stamp	Beswick Number	Doulton Number	Price			
			U.S. $	Can. $	U.K. £	Aust. $
BP-8c	3672	P3672	225.00	300.00	125.00	325.00

KEP AND JEMIMIA™

Modeller:	Martyn Alcock
Length:	4 ½", 11.4 cm
Colour:	Jemima: Pink and blue shawl
	Kep: Brown and white collie
Issued:	2002 in a limited edition of 2,000 (C of A)
Series:	Tableau

Back Stamp	Beswick Number	Doulton Number	Price			
			U.S. $	Can. $	U.K. £	Aust. $
BP-11b	P4901	P4901	275.00	350.00	150.00	375.00

MITTENS, TOM KITTEN AND MOPPET™

Modeller: Amanda Hughes-Lubeck
Length: 7", 17.8 cm
Colour: Pale blue and beige
Issued: 1999 - 1999
Series: Tableau of the Year

Back Stamp	Beswick Number	Doulton Number	Price			
			U.S. $	Can. $	U.K. £	Aust. $
BP-8c	3792	P3792	175.00	250.00	100.00	275.00

MRS. RABBIT AND THE FOUR BUNNIES™

Modeller: Shane Ridge
Height: 4 ½", 11.9 cm
Colour: Mrs Rabbit: Pale blue dress, white apron
Bunnies: Rose cloaks
Peter: Pale blue jacket
Issued: 1997 in a limited edition of 1,997
Series: Tableau of the Year

Back Stamp	Beswick Number	Doulton Number	Price			
			U.S. $	Can. $	U.K. £	Aust. $
BP-8b	3672	P3672	625.00	850.00	350.00	900.00

MRS. TIGGY-WINKLE AND LUCIE™

Modeller: Martyn Alcock
Height: 4", 10.1 cm
Colour: Mrs. Tiggy-Winkle: Brown, pink and cream dress, yellow and blue striped skirt, white apron, red handkerchief, platinum iron and horseshoe,
Lucie: Pink dress, white pinafore
Issued: 1999 in a limited edition of 2,950
Series: Tableau

Back Stamp	Beswick Number	Doulton Number	Price			
			U.S. $	Can. $	U.K. £	Aust. $
BP-9d	3867	P3867	225.00	300.00	125.00	325.00

Note: Commissioned by Peter Rabbit and Friends.

MY DEAR SON THOMAS™

Modeller:	Martyn Alcock
Height:	3 ½", 8.9 cm
Colour:	Blue, white, pink, grey and tan
Issued:	2001 in a limited edition of 3,000

Back Stamp	Beswick Number	Doulton Number	Price U.S. $	Can. $	U.K. £	Aust. $
BP-11b	P4169	P4169	175.00	250.00	100.00	275.00

PETER AND BENJAMIN PICKING APPLES™

Modeller:	Martyn Alcock
Height:	4 ¾", 11.4 cm
Colour:	Blue, brown, tan, red and green
Issued:	2002 in a limited edition of 3,000
Series:	Tabluea

Back Stamp	Beswick Number	Doulton Number	Price U.S. $	Can. $	U.K. £	Aust. $
BP-11b	P4160	P4160	175.00	250.00	100.00	275.00

PETER AND BENJAMIN PICKING UP ONIONS™

Modeller:	Martyn Alcock
Height:	5", 12.7 cm
Colour:	Peter: Pale blue jacket
	Benjamin: Brown jacket
Issued:	2000 in a limited edition of 3,000
Series:	Tableau of the Year

Back Stamp	Beswick Number	Doulton Number	Price U.S. $	Can. $	U.K. £	Aust. $
BP-8c	3930	P3930	225.00	300.00	125.00	325.00

Benjamin Bunny: Large Size, Ears In, Shoes In; First Variation Brown Shoes

BEATRIX POTTER MISCELLANEOUS

CHARACTER JUGS
PLAQUES
STANDS

CHARACTER JUGS

JEMIMA PUDDLE-DUCK
CHARACTER JUG™

Modeller:	Ted Chawner
Height:	4", 10.1 cm
Colour:	Blue, pink and white
Issued:	1989 - 1992

Back Stamp	Beswick Number	Doulton Number	Price			
			U.S. $	Can. $	U.K. £	Aust. $
BP-4	3088	P3088	175.00	250.00	100.00	275.00
BP-6a			135.00	175.00	75.00	185.00

MR. JEREMY FISHER
CHARACTER JUG™

Modeller:	Graham Tongue
Height:	3", 7.6 cm
Colour:	Mauve
Issued:	1987 - 1992

Back Stamp	Beswick Number	Doulton Number	Price			
			U.S. $	Can. $	U.K. £	Aust. $
BP-4	2960	P2960	175.00	250.00	100.00	275.00
BP-6a			135.00	175.00	75.00	185.00

MRS. TIGGY-WINKLE
CHARACTER JUG™

Modeller:	Ted Chawner
Height:	3", 7.6 cm
Colour:	White dress with brown stripes
Issued:	1988 - 1992

Back Stamp	Beswick Number	Doulton Number	Price			
			U.S. $	Can. $	U.K. £	Aust. $
BP-4	3102	P3102	175.00	250.00	100.00	275.00
BP-6a			135.00	175.00	75.00	185.00

OLD MR. BROWN
CHARACTER JUG™

Modeller:	Graham Tongue
Height:	3", 7.6 cm
Colour:	Brown and cream
Issued:	1987 - 1992

Back Stamp	Beswick Number	Doulton Number	Price			
			U.S. $	Can. $	U.K. £	Aust. $
BP-4	2959	P2959	175.00	250.00	100.00	275.00
BP-6a			135.00	175.00	75.00	185.00

PETER RABBIT
CHARACTER JUG™

Modeller:	Graham Tongue
Height:	3", 7.6 cm
Colour:	Brown, blue and white
Issued:	1987 - 1992

Back Stamp	Beswick Number	Doulton Number	Price			
			U.S. $	Can. $	U.K. £	Aust. $
BP-4	3006	P3006	175.00	250.00	100.00	275.00
BP-6a			135.00	175.00	75.00	185.00

TOM KITTEN
CHARACTER JUG™

Modeller:	Ted Chawner
Height:	3", 7.6 cm
Colour:	Brown, blue and white
Issued:	1989 - 1992

Back Stamp	Beswick Number	Doulton Number	Price			
			U.S. $	Can. $	U.K. £	Aust. $
BP-4	3103	P3103	175.00	250.00	100.00	275.00
BP-6a			135.00	175.00	75.00	185.00

PLAQUES

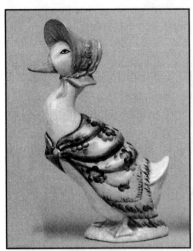

JEMIMA PUDDLE-DUCK PLAQUE™

Modeller: Albert Hallam
Height: 6", 15.2 cm
Colour: White duck, mauve shawl, pale blue bonnet
Issued: 1967 - 1969

Back Stamp	Beswick Number	Doulton Number	Price			
			U.S. $	Can. $	U.K. £	Aust. $
BP-2	2082	P2082	2,100.00	2,800.00	1,200.00	2,900.00

JEMIMA PUDDLE-DUCK WITH FOXY WHISKERED GENTLEMAN PLAQUE™

Modeller: Harry Sales and
             David Lyttleton
Size: 7 ½" x 7 ½",
             19.1 cm x 19.1 cm
Colour: Brown, green, white and blue
Issued: 1977 - 1982

Back Stamp	Beswick Number	Doulton Number	Price			
			U.S. $	Can. $	U.K. £	Aust. $
BP-3	2594	P2594	175.00	250.00	100.00	275.00

MRS. TITTLEMOUSE PLAQUE™

Modeller: Harry Sales
Height: 7 ½" x 7 ½",
             19.1 cm x 19.1 cm
Colour: Blue, pink and green
Issued: 1982 - 1984

Back Stamp	Beswick Number	Doulton Number	Price			
			U.S. $	Can. $	U.K. £	Aust. $
BP-3	2685	P2685	175.00	250.00	100.00	275.00

PETER RABBIT PLAQUE™
First Version

Modeller:	Graham Tongue
Height:	6", 15.2 cm
Colour:	Brown rabbit wearing a blue coat
Issued:	1967 - 1969

Back Stamp	Beswick Number	Doulton Number	U.S. $	Can. $	U.K. £	Aust. $
BP-2	2083	P2083	2,100.00	2,800.00	1,200.00	2,900.00

PETER RABBIT PLAQUE™
Second Version

Modeller:	Harry Sales and David Lyttleton
Size:	7 ½" x 7 ½", 19.1 cm x 19.1 cm
Colour:	Blue, green, brown and orange
Issued:	1979 - 1983

Back Stamp	Beswick Number	Doulton Number	U.S. $	Can. $	U.K. £	Aust. $
BP-3	2650	P2650	175.00	250.00	100.00	275.00

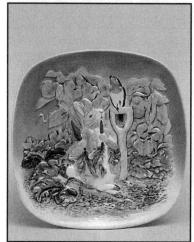

TOM KITTEN PLAQUE™

Modeller:	Graham Tongue
Height:	6", 15.2 cm
Colour:	Brown, blue and white
Issued:	1967 - 1969

Back Stamp	Beswick Number	Doulton Number	U.S. $	Can. $	U.K. £	Aust. $
BP-2	2085	P2085	2,100.00	2,800.00	1,200.00	2,900.00

STANDS

DISPLAY STAND

Modeller:	Andrew Brindley
Size:	12 ½" x 12 ½",
	31.7 cm x 31.7 cm
Colour:	Brown, light brown
Issued:	1970 - 1997

Back Stamp	Beswick Number	Doulton Number	Price			
			U.S. $	Can. $	U.K. £	Aust. $
Beswick	2295	P2295	100.00	135.00	50.00	150.00
Doulton			100.00	135.00	50.00	150.00

TREE LAMP BASE™

Modeller:	Albert Hallam and
	James Hayward
Height:	7", 17.8 cm
Colour:	Brown and green
Issued:	1958 - 1982

Back Stamp	Beswick Number	Doulton Number	Price			
			U.S. $	Can. $	U.K. £	Aust. $
BP-2	1531	P1531	175.00	250.00	100.00	275.00
BP-3			135.00	175.00	75.00	190.00

Note: 1. The above prices are for figureless lamp bases. Those with figures will vary in accordance with the figurine found attached to the base.
2. Lamp bases are known with the black circle backstamp.

BEATRIX POTTER

RESIN STUDIO SCULPTURES

SS1
TIMMY WILLIE™

Designer:	Harry Sales
Modeller:	Graham Tongue
Height:	4 ¼", 10.8 cm
Colour:	Green and brown
Issued:	1985 - 1985
U.S.	**$110.00**
Can.	**$150.00**
U.K.	**£ 60.00**
Aust.	**$165.00**

SS2
FLOPSY BUNNIES™

Designer:	Harry Sales
Modeller:	Graham Tongue
Height:	5", 12.7 cm
Colour:	Browns and green
Issued:	1985 - 1985
U.S.	**$110.00**
Can.	**$150.00**
U.K.	**£ 60.00**
Aust.	**$165.00**

SS3
MR. JEREMY FISHER™

Designer:	Harry Sales
Modeller:	David Lyttleton
Height:	4", 10.1 cm
Colour:	Beige, green and cream
Issued:	1985 - 1985
U.S.	**$110.00**
Can.	**$150.00**
U.K.	**£ 60.00**
Aust.	**$165.00**

SS4
PETER RABBIT™

Designer:	Harry Sales
Modeller:	Graham Tongue
Height:	7", 17.8 cm
Colour:	Browns, blue and green
Issued:	1985 - 1985
U.S.	**$110.00**
Can.	**$150.00**
U.K.	**£ 60.00**
Aust.	**$165.00**

SS11
MRS. TIGGY-WINKLE™

Designer:	Harry Sales
Modeller:	Graham Tongue
Height:	5", 12.7 cm
Colour:	Browns, green, white and blue
Issued:	1985 - 1985
U.S.	**$110.00**
Can.	**$150.00**
U.K.	**£ 60.00**
Aust.	**$165.00**

SS26
YOCK YOCK™
(In The Tub)

Designer:	Harry Sales
Modeller:	David Lyttleton
Height:	2", 5.0 cm
Colour:	Pink and brown
Issued:	1986 - 1986
U.S.	**$325.00**
Can.	**$425.00**
U.K.	**£175.00**
Aust.	**$450.00**

SS27
PETER RABBIT™
(In The Watering Can)

Designer:	Harry Sales
Modeller:	David Lyttleton
Height:	3 ¼", 8.3 cm
Colour:	Browns and blue
Issued:	1986 - 1986
U.S.	**$400.00**
Can.	**$550.00**
U.K.	**£225.00**
Aust.	**$575.00**

BEDTIME CHORUS

1801
PIANIST™

Designer:	Albert Hallam
Height:	3", 7.6 cm
Colour:	Pale blue and yellow
Issued:	1962 - 1969
U.S.	**$175.00**
Can.	**$250.00**
U.K.	**£100.00**
Aust.	**$275.00**

1802
PIANO™

Designer:	Albert Hallam
Height:	3", 7.6 cm
Colour:	Brown and white
Issued:	1962 - 1969
U.S.	**$ 90.00**
Can.	**$120.00**
U.K.	**£ 50.00**
Aust.	**$135.00**

1803
CAT - SINGING™

Designer:	Albert Hallam
Height:	1 ¼", 3.2 cm
Colour:	Ginger stripe
Issued:	1962 - 1971
U.S.	**$ 70.00**
Can.	**$ 95.00**
U.K.	**£ 40.00**
Aust.	**$100.00**

1804
BOY WITHOUT SPECTACLES™

Designer:	Albert Hallam
Height:	3 ½", 8.9 cm
Colour:	Yellow, white and blue
Issued:	1962 - 1969
U.S.	**$225.00**
Can.	**$300.00**
U.K.	**£125.00**
Aust.	**$325.00**

1805
BOY WITH SPECTACLES™

Designer:	Albert Hallam
Height:	3", 7.6 cm
Colour:	Green, white and blue
Issued:	1962 - 1969
U.S.	**$225.00**
Can.	**$300.00**
U.K.	**£125.00**
Aust.	**$325.00**

1824
DOG - SINGING™

Designer:	Albert Hallam
Height:	1 ½", 3.8 cm
Colour:	Tan
Issued:	1962 - 1971
U.S.	**$ 80.00**
Can.	**$110.00**
U.K.	**£ 45.00**
Aust.	**$120.00**

1825
BOY WITH GUITAR™

Designer:	Albert Hallam
Height:	3", 7.6 cm
Colour:	Blue-grey, brown and blue
Issued:	1962 - 1969
U.S.	**$225.00**
Can.	**$300.00**
U.K.	**£125.00**
Aust.	**$325.00**

1826
GIRL WITH HARP™

Designer:	Albert Hallam
Height:	3 ½", 8.9 cm
Colour:	Purple, red and brown
Issued:	1962 - 1969
U.S.	**$225.00**
Can.	**$300.00**
U.K.	**£125.00**
Aust.	**$325.00**

BESWICK BEARS

Beswick Bears

WILLIAM

BB001

BILLY
kicked his ball up high
and it landed "SPLAT"
in the apple pie.
Beswick Bears
BB002

HARRY
slipped – he'd made a mistake.
He dropped the plates,
but saved his cake.
Beswick Bears
BB003

BOBBY
hits his ball in the air,
It comes to land,
he knows not where.
Beswick Bears
BB004

	BB001 WILLIAM™		BB002 BILLY™		BB003 HARRY™		BB004 BOBBY™
Height:	2 ¼", 5.7 cm	Height:	4", 10.1 cm	Height:	3 ¼", 8.3 cm	Height:	4", 10.1 cm
Colour:	Brown bear, blue apron, white and rose book	Colour:	Brown bear, green waistcoat, blue hat, yellow, red and blue ball	Colour:	Brown bear, blue waistcoat, brown hat, white plates	Colour:	Brown bear, blue waistcoat, brown hat, yellow ball, black and red bat
Issued:	1993 - 1993	Issued:	1993 - 1993	Issued:	1993 - 1993	Issued:	1993 - 1993
U.S.	**$ 90.00**	**U.S.**	**$ 75.00**	**U.S.**	**$ 75.00**	**U.S.**	**$ 75.00**
Can.	**$125.00**	**Can.**	**$100.00**	**Can.**	**$100.00**	**Can.**	**$100.00**
U.K.	**£ 50.00**	**U.K.**	**£ 45.00**	**U.K.**	**£ 45.00**	**U.K.**	**£ 45.00**
Aust.	**$135.00**	**Aust.**	**$115.00**	**Aust.**	**$115.00**	**Aust.**	**$115.00**

JAMES
has a gift wrapped up in a bow –
It's a nice little "thank you",
un petit cadeau.
BB005

SUSIE
is playing her new recorder
Any time she'll play to order.
BB006

ANGELA
kneels to pick some flowers
Happily dreaming for
hours and hours.
BB007

CHARLOTTE
tries to keep in the shade,
Twirling her parasol,
a pretty young maid.
BB008

BB005
JAMES™

Height:	3 ¾", 9.5 cm
Colour:	Brown bear, yellow waistcoat, blue hat, blue gift box with pink ribbon
Issued:	1993 - 1993
U.S.	**$ 75.00**
Can.	**$100.00**
U.K.	**£ 45.00**
Aust.	**$115.00**

BB006
SUSIE™

Height:	3 ½", 8.9 cm
Colour:	Brown bear, blue dress, brown recorder
Issued:	1993 - 1993
U.S.	**$ 75.00**
Can.	**$100.00**
U.K.	**£ 45.00**
Aust.	**$115.00**

BB007
ANGELA™

Height:	3 ¼", 8.3 cm
Colour:	Brown bear, yellow dress, white flowers
Issued:	1993 - 1993
U.S.	**$ 75.00**
Can.	**$100.00**
U.K.	**£ 45.00**
Aust.	**$115.00**

BB008
CHARLOTTE™

Height:	4", 10.1 cm
Colour:	Brown bear, pink dress, blue and yellow parasol
Issued:	1993 - 1993
U.S.	**$ 75.00**
Can.	**$100.00**
U.K.	**£ 45.00**
Aust.	**$115.00**

SAM
plays his banjo all day long,
Amusing friends
with a tune and a song.
Beswick Bears
BB009

LIZZY
paints pictures of places and scenes,
Using yellows and blues,
pinks and greens.
Beswick Bears
BB010

EMILY
is in charge of the afternoon tea –
Perhaps she has buns
for you and for me.
Beswick Bears
BB011

SARAH
is sipping her afternoon tea
Perched on the stump
of an old oak tree.
Beswick Bears
BB012

BB009
SAM™
Height: 3 ½", 8.9 cm
Colour: Brown bear, rose
            waistcoat, yellow
            banjo
Issued: 1993 - 1993
U.S. $ 75.00
Can. $100.00
U.K.   £ 45.00
Aust. $115.00

BB010
LIZZY™
Height: 2 ¼", 5.7 cm
Colour: Brown bear, pink
            dress, paint box
Issued: 1993 - 1993
U.S. $ 75.00
Can. $100.00
U.K.   £ 45.00
Aust. $115.00

BB011
EMILY™
Height: 3 ½", 8.9 cm
Colour: Brown bear, pale
            blue dress, brown
            picnic hamper
Issued: 1993 - 1993
U.S. $ 75.00
Can. $100.00
U.K.   £ 45.00
Aust. $115.00

BB012
SARAH™
Height: 3 ¼", 8.3 cm
Colour: Brown bear, green
            dress, white cup
            and saucer
Issued: 1993 - 1993
U.S. $ 75.00
Can. $100.00
U.K.   £ 45.00
Aust. $115.00

JILL BARKLEM'S
BRAMBLY HEDGE

DBH 1
POPPY EYEBRIGHT™
Style One

Designer:	Harry Sales
Modeller:	David Lyttleton
Height:	3 ¼", 8.3 cm
Colour:	Grey-white and pink dress, white apron trimmed with blue flowers
Issued:	1983 - 1997

Doulton Number		Price		
	U.S. $	Can. $	U.K. £	Aust. $
DBH 1	65.00	90.00	40.00	100.00

DBH 2
MR. APPLE™
Style One

Designer:	Harry Sales
Modeller:	David Lyttleton
Height:	3 ¼", 8.3 cm
Colour:	Black trousers, white and blue striped shirt, white apron
Issued:	1983 - 1997

Doulton Number		Price		
	U.S. $	Can. $	U.K. £	Aust. $
DBH 2	65.00	90.00	40.00	100.00

DBH 3
MRS. APPLE™
Style One

Designer:	Harry Sales
Modeller:	David Lyttleton
Height:	3 ¼", 8.3 cm
Colour:	White and blue striped dress, white apron
Issued:	1983 - 1997

Doulton Number		Price		
	U.S. $	Can. $	U.K. £	Aust. $
DBH 3	65.00	90.00	40.00	100.00

BEATRIX POTTER

MRS. TIGGY-WINKLE
TAKES TEA

MRS. TIGGY-WINKLE WASHING

MRS. TITTLEMOUSE
Style One

MRS. TITTLEMOUSE
STYLE TWO

NO MORE TWIST

OLD MR. BOUNCER

OLD MR. BROWN

OLD MR. PRICKLEPIN

PETER AND THE RED POCKET
HANDKERCHIEF

PETER AND THE RED POCKET
HANDKERCHIEF
Small Size, Gold Buttons

PETER AND THE RED POCKET
HANDKERCHIEF
Large Size, Yellow Buttons

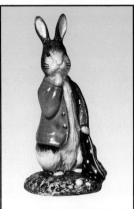

PETER AND THE RED POCKET
HANDKERCHIEF
Large Size, Gold Buttons

BEATRIX POTTER

PETER ATE A RADISH

PETER IN BED

PETER IN THE
GOOSEBERRY NET

PETER IN THE
WATERING CAN

PETER ON HIS BOOK

PETER RABBIT
Small Size, Deep Blue Jacket

PETER RABBIT
Small Size, Light Blue Jacket
Yellow Buttons

PETER RABBIT
Small Size, Light Blue Jacket
Gold Buttons

PETER RABBIT
Large Size, Yellow Buttons

PETER RABBIT DIGGING

PETER RABBIT GARDENING

PETER RABBIT
WITH DAFFODILS

BEATRIX POTTER

PETER WITH POSTBAG

PICKLES

PIGLING BLAND
Deep Maroon Jacket

PIGLING BLAND
Lilac Jacket

PIGLING EATS HIS
PORRIDGE

PIG-WIG

POORLY PETER RABBIT

REBECCAH PUDDLE-DUCK

RIBBY

RIBBY AND
THE PATTY PAN

SALLY HENNY PENNY

SAMUEL WHISKERS

BEATRIX POTTER

SIMPKIN

SIR ISAAC NEWTON

SQUIRREL NUTKIN
Small Size, Red-brown Squirrel

SQUIRREL NUTKIN
Small Size, Golden Brown Squirrel

SQUIRREL NUTKIN
Large Size, Gold Apple Core

SUSAN

SWEET PETER RABBIT

TABITHA TWITCHIT
Blue Striped Top

TABITHA TWITCHIT
White Top

**TABITHA TWITCHIT AND
MISS MOPPET**
Small Size

**TABITHA TWITCHIT AND
MISS MOPPET**
Large Size, Gold Stool Legs

TAILOR OF GLOUCESTER
Small Size

BEATRIX POTTER

TAILOR OF GLOUCESTER
Large Size, Gold Accents

**THE OLD WOMAN WHO
LIVED IN A SHOE**

**THE OLD WOMAN WHO
LIVED IN A SHOE KNITTING**

**THIS PIG HAD A BIT
OF MEAT**

**THOMASINA
TITTLEMOUSE**

TIMMY TIPTOES
Red Jacket

TIMMY TIPTOES
Light Pink Jacket

**TIMMY WILLIE
FETCHING MILK**

**TIMMY WILLIE FROM
JOHNNY TOWN-MOUSE**

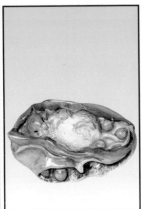

TIMMY WILLIE SLEEPING

TOM KITTEN
Small Size, Deep Blue Outfit

TOM KITTEN
Small Size, Light Blue Outfit
Yellow Buttons

BEATRIX POTTER

TOM KITTEN
Small Size, Light Blue Outfit
Gold Buttons

TOM KITTEN
Large Size, Yellow Buttons

**TOM KITTEN
AND BUTTERFLY**

**TOM KITTEN IN
THE ROCKERY**

TOM THUMB

TOMMY BROCK
Spade Handle Out, Small Eye Patch

TOMMY BROCK
Spade Handle Out, Large Eye Patch

TOMMY BROCK
Spade Handle In, Small Eye Patch

TOMMY BROCK
Spade Handle In, Large Eye Patch

TWO GENTLEMEN RABBITS

YOCK-YOCK IN THE TUB

TABLEAUX

DUCHESS AND RIBBY

FLOPSY AND BENJAMIN BUNNY

FLOPSY, MOPSY AND COTTONTAIL
Style Two

GINGER AND PICKLES

HIDING FROM THE CAT

KEP AND JEMIMA

TABLEAUX

MITTENS, TOM KITTEN AND MOPPET

MRS. RABBIT AND THE FOUR BUNNIES

MRS. TIGGY-WINKLE AND LUCIE

MY DEAR SON THOMAS

PETER AND BENJAMIN PICKING APPLES

PETER AND BENJAMIN PICKING UP ONIONS

BEATRIX POTTER characters, names and images © F. Warne & Co.

DBH 4
LORD WOODMOUSE™
Style One

Designer:	Harry Sales
Modeller:	David Lyttleton
Height:	3 ¼", 8.3 cm
Colour:	Green trousers, brown coat and burgundy waistcoat
Issued:	1983 - 1997

Doulton Number	Price			
	U.S. $	Can. $	U.K. £	Aust. $
DBH 4	65.00	90.00	40.00	100.00

DBH 5
LADY WOODMOUSE™
Style One

Designer:	Harry Sales
Modeller:	David Lyttleton
Height:	3 ¼", 8.3 cm
Colour:	Red and white striped dress, white apron
Issued:	1983 - 1997

Doulton Number	Price			
	U.S. $	Can. $	U.K. £	Aust. $
DBH 5	65.00	90.00	40.00	100.00

DBH 6
DUSTY DOGWOOD™
Style One

Designer:	Harry Sales
Modeller:	David Lyttleton
Height:	3 ¼", 8.3 cm
Colour:	Dark grey suit, rose-pink waistcoat
Issued:	1984 - 1995

Doulton Number	Price			
	U.S. $	Can. $	U.K. £	Aust. $
DBH 6	75.00	100.00	45.00	110.00

DBH 7
WILFRED TOADFLAX™
Style One

Designer:	Harry Sales
Modeller:	David Lyttleton
Height:	3 ¼", 8.3 cm
Colour:	Grey overalls, red and white striped shirt
Issued:	1983 - 1997

Doulton Number	Price			
	U.S. $	Can. $	U.K. £	Aust. $
DBH 7	90.00	125.00	50.00	135.00

DBH 8
PRIMROSE WOODMOUSE™

Designer:	Harry Sales
Modeller:	David Lyttleton
Height:	3 ¼", 8.3 cm
Colour:	Yellow dress with white apron
Issued:	1983 - 1997

Doulton Number	Price			
	U.S. $	Can. $	U.K. £	Aust. $
DBH 8	90.00	125.00	50.00	135.00

DBH 9
OLD MRS. EYEBRIGHT™
Style One

Designer:	Harry Sales
Modeller:	David Lyttleton
Height:	3 ¼", 8.3 cm
Colour:	Mauve skirt, white and pink striped shawl, white apron
Issued:	1984 - 1995

Doulton Number	Price			
	U.S. $	Can. $	U.K. £	Aust. $
DBH 9	135.00	175.00	75.00	190.00

DBH 10A
MR. TOADFLAX™
Style One, First Version (Tail at front, with cushion)

Designer: Harry Sales
Modeller: David Lyttleton
Height: 3 ¼", 8.3 cm
Colour: Blue and white striped shirt,
            pink trousers, burgundy braces,
            multicoloured patchwork quilt
Issued: 1984 - 1984

Doulton Number	Price			
	U.S. $	Can. $	U.K. £	Aust. $
DBH 10A	1,700.00	2,300.00	950.00	2,400.00

DBH 10B
MR. TOADFLAX™
Style One, Second Version (Tail at back, without cushion)

Designer: Harry Sales
Modeller: David Lyttleton
Height: 3 ¼", 8.3 cm
Colour: Blue and white striped shirt,
            pink trousers, burgundy braces
Issued: 1984 - 1985

Doulton Number	Price			
	U.S. $	Can. $	U.K. £	Aust. $
DBH 10B	500.00	650.00	275.00	700.00

DBH 10C
MR. TOADFLAX™
Style One, Third Version (Tail at back, with cushion)

Designer: Harry Sales
Modeller: David Lyttleton
Height: 3 ¼", 8.3 cm
Colour: Blue and white striped shirt, lilac trousers,
            burgundy braces, multicoloured patchwork
            cushion
Issued: 1985 - 1997

Doulton Number	Price			
	U.S. $	Can. $	U.K. £	Aust. $
DBH 10C	75.00	100.00	45.00	110.00

Note: For further illustrations see page 124.

DBH 11
MRS. TOADFLAX™

Designer:	Harry Sales
Modeller:	David Lyttleton
Height:	3 ¼", 8.3 cm
Colour:	Green and white striped dress, white apron
Issued:	1985 - 1995

Doulton Number	Price			
	U.S. $	Can. $	U.K. £	Aust. $
DBH 11	115.00	150.00	65.00	165.00

Note: The contents of the bowl may vary in colour.

DBH 12
CATKIN™

Designer:	Harry Sales
Modeller:	David Lyttleton
Height:	3 ¼", 8.3 cm
Colour:	Yellow dress and white apron
Issued:	1985 - 1994

Doulton Number	Price			
	U.S. $	Can. $	U.K. £	Aust. $
DBH 12	175.00	250.00	100.00	275.00

DBH 13
OLD VOLE™

Designer:	Harry Sales
Modeller:	David Lyttleton
Height:	3 ¼", 8.3 cm
Colour:	Green jacket, blue trousers, yellow waistcoat
Issued:	1985 - 1992

Doulton Number	Price			
	U.S. $	Can. $	U.K. £	Aust. $
DBH 13	400.00	550.00	225.00	600.00

DBH 14
BASIL™
Style One

Designer:	Harry Sales
Modeller:	David Lyttleton
Height:	3 ¼", 8.3 cm
Colour:	Brown waistcoat, green and white striped trousers
Issued:	1985 - 1992

Doulton Number	Price			
	U.S. $	Can. $	U.K. £	Aust. $
DBH 14	350.00	475.00	200.00	525.00

DBH 15
MRS. CRUSTYBREAD™

Designer:	Graham Tongue
Modeller:	Ted Chawner
Height:	3 ¼", 8.3 cm
Colour:	Yellow dress, white apron and cap
Issued:	1987 - 1994

Doulton Number	Price			
	U.S. $	Can. $	U.K. £	Aust. $
DBH 15	350.00	475.00	200.00	525.00

DBH 16
CLOVER™

Designer:	Graham Tongue
Modeller:	Graham Tongue
Height:	3 ¼", 8.3 cm
Colour:	Burgundy dress, white apron
Issued:	1987 - 1997

Doulton Number	Price			
	U.S. $	Can. $	U.K. £	Aust. $
DBH 16	70.00	95.00	40.00	100.00

DBH 17
TEASEL™

Designer:	Graham Tongue
Modeller:	Ted Chawner
Height:	3 ¼", 8.3 cm
Colour:	Blue-grey dungarees, blue and white striped shirt
Issued:	1987 - 1992

Doulton Number	Price			
	U.S. $	Can. $	U.K. £	Aust. $
DBH 17	400.00	550.00	225.00	600.00

DBH 18
STORE STUMP MONEY BOX™

Designer:	Martyn Alcock
Height:	3 ¼", 8.3 cm
Colour:	Browns
Issued:	1987 - 1989

Doulton Number	Price			
	U.S. $	Can. $	U.K. £	Aust. $
DBH 18	350.00	475.00	200.00	525.00

DBH 19
LILY WEAVER™
Style One

Designer:	Graham Tongue
Modeller:	Ted Chawner
Height:	3 ¼", 8.3 cm
Colour:	White, green and mauve
Issued:	1988 - 1993

Doulton Number	Price			
	U.S. $	Can. $	U.K. £	Aust. $
DBH 19	325.00	425.00	175.00	475.00

DBH 20
FLAX WEAVER™
Style One

Designer: Graham Tongue
Modeller: Ted Chawner
Height: 3 ¼", 8.3 cm
Colour: Grey trousers, grey and white striped shirt
Issued: 1988 - 1993

Doulton Number	Price			
	U.S. $	Can. $	U.K. £	Aust. $
DBH 20	350.00	475.00	200.00	525.00

DBH 21
CONKER™

Designer: Graham Tongue
Modeller: Ted Chawner
Height: 3 ¼", 8.3 cm
Colour: Green jacket, yellow waistcoat,
                  green striped trousers
Issued: 1988 - 1994

Doulton Number	Price			
	U.S. $	Can. $	U.K. £	Aust. $
DBH 21	350.00	475.00	200.00	525.00

DBH 22
PRIMROSE ENTERTAINS™

Designer: Graham Tongue
Modeller: Alan Maslankowski
Height: 3 ¼", 8.3 cm
Colour: Green and yellow dress
Issued: 1990 - 1995

Doulton Number	Price			
	U.S. $	Can. $	U.K. £	Aust. $
DBH 22	175.00	225.00	100.00	250.00

DBH 23
WILFRED ENTERTAINS™

Designer:	Graham Tongue
Modeller:	Alan Maslankowski
Height:	3 ¼", 8.3 cm
Colour:	Burgundy and yellow outfit, black hat
Issued:	1990 - 1995

Doulton Number	Price			
	U.S. $	Can. $	U.K. £	Aust $
DBH 23	150.00	200.00	85.00	225.00

DBH 24
MR. SALTAPPLE™
Style One

Designer:	Graham Tongue
Modeller:	Warren Platt
Height:	3 ¼", 8.3 cm
Colour:	Blue and white striped outfit, beige base
Issued:	1993 - 1997

Doulton Number	Price			
	U.S. $	Can. $	U.K. £	Aust. $
DBH 24	85.00	125.00	50.00	135.00

DBH 25
MRS. SALTAPPLE™
Style One

Designer:	Graham Tongue
Modeller:	Warren Platt
Height:	3 ¼", 8.3 cm
Colour:	Rose and cream dress, beige hat and base
Issued:	1993 - 1997

Doulton Number	Price			
	U.S. $	Can. $	U.K. £	Aust. $
DBH 25	85.00	125.00	50.00	135.00

DBH 26
DUSTY AND BABY™

Designer:	Graham Tongue
Modeller:	Martyn Alcock
Height:	3 ¾", 9.5 cm
Colour:	Dusty: Blue striped shirt, beige dungarees
	Baby: White gown
Issued:	1995 - 1997

Doulton	Price			
Number	U.S. $	Can. $	U.K. £	Aust. $
DBH 26	85.00	125.00	50.00	135.00

DBH 30
THE ICE BALL™

Designer:	Shane Ridge
Modeller:	Shane Ridge
Height:	4 ¼", 10.8 cm
Colour:	Green, yellow, pink and white
Issued:	2000 in a limited edition of 3,000 (C of A)
Series:	Tableau

Doulton	Price			
Number	U.S. $	Can. $	U.K. £	Aust. $
DBH 30	175.00	250.00	100.00	300.00

DBH 31
LORD WOODMOUSE™
Style Two

Designer:	Shane Ridge
Modeller:	Shane Ridge
Height:	4 ¼", 10.8 cm
Colour:	Brown, salmon, black, red and yellow
Issued:	2000 - 2002

Doulton	Price			
Number	U.S. $	Can. $	U.K. £	Aust. $
DBH 31	80.00	100.00	40.00	110.00

DBH 32
LADY WOODMOUSE™
Style Two

Designer: Warren Platt
Modeller: Warren Platt
Height: 4 ¼", 10.8 cm
Colour: White, pale blue, red and yellow
Issued: 2000 - 2002

Doulton Number	Price			
	U.S. $	Can. $	U.K. £	Aust. $
DBH 32	80.00	100.00	40.00	110.00

DBH 33
PRIMROSE PICKING BERRIES™

Designer: Shane Ridge
Modeller: Shane Ridge
Height: 3 ½", 8.9 cm
Colour: Yellow, white and purple
Issued: 2000 - 2002

Doulton Number	Price			
	U.S. $	Can. $	U.K. £	Aust. $
DBH 33	55.00	70.00	30.00	75.00

DBH 34
WILFRED CARRIES THE PICNIC™

Designer: Shane Ridge
Modeller: Shane Ridge
Height: 3 ½", 8.9 cm
Colour: Blue, brown and red
Issued: 2000 - 2002

Doulton Number	Price			
	U.S. $	Can. $	U.K. £	Aust. $
DBH 34	55.00	70.00	30.00	75.00

DBH 35
WILFRED AND THE TOY CHEST (Money Box)™

Designer:	Martyn Alcock
Modeller:	Martyn Alcock
Height:	3 ¾", 9.5 cm
Colour:	Green, yellow, red and black
Issued:	2000 - 2002

| Doulton Number | Price | | | |
	U.S. $	Can. $	U.K. £	Aust. $
DBH 35	125.00	175.00	70.00	185.00

DBH 36
POPPY EYEBRIGHT™
Style Two

Designer:	Warren Platt
Modeller:	Warren Platt
Height:	4", 10.1 cm
Colour:	White skirt with red polka-dot; blue blouse; white apron
Issued:	2001 - 2002

| Doulton Number | Price | | | |
	U.S. $	Can. $	U.K. £	Aust. $
DBH 36	75.00	100.00	40.00	110.00

DBH 37
DUSTY DOGWOOD™
Style Two

Designer:	Martyn Alcock
Modeller:	Martyn Alcock
Height:	4", 10.1 cm
Colour:	Blue and white striped shirt; white, yellow and orange pants; white apron and neckerchief, tan sack
Issued:	2001 - 2002

| Doulton Nunber | Price | | | |
	U.S. $	Can. $	U.K. £	Aust. $
DBH 37	75.00	100.00	40.00	110.00

DBH 38
BASIL™
Style Two

Designer:	Shane Ridge
Modeller:	Shane Ridge
Height:	3 ½", 8.9 cm
Colour:	Red waistcoat, green and white striped trousers
Issued:	2001 - 2002

Doulton Number	Price			
	U.S. $	Can. $	U.K. £	Aust. $
DBH 38	75.00	100.00	40.00	110.00

DBH 39
MR. SALTAPPLE™
Style Two

Designer:	Shane Ridge
Modeller:	Shane Ridge
Height:	4", 10.1 cm
Colour:	Blue shirt, brown overalls and basket, green neckerchief
Issued:	2001 - 2002
Series:	Sea Story

Doulton Number	Price			
	U.S. $	Can. $	U.K. £	Aust. $
DBH 39	75.00	100.00	40.00	110.00

DBH 40
MRS. SALTAPPLE™
Style Two

Designer:	Martyn Alcock
Modeller:	Martyn Alcock
Height:	3 ½", 8.9 cm
Colour:	Lilac and white dress; pale yellow bonnet with purple ribbon; brown basket
Issued:	2001 - 2002
Series:	Sea Story

Doulton Number	Price			
	U.S. $	Can. $	U.K. £	Aust. $
DBH 40	75.00	100.00	40.00	110.00

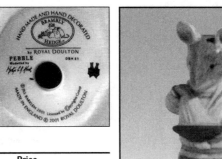

DBH 41
PEBBLE™

Designer:	Martyn Alcock
Modeller:	Martyn Alcock
Height:	3 ¼", 8.3 cm
Colour:	Blue and white striped sailor suit; red boat
Issued:	2001 - 2002
Series:	Sea Story

Doulton Number	Price			
	U.S. $	Can. $	U.K. £	Aust. $
DBH 41	60.00	85.00	35.00	95.00

DBH 42
SHELL™

Designer:	Warren Platt
Modeller:	Warren Platt
Height:	3 ½", 8.9 cm
Colour:	Pink and white dress; pale yellow bonnet
Issued:	2001 - 2002
Series:	Sea Story

Doulton Number	Price			
	U.S. $	Can. $	U.K. £	Aust. $
DBH 42	60.00	85.00	35.00	95.00

DBH 43
SHRIMP™

Designer:	Warren Platt
Modeller:	Warren Platt
Height:	3", 7.6 cm
Colour:	White dress and hat, pink ribbons
Issued:	2001 - 2002
Series:	Sea Story

Doulton Number	Price			
	U.S. $	Can. $	U.K. £	Aust. $
DBH 43	60.00	85.00	35.00	95.00

DBH 44
THE BRIDE AND GROOM™

Designer:	Martyn Alcock
Modeller:	Martyn Alcock
Height:	4 ¼", 10.8 cm
Colour:	Bride: (Poppy Eyebright) White skirt, pink and white striped sleeves, white apron trimmed with flowers; multicoloured bouquet
	Groom: (Dusty Dogwood) Dark grey suit, lavender waistcoat
Issued:	2001 - 2002

Doulton Number		Price		
	U.S. $	Can. $	U.K. £	Aust. $
DBH 44	135.00	175.00	75.00	200.00

DBH 45
HAPPY BIRTHDAY WILFRED™

Designer:	Martyn Alcock
Modeller:	Martyn Alcock
Height:	3", 7.6 cm
Colour:	Multicoloured quilt, brown bed; brown mouse wearing red and white striped sweater; pink and white table cloth
Issued:	2001 in a limited edition of 3,000 (C of A)
Series:	Tableau

Doulton Number		Price		
	U.S. $	Can. $	U.K. £	Aust. $
DBH 45	225.00	300.00	125.00	325.00

DBH 46
MR. TOADFLAX™
Style Two

Designer:	Warren Platt
Modeller:	Warren Platt
Height:	3 ¼", 8.3 cm
Colour:	Mauve trousers, blue and white striped shirt; red suspenders
Issued:	2002 - 2002

Doulton Number		Price		
	U.S. $	Can. $	U.K. £	Aust. $
DBH 46	75.00	100.00	40.00	110.00

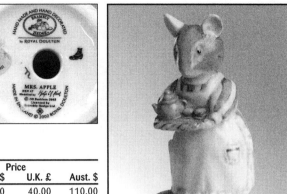

DBH 47
MRS. APPLE™
Style Two

Designer:	Martyn Alcock
Modeller:	Martyn Alcock
Height:	4", 10.1 cm
Colour:	Blue and white striped dress; white apron; green tea set
Issued:	2002 - 2002

Doulton Number	Price			
	U.S. $	Can. $	U.K. £	Aust. $
DBH 47	75.00	100.00	40.00	110.00

DBH 48
HEADING HOME™

Designer:	Martyn Alcock
Modeller:	Martyn Alcock
Height:	3 ½", 8.9 cm
Colour:	Blue and white striped dress; white apron; yellow straw hat; brown wheel barrow
Issued:	2003 to the present
Series:	Spring Story

Doulton Number	Price			
	U.S. $	Can. $	U.K. £	Aust. $
DBH 48	–	–	35.00	–

DBH 49
WILFRED'S BIRTHDAY CAKE™

Designer:	Warren Platt
Modeller:	Warren Platt
Height:	3 ¼", 8.3 cm
Colour:	Red and white striped shirt; blue overalls; pink and white cake
Issued:	2003 to the present
Series:	Spring Story

Doulton Number	Price			
	U.S. $	Can. $	U.K. £	Aust. $
DBH 49	–	–	25.00	–

DBH 50
WHERE ARE BASIL'S TROUSERS?™
Height: 3 ¼", 8.3 cm
Colour: Multicoloured quilt and cushion;
             pink sofa; brown table
Issued: 2003 to the present
Series: Spring Story

Doulton Number	Price			
	U.S. $	Can. $	U.K. £	Aust. $
DBH 50	–	–	35.00	–

DBH 51
DUSTY'S BUNS™
Height: 3 ½", 8.9 cm
Colour: Blue and white striped shirt; yellow trousers,
             white apron and neckerchief
Issued: 2003 to the present
Series: Spring Story

Doulton Number	Price			
	U.S. $	Can. $	U.K. £	Aust. $
DBH 51	–	–	25.00	–

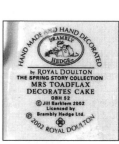

DBH 52
MRS. TOADFLAX DECORATES CAKE™
Height: 3 ¾", 9.5 cm
Colour: Cream dress with orange and yellow
             stars; cream apron; pink and white
             cake; tan table
Issued: 2003 to the present
Series: Spring Story

Doulton Number	Price			
	U.S. $	Can. $	U.K. £	Aust. $
DBH 52	–	–	40.00	–

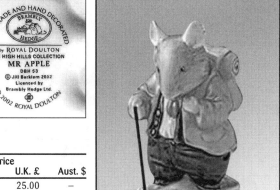

DBH 53
MR. APPLE™
Style Two

Height:	3 ½", 8.9 cm
Colour:	Black trousers and waistcoat; blue and white striped shirt; red neckerchief; brown jacket; yellow knapsack
Issued:	2003 to the present
Series:	High Hills Collection

Doulton Number	U.S. $	Can. $	Price U.K. £	Aust. $
DBH 53	–	–	25.00	–

DBH 54
LILY WEAVER™
Style Two

Height:	3 ¾", 9.5 cm
Colour:	Brown coat, yellow dress and knapsack, straw hat, brown basket
Issued:	2003 to the present
Series:	High Hills Collection

Doulton Number	U.S. $	Can. $	Price U.K. £	Aust. $
DBH 54	–	–	25.00	–

DBH 55
FLAX WEAVER™
Style Two

Height:	4 ¼", 10.8 cm
Colour:	Blue jacket and trousers; orange and red striped shirt; red neckerchief
Issued:	2003 to the present
Series:	High Hills Collection

Doulton Number	U.S. $	Can. $	Price U.K. £	Aust. $
DBH 55	–	–	25.00	–

DBH 56
WILFRED TOADFLAX™
Style Two

Height:	2 ½", 6.4 cm
Colour:	Blue overalls, red and white striped shirt and hat; purple coat; yellow knapsack
Issued:	2003 to the present
Series:	High Hills Collection

Doulton Number	Price			
	U.S. $	Can. $	U.K. £	Aust. $
DBH 56	–	–	25.00	–

DBH 57
ON THE LEDGE™

Height:	4 ¾", 12.1 cm
Colour:	Wilfred: Purple coat, blue overalls; red and white striped shirt and hat
	Mr. Apple: Tan coat, black trousers and waistcoat; blue and white striped shirt; red neckerchief
Issued:	2003 to the present
Series:	High Hills Collection

Doulton Number	Price			
	U.S. $	Can. $	U.K. £	Aust. $
DBH 57	–	–	40.00	–

DBH58
LILY WEAVER SPINNING™

Height:	4 ¼", 10.8 cm
Colour:	Mustard skirt, brown top, pink, yellow and white striped sleeves; white apron, cap and neckerchief; brown spinning wheel
Issued:	2003 to the present
Series:	High Hills Collection

Doulton Number	Price			
	U.S. $	Can. $	U.K. £	Aust. $
DBH 58	–	–	40.00	–

DBH 59
TEA AT HORNBEAM TREE™

Height:	4", 10.1 cm
Colour:	White skirt with yellow and orange design, green blouse with grey dots, white apron, white bonnet with yellow ribbon, tray with blue and white striped crockery
Issued:	2003 to the present
Series:	High Hills Collection

Doulton Number		Price			
		U.S. $	Can. $	U.K. £	Aust. $
DBH 59		–	–	25.00	–

DBH 60
A CHEERFUL BLAZE™

Height:	3 ½", 8.9 cm
Colour:	Browns, green, red, and blue
Issued:	2003 to the present
Series:	High Hills Collection

Doulton Number		Price			
		U.S. $	Can. $	U.K. £	Aust. $
DBH 60		–	–	50.00	–

DBH 61
SHOOTING THE RAPIDS™

Height:	3 ¾", 9.5 cm
Colour:	Browns, purple, blues and white
Issued:	2003 in a limited edition of 2,000
Series:	High Hills Collection

Doulton Number		Price			
		U.S. $	Can. $	U.K. £	Aust. $
DBH 61		–	–	65.00	–

DBH 62
OLD MRS. EYEBRIGHT™
Style Two

Height: 3 ¾", 9.5 cm
Colour: Pink, purple and brown
Issued: 2004 to the present
Series: Autumn Collection

| Doulton | Price | | | |
Number	U.S. $	Can. $	U.K. £	Aust. $
DBH 62	75.00	100.00	40.00	110.00

DBH 63
YOU'RE SAFE™

Height: 4", 10.1 cm
Colour: Green, pink and grey
Issued: 2004 to the present
Series: Autumn Collection

| Doulton | Price | | | |
Number	U.S. $	Can. $	U.K. £	Aust. $
DBH 63	–	–	35.00	–

DBH 64
IN THE WOODS™

Height: 4", 10.1 cm
Colour: Pink, blue and brown
Issued: 2004 to the present
Series: Autumn Collection

| Doulton | Price | | | |
Number	U.S. $	Can. $	U.K. £	Aust. $
DBH 64	–	–	25.00	–

DBH 65
IN THE BRAMBLES™

Height:	3 ½", 8.9 cm
Colour:	Yellow, brown, red and green
Issued:	2004 to the present
Series:	Autumn Collection

Doulton Number	Price			
	U.S. $	Can. $	U.K. £	Aust. $
DBH 65	–	–	35.00	–

DBH 66
OFF TO PICK MUSHROOMS™

Height:	4 ¼", 10.8 cm
Colour:	Pink, brown, red and green
Issued:	2004 to the present
Series:	Autumn Collection

Doulton Number	Price			
	U.S. $	Can. $	U.K. £	Aust. $
DBH 66	–	–	40.00	–

DBH 67
LET'S MAKE A SNOWMOUSE™

Height:	3 ½", 8.9 cm
Colour:	Grey, red and brown
Issued:	2004 to the present
Series:	Winter Story

Doulton Number	Price			
	U.S. $	Can. $	U.K. £	Aust. $
DBH 67	–	–	27.00	–

DBH 68
HOT BUTTERED TOAST FOR BREAKFAST™

Height:	7", 17.8 cm
Colour:	Pink, white, brown, grey, yellow and red
Issued:	2004 to the present
Series:	Winter Story

Doulton Number		Price			
		U.S. $	Can. $	U.K. £	Aust. $
DBH 68		–	–	35.00	–

DBH 69
HOME FOR SUPPER™

Height:	4 ¼", 10.8 cm
Colour:	Browns, grey, dark purple and red
Issued:	2004 to the present
Series:	Winter Story

Doulton Number		Price			
		U.S. $	Can. $	U.K. £	Aust. $
DBH 69		–	–	35.00	–

THE CAT'S CHORUS

CC1
PURRFECT PITCH™

Modeller:	Shane Ridge
Height:	4", 10.1 cm
Colour:	White cat; black dress and hair, red gloves and shoes
Issued:	1998 - 2001
U.S.	**$ 70.00**
Can.	**$ 95.00**
U.K.	**£ 40.00**
Aust.	**$100.00**

CC2
CALYPSO KITTEN™

Modeller:	Shane Ridge
Height:	4", 10.1 cm
Colour:	Black cat, patterned yellow shirt, beige trousers, red and yellow drum
Issued:	1998 - 2001
U.S.	**$ 70.00**
Can.	**$ 95.00**
U.K.	**£ 40.00**
Aust.	**$100.00**

CC3
ONE COOL CAT™

Modeller:	Shane Ridge
Height:	4", 10.1 cm
Colour:	Ginger cat, blue suit with black trim, black shoes, yellow saxophone
Issued:	1998 - 2001
U.S.	**$ 70.00**
Can.	**$ 95.00**
U.K.	**£ 40.00**
Aust.	**$100.00**

CC4
RATCATCHER BILK

Modeller:	Shane Ridge
Height:	4", 10.1 cm
Colour:	White cat, blue shirt and hat, yellow waistcoat, black trousers and clarinet
Issued:	1998 - 2001
U.S.	**$ 70.00**
Can.	**$ 95.00**
U.K.	**£ 40.00**
Aust.	**$100.00**

CC5
TRAD JAZZ TOM™

Modeller:	Shane Ridge
Height:	4", 10.1 cm
Colour:	Grey cat, trousers and waistcoat, lemon shirt, black hat, yellow trumpet
Issued:	1998 - 2001
U.S.	**$ 70.00**
Can.	**$ 95.00**
U.K.	**£ 40.00**
Aust.	**$100.00**

CC6
CATWALKING BASS™

Modeller:	Shane Ridge
Height:	4", 10.1 cm
Colour:	White cat, yellow jacket, green shirt, red trousers, black hat, tan bass
Issued:	1998 - 2001
U.S.	**$ 70.00**
Can.	**$ 95.00**
U.K.	**£ 40.00**
Aust.	**$100.00**

CC7
FELINE FLAMENCO™

Modeller:	Shane Ridge
Height:	4", 10.1 cm
Colour:	Ginger cat, lemon shirt, black trousers and waistcoat, red/ white cumberbund, tan guitar
Issued:	1998 - 2001
U.S.	**$ 70.00**
Can.	**$ 95.00**
U.K.	**£ 40.00**
Aust.	**$100.00**

CC8
BRAVURA BRASS™

Modeller:	Shane Ridge
Height:	4", 10.1 cm
Colour:	Ginger cat, black suit and shoes, white shirt, yellow french horn
Issued:	1998 - 2001
U.S.	**$ 70.00**
Can.	**$ 95.00**
U.K.	**£ 40.00**
Aust.	**$100.00**

CC9
FAT CAT™

Modeller:	Shane Ridge
Height:	3 ¾", 9.5 cm
Colour:	Brown, yellow and blue
Issued:	1999 - 2001
U.S.	**$ 70.00**
Can.	**$ 95.00**
U.K.	**£ 40.00**
Aust.	**$100.00**

CC10
GLAM GUITAR™

Modeller:	Shane Ridge
Height:	4 ¼", 10.8 cm
Colour:	Red, yellow and white
Issued:	1999 - 2001
U.S.	**$ 70.00**
Can.	**$ 95.00**
U.K.	**£ 40.00**
Aust.	**$100.00**

"Purrfect Pitch"

COMPTON & WOODHOUSE

TEDDY BEARS

ARCHIE™

Height:	4 ½", 11.9 cm
Colour:	Brown bear; light blue waistcoat; red and white spotted handkerchief
Issued:	1997
U.S.	**$ 90.00**
Can.	**$120.00**
U.K.	**£ 50.00**
Aust.	**$130.00**

BENJAMIN™

Height:	4 ½", 11.9 cm
Colour:	Brown bear wearing a bright yellow scarf
Issued:	1996
U.S.	**$ 90.00**
Can.	**$120.00**
U.K.	**£ 50.00**
Aust.	**$130.00**

BERTIE™

Height:	4 ½", 11.9 cm
Colour:	Dark brown bear; straw hat with red and purple band; yellow cane
Issued:	1997
U.S.	**$ 90.00**
Can.	**$120.00**
U.K.	**£ 50.00**
Aust.	**$130.00**

HENRY™

Height:	4 ½", 11.9 cm
Colour:	Dark brown bear; purple tie, brown satchel
Issued:	1998
U.S.	**$ 90.00**
Can.	**$120.00**
U.K.	**£ 50.00**
Aust.	**$130.00**

COUNTRY COUSINS

SWEET
SUZIE
"Thank you"
PM 2101

PETER
*"Once upon
a time"*
PM 2102

HARRY
*"A new home
for Fred"*
PM 2103

MICHAEL
*"Happily
ever after"*
PM 2104

PM 2101		PM 2102		PM 2103		PM 2104	
SWEET SUZIE™		**PETER**™		**HARRY**™		**MICHAEL**™	
Thank You		Once Upon A Time		A New Home for Fred		Happily Ever After	
Designer:	Unknown	Designer:	Unknown	Designer:	Unknown	Designer:	Unknown
Height:	2 ¾", 7.0 cm	Height:	2 ½", 5.6 cm	Height:	2", 5.0 cm	Height:	2 ½", 6.4 cm
Colour:	Brown rabbit wearing a brown and yellow pinafore	Colour:	Brown hedgehog wearing a blue suit and a white bowtie	Colour:	Brown hedgehog wearing a blue and white jumper and brown trousers	Colour:	Brown rabbit wearing a green jacket
Issued:	1994 - 1994	Issued:	1994 - 1994	Issued:	1994 - 1994	Issued:	1994 - 1994
U.S.	**$45.00**	**U.S.**	**$45.00**	**U.S.**	**$45.00**	**U.S.**	**$45.00**
Can.	**$60.00**	**Can.**	**$60.00**	**Can.**	**$60.00**	**Can.**	**$60.00**
U.K.	**£25.00**	**U.K.**	**£25.00**	**U.K.**	**£25.00**	**U.K.**	**£25.00**
Aust.	**$65.00**	**Aust.**	**$65.00**	**Aust.**	**$65.00**	**Aust.**	**$65.00**

BERTRAM
"Ten out of ten"
PM 2105

LEONARDO
"Practice makes perfect"
PM 2106

LILY
"Flowers picked just for you"
PM 2107

PATRICK
"This way's best"
PM 2108

PM 2105
BERTRAM™
Ten Out of Ten

Height:	3", 7.6 cm
Colour:	Brown owl wearing a green and blue striped waistcoat, a red bow tie and blue mortar board with red tassel
Issued:	1994 - 1994
U.S.	**$45.00**
Can.	**$60.00**
U.K.	**£25.00**
Aust.	**$65.00**

PM 2106
LEONARDO
Practice Makes Perfect

Height:	2 ¾", 7.0 cm
Colour:	Brown owl wearing a brown hat; white palette and blue paintbrush
Issued:	1994 - 1994
U.S.	**$45.00**
Can.	**$60.00**
U.K.	**£25.00**
Aust.	**$65.00**

PM 2107
LILY
Flowers Picked Just for You™

Height:	3", 7.6 cm
Colour:	Brown hedgehog wearing a pink dress with matching bonnet with white ribbon, yellow pinafore with white collar
Issued:	1994 - 1994
U.S.	**$45.00**
Can.	**$60.00**
U.K.	**£25.00**
Aust.	**$65.00**

PM 2108
PATRICK™
This Way's Best

Height:	3", 7.6 cm
Colour:	Brown owl wearing a blue and yellow checked waistcoat, white collar and blue bow tie, yellow hat with red band
Issued:	1994 - 1994
U.S.	**$45.00**
Can.	**$60.00**
U.K.	**£25.00**
Aust.	**$65.00**

PM 2109
JAMIE™
Hurrying Home

Height:	3", 7.6 cm
Colour:	Brown hedgehog wearing a pink sailor top with white stripes, blue trousers
Issued:	1994 - 1994
U.S.	**$45.00**
Can.	**$60.00**
U.K.	**£25.00**
Aust.	**$65.00**

PM 2111
MUM AND LIZZIE™
Let's Get Busy

Height:	3 ¼", 8.3 cm
Colour:	Large brown rabbit wearing a blue dress and white pinafore
	Small brown rabbit wearing a white pinafore
Issued:	1994 - 1994
U.S.	**$60.00**
Can.	**$85.00**
U.K.	**£35.00**
Aust.	**$90.00**

PM 2112
MOLLY AND TIMMY™
Picnic Time

Height:	2 ¾", 7 cm
Colour:	Large brown mouse wearing pink dress, yellow bonnet, and blue pinafore,
	Small brown mouse wearing yellow dungarees, white top, blue hat
Issued:	1994 - 1994
U.S.	**$60.00**
Can.	**$85.00**
U.K.	**£35.00**
Aust.	**$90.00**

PM 2113
POLLY AND SARAH™
Good News!

Height:	3 ¼", 8.3 cm
Colour:	Brown rabbit wearing blue dress and pink apron
	Brown hedgehog wearing blue dress and scarf, green jacket, white pinafore
Issued:	1994 - 1994
U.S.	**$60.00**
Can.	**$85.00**
U.K.	**£35.00**
Aust.	**$90.00**

BESWICK INTERNATIONAL
COUNTRY COUSINS
BILL & TED
"Working
together"
PM 2114
Made in China © 1994

BESWICK INTERNATIONAL
COUNTRY COUSINS
**JACK
& DAISY**
"How does your
garden grow?"
PM 2115
Made in China © 1994

BESWICK INTERNATIONAL
COUNTRY COUSINS
**ALISON
& DEBBIE**
"Friendship
is fun"
PM 2116
Made in China © 1994

BESWICK INTERNATIONAL
COUNTRY COUSINS
**ROBERT
& ROSIE**
"Perfect Partners"
PM 2119
Made in China © 1994

PM 2114	PM 2115	PM 2116	PM 2119
BILL AND TED™	**JACK AND DAISY™**	**ALISON AND DEBBIE™**	**ROBERT AND ROSIE™**
Working Together	How Does Your Garden Grow?	Friendship is Fun	Perfect Partners
Height: 3 ¼", 8.3 cm	Height: 2 ¾", 7 cm	Height: 2 ¾", 7 cm	Height: 3 ¼", 8.3 cm
Colour: Brown mouse in blue dungarees Brown hedgehog in green dungarees	Colour: Male - brown mouse, white shirt, blue dungarees Female - brown mouse, pink and white striped dress, white pinafore	Colour: Rabbit - brown, pink dress, white pinafore Squirrel - brown, blue dress, pink apron	Colour: Male - brown squirrel, blue dungarees, blue hat with red band Female - brown squirrel, pink dress with white collar, yellow hat
Issued: 1994 - 1994	Issued: 1994 - 1994	Issued: 1994 - 1994	Issued: 1994 - 1994
U.S. $60.00	**U.S.** $60.00	**U.S.** $60.00	**U.S.** $60.00
Can. $85.00	**Can.** $85.00	**Can.** $85.00	**Can.** $85.00
U.K. £35.00	**U.K.** £35.00	**U.K.** £35.00	**U.K.** £35.00
Aust. $90.00	**Aust.** $90.00	**Aust.** $90.00	**Aust.** $90.00

PM 2120
SAMMY™
Treasure Hunting

Height:	2 ¼", 5.7 cm
Colour:	Brown squirrel wearing a green shirt, blue sack
Issued:	1994 - 1994

Back Stamp	Beswick Number	Price			
		U.S. $	Can. $	U.K. £	Aust. $
BK-1	PM2120	45.00	60.00	25.00	65.00

Patrick "This Way's Best"

DAVID HAND'S ANIMALAND

1148
DINKUM PLATYPUS™

Designer: Arthur Gredington
Height: 4 ¼", 10.8 cm
Colour: Brown and beige platypus,
           green base
Issued: 1949 - 1955

Beswick Number	Price			
	U.S. $	Can. $	U.K. £	Aust. $
1148	350.00	475.00	200.00	525.00

1150
ZIMMY LION™

Designer: Arthur Gredington
Height: 3 ¾", 9.5 cm
Colour: Brown lion with white face
Issued: 1949 - 1955

Beswick Number	Price			
	U.S. $	Can. $	U.K. £	Aust. $
1150	550.00	725.00	300.00	775.00

1151
FELIA™

Designer: Arthur Gredington
Height: 4", 10.1 cm
Colour: Green cat
Issued: 1949 - 1955

Beswick Number	Price			
	U.S. $	Can. $	U.K. £	Aust. $
1151	625.00	850.00	350.00	900.00

1152
GINGER NUTT™

Designer:	Arthur Gredington
Height:	4", 10.1 cm
Colour:	Brown and beige squirrel, green base
Issued:	1949 - 1955

Beswick Number	Price			
	U.S. $	Can. $	U.K. £	Aust. $
1152	725.00	950.00	400.00	1,000.00

1153
HAZEL NUTT™

Designer:	Arthur Gredington
Height:	3 ¾", 9.5 cm
Colour:	Brown and beige squirrel, green base
Issued:	1949 - 1955

Beswick Number	Price			
	U.S. $	Can. $	U.K. £	Aust. $
1153	725.00	950.00	400.00	1,000.00

1154
OSCAR OSTRICH™

Designer:	Arthur Gredington
Height:	3 ¾", 9.5 cm
Colour:	Beige and mauve ostrich, brown base
Issued:	1949 - 1955

Beswick Number	Price			
	U.S. $	Can. $	U.K. £	Aust. $
1154	800.00	1,075.00	450.00	1,150.00

1155
DUSTY MOLE™

Designer:	Arthur Gredington
Height:	3 ½", 8.9 cm
Colour:	Blue mole, white face
Issued:	1949 - 1955

Beswick Number				
	Price			
	U.S. $	Can. $	U.K. £	Aust. $
1155	500.00	650.00	275.00	700.00

1156
LOOPY HARE™

Designer:	Arthur Gredington
Height:	4 ¼", 10.8 cm
Colour:	Brown and beige hare
Issued:	1949 - 1955

Beswick Number				
	Price			
	U.S. $	Can. $	U.K. £	Aust. $
1156	625.00	850.00	350.00	900.00

ENGLISH COUNTRY FOLK

ECF 1	ECF 2	ECF 3	ECF 4
HUNTSMAN FOX	**FISHERMAN OTTER**	**GARDENER RABBIT**	**GENTLEMAN PIG**

ECF 1
HUNTSMAN FOX™
Beswick No.: 9150
Designer: A. Hughes-Lubeck
Height: 5 ¾", 14.6 cm
Colour: Dark green jacket and cap, blue-grey trousers, green wellingtons
Issued: 1993 - 1998

U.S.	$100.00
Can.	$135.00
U.K.	£ 55.00
Aust.	$145.00

ECF 2
FISHERMAN OTTER™
Beswick No.: 9152
Designer: Warren Platt
Height: 5 ¾", 14.6 cm
Colour: Yellow shirt and hat, dark green waistcoat, blue-grey trousers
Issued: 1993 - 1998

U.S.	$100.00
Can.	$135.00
U.K.	£ 55.00
Aust.	$145.00

ECF 3
GARDENER RABBIT™
First Variation
Beswick No.: 9155
Designer: Warren Platt
Height: 6", 15.0 cm
Colour: White shirt, red pullover, blue trousers, grey hat
Issued: 1993 - 1999
Varieties: ECF 12

U.S.	$100.00
Can.	$135.00
U.K.	£ 55.00
Aust.	$145.00

ECF 4
GENTLEMAN PIG™
First Variation
Beswick No.: 9149
Designer: A. Hughes-Lubeck
Height: 5 ¾", 14.6 cm
Colour: Dark brown suit, yellow waistcoat
Issued: 1993 - 1999
Varieties: ECF 10

U.S.	$100.00
Can.	$135.00
U.K.	£ 55.00
Aust.	$145.00

ECF 5
SHEPHERD SHEEPDOG

ECF 6
HIKER BADGER

ECF 7
MRS RABBIT BAKING

ECF 8
THE LADY PIG

ECF 5
SHEPHERD SHEEPDOG™
Beswick No.: 9156
Designer: Warren Platt
Height: 6 ¾", 17.2 cm
Colour: Yellow smock
Issued: 1993 - 1999

U.S.	**$100.00**
Can.	**$135.00**
U.K.	**£ 55.00**
Aust.	**$145.00**

ECF 6
HIKER BADGER™
First Variation
Beswick No.: 9157
Designer: Warren Platt
Height: 5 ¼", 13.3 cm
Colour: Yellow shirt, blue
        waistcoat, red cap
        and socks
Issued: 1993 - 1999
Varieties: ECF 9

U.S.	**$100.00**
Can.	**$135.00**
U.K.	**£ 55.00**
Aust.	**$145.00**

ECF 7
MRS. RABBIT BAKING™
First Variation
Beswick No.: Unknown
Designer: Martyn Alcock
Height: 5 ½", 14.0 cm
Colour: Mauve dress, white
        apron and cap
Issued: 1994 - 1999
Varieties: ECF 13

U.S.	**$100.00**
Can.	**$135.00**
U.K.	**£ 55.00**
Aust.	**$145.00**

ECF 8
THE LADY PIG™
First Variation
Designer: A. Hughes-Lubeck
Height: 5 ½", 14.0 cm
Colour: Green jacket, skirt
        and hat, brown
        umbrella
Issued: 1995 - 1999
Varieties: ECF 11

U.S.	**$100.00**
Can.	**$135.00**
U.K.	**£ 55.00**
Aust.	**$145.00**

ECF 9
HIKER BADGER™
Second Variation

Beswick No.: 9157
Designer: Warren Platt
Height: 5 ¼", 13.3 cm
Colour: Green, red, black
Issued: 1997 in a special
edition of 1,000
Varieties: ECF 6

U.S.	**$135.00**
Can.	**$175.00**
U.K.	**£ 75.00**
Aust.	**$190.00**

ECF 10
GENTLEMAN PIG™
Second Variation

Beswick No.: 9149
Designer: A. Hughes-Lubeck
Height: 5 ¾", 14.6 cm
Colour: Light brown
Issued: 1998 in a limited
edition of 2,000
Varieties: ECF 4

U.S.	**$110.00**
Can.	**$150.00**
U.K.	**£ 60.00**
Aust.	**$165.00**

ECF 11
THE LADY PIG™
Second Variation

Beswick No.: Unknown
Designer: A. Hughes-Lubeck
Height: 5 ½", 14.0 cm
Colour: Browns
Issued: 1998 in a limited
edition of 2,000
Varieties: ECF 8

U.S.	**$110.00**
Can.	**$150.00**
U.K.	**£ 60.00**
Aust.	**$165.00**

ECF 12
GARDENER RABBIT™
Second Variation

Beswick No.: 9155
Designer: Warren Platt
Height: 6", 15.0 cm
Colour: Black and slate
Issued: 1998 in a limited
edition of 2,000
Varieties: ECF 3

U.S.	**$110.00**
Can.	**$150.00**
U.K.	**£ 60.00**
Aust.	**$165.00**

ECF 13
MRS. RABBIT BAKING™
Second Variation

Beswick No.: Unknown
Designer: Martyn Alcock
Height: 5 ½", 14.0 cm
Colour: Grey, yellow, rust
Issued: 1998 in a limited
edition of 2,000
Varieties: ECF 7

U.S.	**$110.00**
Can.	**$150.00**
U.K.	**£ 60.00**
Aust.	**$165.00**

ENID BLYTON'S
NODDY™ COLLECTION

3676
BIG EARS™

Designer:	Enid Blyton
Modeller:	Andy Moss
Height:	5", 12.7 cm
Colour:	Red, white, dark blue and yellow
Issued:	1997 in a special edition of 1,500

U.S.	**$225.00**
Can.	**$300.00**
U.K.	**£125.00**
Aust.	**$325.00**

3678
NODDY™

Designer:	Enid Blyton
Modeller	Andy Moss
Height:	5", 12.7 cm
Colour:	Red, blue and light brown
Issued:	1997 in a special edition of 1,500

U.S.	**$225.00**
Can.	**$300.00**
U.K.	**£125.00**
Aust.	**$325.00**

3679
MR. PLOD™

Designer:	Enid Blyton
Modeller:	Andy Moss
Height:	5", 12.7 cm
Colour:	Navy and yellow
Issued:	1998 in a special edition of 1,500

U.S.	**$225.00**
Can.	**$300.00**
U.K.	**£125.00**
Aust.	**$325.00**

3770
TESSIE BEAR™

Designer:	Enid Blyton
Modeller:	Andy Moss
Height:	5", 12.7 cm
Colour:	Yellow, pink, green and white
Issued:	1998 in a special edition of 1,500

U.S.	**$225.00**
Can.	**$300.00**
U.K.	**£125.00**
Aust.	**$325.00**

NODDY AND BIG EARS™

Designer:	Enid Blyton
Modeller:	Andy Moss
Height:	3 ½", 8.9 cm
Colour:	Red, yellow, blue, brown and black
Issued:	2002 in a limited edition of 750 (C of A)

Doulton	Price			
Number	U.S. $	Can. $	U.K. £	Aust. $
–	350.00	475.00	200.00	525.00

RUPERT BEAR

BESWICK SERIES 1980 - 1986

2694
RUPERT BEAR™
Style One
Designer: Harry Sales
Height: 4 ¼", 10.8 cm
Colour: Red sweater,
           yellow check
           trousers and scarf
Issued: 1980 - 1986

U.S.   **$550.00**
Can.   **$725.00**
U.K.   **£300.00**
Aust. **$775.00**

2710
ALGY PUG™
Designer: Harry Sales
Height: 4", 10.1 cm
Colour: Grey jacket,
           yellow waistcoat,
           brown trousers
Issued: 1981 - 1986

U.S.   **$350.00**
Can.   **$475.00**
U.K.   **£200.00**
Aust. **$525.00**

2711
PONG PING™
Designer: Harry Sales
Height: 4 ¼", 10.8 cm
Colour: Dark green jacket,
           gold trousers
Issued: 1981 - 1986

U.S.   **$350.00**
Can.   **$475.00**
U.K.   **£200.00**
Aust. **$525.00**

2720
BILL BADGER™
Style One
Designer: Harry Sales
Height: 2 ¾", 7.0 cm
Colour: Dark grey jacket,
           light grey trousers
           and red bowtie
Issued: 1981 - 1986

U.S.   **$400.00**
Can.   **$550.00**
U.K.   **£225.00**
Aust. **$600.00**

2779
RUPERT BEAR
SNOWBALLING™
Designer: Harry Sales
Height: 4 ¼", 10.8 cm
Colour: Red coat, yellow
           with brown check
           trousers and scarf
Issued: 1982 - 1986

U.S.   **$ 800.00**
Can.   **$1,075.00**
U.K.   **£ 450.00**
Aust. **$1,150.00**

RUPERT BEAR
ROYAL DOULTON SERIES 1998 - 2000

BILL BADGER™
Style Two

Modeller:	Martyn Alcock
Height:	5", 12.7 cm
Colour:	Turquoise, yellow and purple
Issued:	2000 in a limited edition of 1,920
Comm. by:	Doulton-Direct

U.S.	**$135.00**
Can.	**$175.00**
U.K.	**£ 75.00**
Aust.	**$190.00**

EDWARD TRUNK™

Modeller:	Martyn Alcock
Height:	5 ¼", 13.3 cm
Colour:	Blue coat, red scarf, yellow check trousers
Issued:	2000 in a limited edition of 1,920
Comm. by:	Doulton-Direct

U.S.	**$135.00**
Can.	**$175.00**
U.K.	**£ 75.00**
Aust.	**$190.00**

PODGY PIG™

Modeller:	Martyn Alcock
Height:	5 ¾", 14.6 cm
Colour:	Brown suit, red scarf, black socks, white shoes
Issued:	1998 in a limited edition of 1,920

U.S.	**$135.00**
Can.	**$175.00**
U.K.	**£ 75.00**
Aust.	**$190.00**

RUPERT BEAR™
Style Two

Designer:	Martyn Alcock
Height:	5 ¾", 14.6 cm
Colour:	Red sweater, yellow check trousers and scarf
Issued:	1998 in a limited edition of 1,920

U.S.	**$225.00**
Can.	**$300.00**
U.K.	**£125.00**
Aust.	**$325.00**

RUPERT BEAR AND ALGY PUG
GO-CARTING™

Modeller:	Martyn Alcock
Size:	4 ½" x 5"
Colour:	Red, yellow, blue burgundy, brown
Issued:	2000 in a limited edition of 2,500
Comm. by:	Doulton-Direct

U.S.	**$275.00**
Can.	**$350.00**
U.K.	**£150.00**
Aust.	**$400.00**

RUPERT WITH SATCHEL™

Modeller:	Martyn Alcock
Height:	5", 12.7 cm
Colour:	Red, yellow, white, brown
Issued:	2000 in a limited edition of 2,000
Comm. by:	Doulton-Direct

U.S.	**$350.00**
Can.	**$475.00**
U.K.	**£200.00**
Aust.	**$525.00**

RUPERT BEAR
ROYAL DOULTON SERIES 2004 TO DATE

RB 1
RUPERT'S TOY RAILWAY
Height: 4 ¼", 10.8 cm
Colour: Red, dark blue,
          light blue, purple
          and black
Issued: 2004 in a limited
          edition of 2,500
U.S.   –
Can.   –
U.K.   £95.00
Aust. –

RB 2
PRETENDING TO BE AN
OUTLAW
(Edward Trunk)
Height: 5 ¼", 13.3 cm
Colour: Blue coat, red
          waistcoat, yellow
          check trousers
Issued: 2004 to the present
U.S.   –
Can.   –
U.K.   £30.00
Aust. –

RB 3
LEADING THE WAY
(Ping Pong)
Height: 5 ¼", 13.3 cm
Colour: Black top with
          blue details, brown
          trousers
Issued: 2004 to the present
U.S.   –
Can.   –
U.K.   £30.00
Aust. –

RB 4
RUPERT RIDES HOME
Height: 6", 15.0 cm
Colour: Red, yellow, green
          and pink
Issued: 2004 in a limited
          edition of 2,500
U.S.   –
Can.   –
U.K.   £80.00
Aust. –

RB 5
TEMPTED TO TRESPASS
Height: 5 ¼", 13.3 cm
Colour: White, browns, red,
          yellow, blue, light
          purple and black
Issued: 2004 in a limited
          edition of 2,500
U.S.   –
Can.   –
U.K.   £60.00
Aust. –

RB 6
LOOKING LIKE ROBIN HOOD
(Algy Pug)
Height: 5 ¼", 13.3 cm
Colour: Blue coat, yellow
          waistcoat, red
          trousers
Issued: 2004 to the present
U.S. $55.00
Can. $70.00
U.K.   £30.00
Aust. $85.00

RB 7
FINISHING ARROWS AND
STRINGING HIS BOW
(Rupert)
Height: 5", 12.7 cm
Colour: Red sweater, yellow
          checked trousers
          and scarf
Issued: 2004 to the present
U.S.   –
Can.   –
U.K.   £30.00
Aust. –

RB 8
RUPERT'S SILVER TRUMPET
Height: 5", 12.7 cm
Colour: White, red, yellow,
          black, beige and
          silver
Issued: 2004 to the present
U.S.   –
Can.   –
U.K.   £30.00
Aust. –

RB 9
PODGY LANDS WITH A BUMP

Height:	3 ¼", 8.3 cm
Colour:	White, light brown, yellow, red, black and green
Issued:	2004 to the present
U.S.	–
Can.	–
U.K.	**£30.00**
Aust.	–

RB 10
BINGO'S HUGE FIREWORK

Height:	4 ¾", 12.1 cm
Colour:	White, blue-grey, brown, pink, black and yellow
Issued:	2004 to the present
U.S.	–
Can.	–
U.K.	**£30.00**
Aust.	–

RB 11
RUPERT, BILL AND THE MYSTERIOUS CAR

Height:	4 ½", 11.9 cm
Colour:	White, green, blue, red, yellow, brown and black
Issued:	2004 in a limited edition of 2,500
U.S.	–
Can.	–
U.K.	**£80.00**
Aust.	–

Rupert's Toy Railway, 2004 limited edition of 2,500.

FOOTBALLING FELINES

FF2
MEE-OUCH

Designer:	Andy Moss
Height:	3 ¼", 8.3 cm
Colour:	Blue shirt/socks, white shorts
Issued:	1998 in a special edition of 1,500

U.S.	**$ 70.00**
Can.	**$ 95.00**
U.K.	**£ 40.00**
Aust.	**$100.00**

Note: FF1 not issued.

FF3
KITCAT

Designer:	Andy Moss
Height:	4 ¼", 10.8 cm
Colour:	Red shirt/socks, white shorts
Issued:	1998 in a special edition of 1,500

U.S.	**$ 70.00**
Can.	**$ 95.00**
U.K.	**£ 40.00**
Aust.	**$100.00**

FF4
DRIBBLE

Designer:	Andy Moss
Height:	4 ¼", 10.8 cm
Colour:	White shirt/socks, black shorts
Issued:	1998 in a special edition of 1,500

U.S.	**$ 70.00**
Can.	**$ 95.00**
U.K.	**£ 40.00**
Aust.	**$100.00**

FF5
THROW IN

Designer:	Andy Moss
Height:	6", 15.0 cm
Colour:	Yellow shirt/socks, white shorts
Issued:	1999 in a special edition of 1,500

U.S.	**$ 70.00**
Can.	**$ 95.00**
U.K.	**£ 40.00**
Aust.	**$100.00**

FF6
REFFEREE: RED CARD

Designer:	Andy Moss
Height:	6 ¼", 15.9 cm
Colour:	Black uniform; black and white socks
Issued:	1999 in a special edition of 1,500

U.S.	**$ 70.00**
Can.	**$ 95.00**
U.K.	**£ 40.00**
Aust.	**$100.00**

HANNA-BARBERA

THE FLINTSTONES
TOP CAT

THE FLINTSTONES
1996-1997

3577
PEBBLES FLINTSTONE™

Designer: Simon Ward
Height: 3 ½", 8.9 cm
Colour: Green dress, blue pants, red hair, light brown base
Issued: 1997 in a limited edition of 2,000

U.S.	**$ 90.00**
Can.	**$120.00**
U.K.	**£ 50.00**
Aust.	**$130.00**

3579
BAMM-BAMM RUBBLE™

Designer: Simon Ward
Height: 3", 7.6 cm
Colour: Light and dark brown pants, white hair, yellow club
Issued: 1997 in a limited edition of 2,000

u.s.	**$ 90.00**
Can.	**$120.00**
U.K.	**£ 50.00**
Aust.	**$130.00**

3583
WILMA FLINTSTONE™

Designer: Simon Ward
Height: 4 ¾", 12.1 cm
Colour: White dress, red hair, light brown base
Issued: 1996 in a limited edition of 2,000

U.S.	**$ 90.00**
Can.	**$120.00**
U.K.	**£ 50.00**
Aust.	**$130.00**

3584
BETTY RUBBLE™

Designer: Simon Ward
Height: 4", 10.1 cm
Colour: Blue dress, black hair, light brown base
Issued: 1996 in a limited edition of 2,000

U.S.	**$ 90.00**
Can.	**$120.00**
U.K.	**£ 50.00**
Aust.	**$130.00**

3587
BARNEY RUBBLE™

Designer: Simon Ward
Height: 3 ½", 8.9 cm
Colour: Reddish brown shirt, yellow hair, light brown base
Issued: 1996 in a limited edition of 2,000

U.S.	**$ 90.00**
Can.	**$120.00**
U.K.	**£ 50.00**
Aust.	**$130.00**

3588
FRED FLINTSTONE™

Designer: Simon Ward
Height: 4 ¾", 12.1 cm
Colour: Light brown shirt with dark patches, black hair, blue tie
Issued: 1996 in a limited edition of 2,000

U.S.	**$110.00**
Can.	**$150.00**
U.K.	**£ 60.00**
Aust.	**$165.00**

3590
DINO™

Designer: Simon Ward
Height: 4 ¾", 12.1 cm
Colour: Purple, white and black
Issued: 1997 in a limited edition of 2,000

U.S.	**$115.00**
Can.	**$155.00**
U.K.	**£ 65.00**
Aust.	**$170.00**

TOP CAT
1996-1998

3581
TOP CAT™
Designer:	Andy Moss
Height:	4 ½", 11.9 cm
Colour:	Yellow cat wearing a mauve waistcoat
Issued:	1996 in a limited edition of 2,000
Series:	Top Cat

U.S.	**$175.00**
Can.	**$250.00**
U.K.	**£100.00**
Aust.	**$275.00**

3586
CHOO-CHOO™
Designer:	Andy Moss
Height:	4 ½", 11.9 cm
Colour:	Pink cat wearing a white shirt
Issued:	1996 in a limited edition of 2,000
Series:	Top Cat

U.S.	**$110.00**
Can.	**$150.00**
U.K.	**£ 60.00**
Aust.	**$165.00**

3624
FANCY FANCY™
Designer:	Andy Moss
Height:	4 ½", 11.9 cm
Colour:	Pink cat, black tip on tail, white scarf
Issued:	1997 in a limited edition of 2,000
Series:	Top Cat

U.S.	**$110.00**
Can.	**$150.00**
U.K.	**£ 60.00**
Aust.	**$165.00**

3627
BENNY™
Designer:	Andy Moss
Height:	3 ¾", 8.5 cm
Colour:	Lilac cat wearing a white jacket
Issued:	1997 in a limited edition of 2,000
Series:	Top Cat

U.S.	**$ 80.00**
Can.	**$110.00**
U.K.	**£ 45.00**
Aust.	**$120.00**

3671
OFFICER DIBBLE™
Designer:	Andy Moss
Height:	6 ¾", 17.5 cm
Colour:	Dark blue police officer's uniform
Issued:	1998 in a limited edition of 2,000

U.S.	**$200.00**
Can.	**$265.00**
U.K.	**£110.00**
Aust.	**$275.00**

3673
SPOOK™
Designer:	Andy Moss
Height:	4 ½", 11.9 cm
Colour:	Beige cat wearing black tie
Issued:	1998 in a limited edition of 2,000

U.S.	**$110.00**
Can.	**$150.00**
U.K.	**£ 60.00**
Aust.	**$165.00**

3674
BRAIN™
Designer:	Andy Moss
Height:	4", 10.1 cm
Colour:	Yellow cat wearing a purple shirt
Issued:	1998 in a limited edition of 2,000

U.S.	**$110.00**
Can.	**$150.00**
U.K.	**£ 60.00**
Aust.	**$165.00**

Spook

HARRY POTTER™

HP 1
THE REMEMBRALL™
RECOVERY

Height: 4", 10.1 cm
Colour: Black, blue and
            brown
Issued: 2001 - 2003

U.S. $ 70.00
Can. $ 90.00
U.K.   £ 40.00
Aust. $100.00

HP 2
HARRY CASTS A MAGICAL
SPELL™

Height: 4 ½", 11.9 cm
Colour: Black, blue, red
            beige and brown
Issued: 2001 - 2003

U.S. $ 70.00
Can. $ 90.00
U.K.   £ 40.00
Aust. $100.00

HP 3
HERMIONE STUDIES FOR
POTIONS CLASS™

Height: 5", 12.7 cm
Colour: Black, blue,
            pink, green,
            brown and gold
Issued: 2001 - 2003

U.S. $ 70.00
Can. $ 90.00
U.K.   £ 40.00
Aust. $100.00

HP 4
RON FOLLOWS THE WEASLEY
FAMILY TRADITION™

Height: 5 ¼", 13.3 cm
Colour: Black, blue and
            purple
Issued: 2001 - 2002

U.S. $ 70.00
Can. $ 90.00
U.K.   £ 40.00
Aust. $100.00

HP 5
PROFESSOR SEVERUS SNAPE™

Height: 6 ¼" 15.9 cm
Colour: Black
Issued: 2001 - 2002

U.S. $ 70.00
Can. $ 90.00
U.K.   £ 40.00
Aust. $100.00

HP 6
HEADMASTER ALBUS
DUMBLEDORE™

Height: 6 ½", 16.5 cm
Colour: Purple, green,
            white and brown
Issued: 2001 - 2003

U.S. $ 70.00
Can. $ 90.00
U.K.   £ 40.00
Aust. $100.00

HP 7
WIZARD-IN-TRAINING™

Height: 5 ¼", 13.3 cm
Colour: Black, blue, red,
            white, brown and
            gold
Issued: 2001 - 2003

U.S. $ 70.00
Can. $ 90.00
U.K.   £ 40.00
Aust. $100.00

HP 8
THE FRIENDSHIP BEGINS™

Height: 5 ¼", 13.3 cm
Colour: Blue, red, white,
            purple, green and
            brown
Issued: 2001 in a limited
            edition of 5,000

U.S. $135.00
Can. $175.00
U.K.   £ 75.00
Aust. $200.00

HP 9
HARRY'S 11TH BIRTHDAY™

Height:	6 ¼", 15.9 cm
Colour:	Brown, white, red, blue, olive green and pink
Issued:	2001 in a limited edition of 5,000
U.S.	**$175.00**
Can.	**$250.00**
U.K.	**£100.00**
Aust.	**$275.00**

HP 10
STRUGGLING THROUGH POTIONS CLASS™

Height:	3 ¾", 9.5 cm
Colour:	Black, green, red and tan
Issued:	2002 -2003
U.S.	**$110.00**
Can.	**$150.00**
U.K.	**£ 60.00**
Aust.	**$175.00**

HP 11
SLYTHERIN OR GRYFFINDOR™

Height:	4 ¾", 12.1 cm
Colour:	Black, blue, red and beige
Issued:	2002 - 2003
U.S.	**$ 70.00**
Can.	**$ 90.00**
U.K.	**£ 40.00**
Aust.	**$100.00**

HP 12
RON AND SCRABBERS™

Height:	4 ½", 11.9 cm
Colour:	Purple, blue and green
Issued:	2002 - 2003
U.S.	**$ 70.00**
Can.	**$ 90.00**
U.K.	**£ 40.00**
Aust.	**$100.00**

HP 13
HERMIONE LEARNS TO LEVITATE™

Height:	4 ½", 11/9 cm
Colour:	Black, pink, blue and brown
Issued:	2002 - 2003
U.S.	**$ 70.00**
Can.	**$ 90.00**
U.K.	**£ 40.00**
Aust.	**$100.00**

HP 14
PROFESSOR McGONAGALL™

Height:	5 ¼", 13.3 cm
Colour:	Dark green
Issued:	2002 - 2003
U.S.	**$ 70.00**
Can.	**$ 90.00**
U.K.	**£ 40.00**
Aust.	**$100.00**

HP 15
PROFESSOR QUIRRELL™

Height:	5", 12.7 cm
Colour:	Dark blue and purple
Issued:	2002 - 2003
U.S.	**$ 70.00**
Can.	**$ 90.00**
U.K.	**£ 40.00**
Aust.	**$100.00**

HP 16
HEDWIG™

Height:	3 ½", 8.9 cm
Colour:	White, yellow and beige
Issued:	2002 - 2003
U.S.	**$ 70.00**
Can.	**$ 90.00**
U.K.	**£ 40.00**
Aust.	**$100.00**

HP 17
THE BIRTH OF NORBERT™

Height:	4 ¼", 10.8 cm
Colour	Green, grey, purple and brown
Issued:	2002 - 2003
U.S.	**$ 70.00**
Can.	**$ 90.00**
U.K.	**£ 40.00**
Aust.	**$100.00**

HP 18
THE MIRROR HOLDS THE ANSWER™

Height:	10", 25.4 cm
Colour:	Gold, black, blue, yellow and grey
Issued:	2002 in a limited edition of 5,000
U.S.	**$160.00**
Can.	**$215.00**
U.K.	**£ 90.00**
Aust.	**$230.00**

HP 19
THE JOURNEY TO HOGWARTS™

Height:	3 ½", 8.9 cm
Colour:	Black, brown and blue
Issued:	2002 in a limited edition of 5,000
U.S.	**$175.00**
Can.	**$250.00**
U.K.	**£100.00**
Aust.	**$275.00**

HP 20
MADAME HOOCH™

Height:	5 ¼", 13.3 cm
Colour:	Black and white
Issued:	2002 - 2003
Comm. by:	Doulton-Direct
U.S.	**$ 70.00**
Can.	**$ 90.00**
U.K.	**£ 40.00**
Aust.	**$100.00**

HP 21
PROFESSOR SPROUT™

Height:	5", 12.7 cm
Colour:	Olive green and orange
Issued:	2002 - 2003
Comm. by:	Doulton-Direct
U.S.	**$60.00**
Can.	**$85.00**
U.K.	**£35.00**
Aust.	**$90.00**

HP 22
HARRY POTTER™ PLAYING QUIDDITCH

Height:	4 ¾", 12.1 cm
Colour:	Red, teal blue, black and brown
Issued:	2002 - 2003
Comm. by:	Doulton-Direct
U.S.	**$ 90.00**
Can.	**$120.00**
U.K.	**£ 50.00**
Aust.	**$135.00**

HP 23
DOBBY™

Height:	2 ¼", 5.7 cm
Colour:	Blue and lilac
Issued:	2002 - 2003
Comm. by:	Doulton-Direct
U.S.	**$ 90.00**
Can.	**$120.00**
U.K.	**£ 50.00**
Aust.	**$135.00**

HP 24
DURSLEY FAMILY™

Height:	6", 15.0 cm
Colour:	Black, blue, red, green, white, yellow and brown
Issued:	2002 in a limited edition of 1,000
Comm. by:	Doulton-Direct
U.S.	**$175.00**
Can.	**$250.00**
U.K.	**£100.00**
Aust.	**$275.00**

HP 25
WHOMPING WILLOW™

Height:	9 ½", 24.0 cm
Colour:	Brown, green and turquoise
Issued:	2002 in a limited edition of 1,000
Comm. by:	Doulton-Direct

U.S.	**$ 750.00**
Can.	**$ 975.00**
U.K.	**£ 400.00**
Aust.	**$1,000.00**

HP 26
RESCUE IN THE FORBIDDEN FOREST™

Height:	7 ¼", 18.4 cm
Colour:	Cream, brown, black and blue
Issued:	2002 in a limited edition of 5,000
Comm. by:	Doulton-Direct

U.S.	**$150.00**
Can.	**$200.00**
U.K.	**£ 85.00**
Aust.	**$225.00**

Harry's 11th Birthday

THE HERBS
(Parsley and the Herbs)

H 1
PARSLEY THE LION™

Beswick No.: 4058
Designer: Ivor Wood
Modeller: Shane Ridge
Height: 3 ¾", 9.5 cm
Colour: Greens, yellow and white
Issued: 2001 in a limited edition of 2,500
Comm. by: Doulton-Direct

U.S.	**$110.00**
Can.	**$150.00**
U.K.	**£ 60.00**
Aust.	**$165.00**

H 2
BAYLEAF THE GARDENER™

Beswick No.: 4059
Designer: Ivor Wood
Modeller: Shane Ridge
Height: 5 ¾", 14.6 cm
Colour: Red, white, brown, cream, grey, black
Issued: 2001 in a limited edition of 2,500
Comm. by: Doulton-Direct

U.S.	**$110.00**
Can.	**$150.00**
U.K.	**£ 60.00**
Aust.	**$165.00**

H 3
DILL THE DOG™

Beswick No.: 4057
Designer: Ivor Wood
Modeller: Shane Ridge
Height: 3 ½", 8.9 cm
Colour: Brown, grey, yellow and cream
Issued: 2001 in a limited edition of 2,500
Comm. by: Doulton-Direct

U.S.	**$110.00**
Can.	**$150.00**
U.K.	**£ 60.00**
Aust.	**$165.00**

H 4
SAGE THE OWL™

Beswick No.: 4056
Designer: Ivor Wood
Modeller: Shane Ridge
Height: 3", 7.5 cm
Colour: Green, brown, yellow and white
Issued: 2001 in a limited edition of 2,500
Comm. by: Doulton-Direct

U.S.	**$110.00**
Can.	**$150.00**
U.K.	**£ 60.00**
Aust.	**$165.00**

HIPPOS ON HOLIDAY

HH1
GRANDMA™

Modeller:	A. Hughes-Lubeck
Height:	5", 12.7 cm
Colour:	Orange, grey, black and brown
Issued:	1999 in a limited edition of 3,500

U.S.	**$ 70.00**
Can.	**$ 95.00**
U.K.	**£ 40.00**
Aust.	**$100.00**

HH2
GRANDPA™

Modeller:	Warren Platt
Height:	5", 12.7 cm
Colour:	White jacket and cap, blue trousers
Issued:	1999 in a limited edition of 3,500

U.S.	**$ 70.00**
Can.	**$ 95.00**
U.K.	**£ 40.00**
Aust.	**$100.00**

HH3
MA™

Modeller:	A. Hughes-Lubeck
Height:	5", 12.7 cm
Colour:	Purple, grey, pink and yellow
Issued:	1999 in a limited edition of 3,500

U.S.	**$ 70.00**
Can.	**$ 95.00**
U.K.	**£ 40.00**
Aust.	**$100.00**

HH4
PA™

Modeller:	Martyn Alcock
Height:	5", 12.7 cm
Colour:	Yellow, green and grey
Issued:	1999 in a limited edition of 3,500

U.S.	**$ 70.00**
Can.	**$ 95.00**
U.K.	**£ 40.00**
Aust.	**$100.00**

HH5
HARRIET™

Modeller:	Martyn Alcock
Height:	5", 12.7 cm
Colour:	Pink and grey
Issued:	1999 in a limited edition of 3,500

U.S.	**$ 70.00**
Can.	**$ 95.00**
U.K.	**£ 40.00**
Aust.	**$100.00**

HH6
HUGO™

Modeller:	Warren Platt
Height:	4", 10.1 cm
Colour:	Grey, white, blue and yellow
Issued:	1999 in a limited edition of 3,500

U.S.	**$ 70.00**
Can.	**$ 95.00**
U.K.	**£ 40.00**
Aust.	**$100.00**

JANE HISSEY'S
OLD BEAR™
AND FRIENDS

OB4601
OLD BEAR™

Designer:	Jane Hissey
Modeller:	Paul Gurney
Height:	4", 10.1 cm
Colour:	Light brown bear
Issued:	1997 - 2001

U.S.	**$ 75.00**
Can.	**$100.00**
U.K.	**£ 45.00**
Aust.	**$110.00**

OB4602
TIME FOR BED™

Designer:	Jane Hissey
Modeller:	Paul Gurney
Height:	4", 10.1 cm
Colour:	Golden brown giraffe; light brown bear; blue and white striped pyjamas, yellow toothbrush
Issued:	1997 - 1999

U.S.	**$ 75.00**
Can.	**$100.00**
U.K.	**£ 45.00**
Aust.	**$110.00**

OB4603
BRAMWELL BROWN HAS A GOOD IDEA™

Designer:	Jane Hissey
Modeller:	Paul Gurney
Height:	4", 10.1 cm
Colour:	Brown bear, beige teddy bear wearing red trousers, green and white base
Issued:	1997 - 1998

U.S.	**$ 75.00**
Can.	**$100.00**
U.K.	**£ 45.00**
Aust.	**$110.00**

OB4604
DON'T WORRY, RABBIT™

Designer:	Jane Hissey
Modeller:	Paul Gurney
Height:	4", 10.1 cm
Colour:	Light brown bear, beige rabbit, yellow and red blocks, green base
Issued:	1997 - 2000

U.S.	**$ 75.00**
Can.	**$100.00**
U.K.	**£ 45.00**
Aust.	**$110.00**

OB4605
THE LONG RED SCARF™

Designer:	Jane Hissey
Modeller:	Paul Gurney
Height:	4", 10.1 cm
Colour:	Golden brown giraffe wearing long red scarf, dark brown bear
Issued:	1997 - 1999

U.S.	**$ 75.00**
Can.	**$100.00**
U.K.	**£ 45.00**
Aust.	**$110.00**

OB4606
WAITING FOR SNOW™

Designer:	Jane Hissey
Modeller:	Paul Gurney
Height:	4", 10.1 cm
Colour:	Golden brown giraffe, light brown bear, white duck with brown beak
Issued:	1997 - 1999

U.S.	**$ 75.00**
Can.	**$100.00**
U.K.	**£ 45.00**
Aust.	**$110.00**

OB4607
THE SNOWFLAKE BISCUITS™

Designer:	Jane Hissey
Modeller:	Paul Gurney
Height:	4", 10.1 cm
Colour:	Golden brown, red, light brown white, black and brown
Issued:	1997 - 2001

U.S.	**$ 75.00**
Can.	**$100.00**
U.K.	**£ 45.00**
Aust.	**$110.00**

OB4608
WELCOME HOME OLD BEAR™

Designer:	Jane Hissey
Modeller:	Paul Gurney
Height:	4", 10.1 cm
Colour:	Brown bear with two light brown bears and a white duck
Issued:	1997 - 2001

U.S.	**$ 75.00**
Can.	**$100.00**
U.K.	**£ 45.00**
Aust.	**$110.00**

OB4609
RUFF'S PRIZE™

Designer:	Jane Hissey
Modeller:	Paul Gurney
Height:	2 ½", 6.5 cm
Colour:	Light brown, dark brown and red
Issued:	1997 - 1999
U.S.	**$ 75.00**
Can.	**$100.00**
U.K.	**£ 45.00**
Aust.	**$110.00**

OB4610
TIME FOR A CUDDLE, HUG ME TIGHT™

Designer:	Jane Hissey
Modeller:	Paul Gurney
Height:	3 ½", 8.9 cm
Colour:	Golden brown, light brown, blue and white
Issued:	1997 - 2000
U.S.	**$ 75.00**
Can.	**$100.00**
U.K.	**£ 45.00**
Aust.	**$110.00**

OB4611
DON'T FORGET OLD BEAR™

Designer:	Jane Hissey
Modeller:	Paul Gurney
Height:	3", 7.6 cm
Colour:	Brown bear in brown box, red book covers
Issued:	1998 - 2001
U.S.	**$ 75.00**
Can.	**$100.00**
U.K.	**£ 45.00**
Aust.	**$110.00**

OB4612
HOLD ON TIGHT™

Designer:	Jane Hissey
Modeller:	Paul Gurney
Height:	3", 7.6 cm
Colour:	White, blue, light brown, blue and white
Issued:	1998 - 2001
U.S.	**$ 75.00**
Can.	**$100.00**
U.K.	**£ 45.00**
Aust.	**$110.00**

OB4613
RESTING WITH CAT™

Designer:	Jane Hissey
Modeller:	Paul Gurney
Height:	2 ½", 6.4 cm
Colour:	Black cat with red inner ears and necktie, light brown bear wearing red trousers
Issued:	1998 - 2001
U.S.	**$ 75.00**
Can.	**$100.00**
U.K.	**£ 45.00**
Aust.	**$110.00**

OB4614
LOOKING FOR A SAILOR™

Designer:	Jane Hissey
Modeller:	Paul Gurney
Height:	5", 12.7 cm
Colour:	Red and blue horse, light brown bear
Issued:	1998 - 2001
U.S.	**$ 75.00**
Can.	**$100.00**
U.K.	**£ 45.00**
Aust.	**$110.00**

OB4615
TOO MUCH FOOD™

Designer:	Jane Hissey
Modeller:	Paul Gurney
Height:	4", 10.1 cm
Colour:	Golden brown bear on a brown basket, light brown bear wearing red trousers
Issued:	1998 - 2001
U.S.	**$ 75.00**
Can.	**$100.00**
U.K.	**£ 45.00**
Aust.	**$110.00**

OB4616
NEST OF SOCKS™

Designer:	Jane Hissey
Modeller:	Paul Gurney
Height:	2 ¾", 7.0 cm
Colour:	Pale brown, blue, green, white yellow and red
Issued:	2000 - 2001
U.S.	**$ 75.00**
Can.	**$100.00**
U.K.	**£ 45.00**
Aust.	**$110.00**

OB4617
SNOW DECORATIONS™

Designer:	Jane Hissey
Modeller:	Paul Gurney
Height:	3 ½", 8.9 cm
Colour:	Brown bear
Issued:	2000 - 2001
U.S.	**$ 75.00**
Can.	**$100.00**
U.K.	**£ 45.00**
Aust.	**$125.00**

OB4618
STORYTIME™

Designer:	Jane Hissey
Modeller:	Paul Gurney
Height:	2 ½", 6.4 cm
Colour:	Black, beige, red, light blue, and white
Issued:	2000 - 2001
U.S.	**$ 75.00**
Can.	**$100.00**
U.K.	**£ 45.00**
Aust.	**$125.00**

OB4619
DUCK™

Designer:	Jane Hissey
Modeller:	Paul Gurney
Height:	3", 7.6 cm
Colour:	White, brown and yellow duck, multicoloured quilt
Issued:	2000 - 2001
U.S.	**$120.00**
Can.	**$150.00**
U.K.	**£ 60.00**
Aust.	**$175.00**

OB4620
UP, UP AND AWAY™

Designer:	Jane Hissey
Modeller:	Paul Gurney
Height:	3 ½", 8.9 cm
Colour:	White, red, brown, blue and silver
Issued:	2000 - 2001
U.S.	**$ 75.00**
Can.	**$100.00**
U.K.	**£ 45.00**
Aust.	**$125.00**

JOAN WALSH ANGLUND

2272
ANGLUND BOY™

Designer:	Albert Hallam
Height:	4 ½", 11.9 cm
Colour:	Green dungarees, brown hat
Issued:	1970 - 1971
U.S.	**$135.00**
Can.	**$175.00**
U.K.	**£ 75.00**
U.S.	**$200.00**

2293
ANGLUND GIRL WITH DOLL™

Designer:	Albert Hallam
Height:	4 ½", 11.9 cm
Colour:	Green dress and bow, white apron
Issued:	1970 - 1971
U.S.	**$135.00**
Can.	**$175.00**
U.K.	**£ 75.00**
Aust.	**$200.00**

2317
ANGLUND GIRL WITH FLOWERS™

Designer:	Albert Hallam
Height:	4 ¾", 12.1 cm
Colour:	White dress, blue leggings, straw hat with blue ribbon
Issued:	1971 - 1971
U.S.	**$135.00**
Can.	**$175.00**
U.K.	**£ 75.00**
Aust.	**$200.00**

KITTY MACBRIDE

Kitty MacBride ©
"A Family Mouse"
2526
BESWICK
ENGLAND

Kitty MacBride ©
"A Double Act"
2527
BESWICK
ENGLAND

Kitty MacBride ©
"The Racegoer"
2528
BESWICK
ENGLAND

Kitty MacBride ©
"A Good Read"
2529
BESWICK
ENGLAND

2526
A FAMILY MOUSE™

Designer:	Graham Tongue
Height:	3 ½", 8.9 cm
Colour:	Brown, mauve, turquoise, light and dark green
Issued:	1975 - 1983
U.S.	**$135.00**
Can.	**$175.00**
U.K.	**£ 75.00**
Aust.	**$200.00**

2527
A DOUBLE ACT™

Designer:	Graham Tongue
Height:	3 ½", 8.9 cm
Colour:	Yellow, orange, brown, green and blue
Issued:	1975 - 1983
U.S.	**$135.00**
Can.	**$175.00**
U.K.	**£ 75.00**
Aust.	**$200.00**

2528
THE RACEGOER™

Designer:	David Lyttleton
Height:	3 ½", 8.9 cm
Colour:	Brown, yellow, and green
Issued:	1975 - 1983
U.S.	**$135.00**
Can.	**$175.00**
U.K.	**£ 75.00**
Aust.	**$200.00**

2529
A GOOD READ™

Designer:	David Lyttleton
Height:	2 ½", 6.4 cm
Colour:	Yellow, blue, brown and white
Issued:	1975 - 1983
U.S.	**$300.00**
Can.	**$400.00**
U.K.	**£165.00**
Aust.	**$425.00**

2530	2531	2532	2533
LAZYBONES™	**A SNACK**™	**STRAINED RELATIONS**™	**JUST GOOD FRIENDS**™
Designer: David Lyttleton	Designer: David Lyttleton	Designer: David Lyttleton	Designer: David Lyttleton
Height: 1 ½", 3.8 cm	Height: 3 ¼", 8.3 cm	Height: 3", 7.6 cm	Height: 3", 7.6 cm
Colour: Blue, black, brown, green and white	Colour: Brown, blue, yellow and green	Colour: Brown, blue and green	Colour: Brown, yellow, blue, red and green
Issued: 1975 - 1983	Issued: 1975 - 1983	Issued: 1975 - 1983	Issued: 1975 - 1983
U.S. $135.00	U.S. $135.00	U.S. $135.00	U.S. $175.00
Can. $175.00	Can. $175.00	Can. $175.00	Can. $250.00
U.K. £ 75.00	U.K. £ 75.00	U.K. £ 75.00	U.K. £100.00
Aust. $200.00	Aust. $200.00	Aust. $200.00	Aust. $275.00

Backstamp not
available
at press time

Backstamp not
available
at press time

2565
THE RING™

Designer:	David Lyttleton
Height:	3 ¼", 8.3 cm
Colour:	Brown, white, purple and yellow
Issued:	1976 - 1983

U.S.	**$225.00**
Can.	**$300.00**
U.K.	**£125.00**
Aust.	**$325.00**

2566
GUILTY SWEETHEARTS™

Designer:	David Lyttleton
Height:	2 ¼", 5.7 cm
Colour:	Brown, yellow, green and white
Issued:	1976 - 1983

U.S.	**$225.00**
Can.	**$300.00**
U.K.	**£125.00**
Aust.	**$325.00**

2589
ALL I DO IS THINK OF YOU™

Designer:	David Lyttleton
Height:	2 ½", 6.4 cm
Colour:	Brown, yellow and white
Issued:	1976 - 1983

U.S.	**$550.00**
Can.	**$725.00**
U.K.	**£300.00**
Aust.	**$775.00**

LITTLE LIKEABLES

LL1
FAMILY GATHERING™
(Hen and Two Chicks)

Designer:	Diane Griffiths
Height:	4 ½", 11.9 cm
Colour:	White hen and chicks with yellow beaks; gold comb on hen
Issued:	1985 - 1987

U.S.	**$ 80.00**
Can.	**$110.00**
U.K.	**£ 45.00**
Aust.	**$120.00**

LL2
WATCHING THE WORLD GO BY™
(Frog)

Designer:	Robert Tabbenor
Height:	3 ¾", 9.5 cm
Colour:	White frog, black and green eyes
Issued:	1985 - 1987

U.S.	**$ 80.00**
Can.	**$110.00**
U.K.	**£ 45.00**
Aust.	**$120.00**

LL3
HIDE AND SLEEP™
(Pig and Two Piglets)

Designer:	Robert Tabbenor
Height:	3 ¼", 8.3 cm
Colour:	White pigs with pink noses, ears and tails
Issued:	1985 - 1987

U.S.	**$ 80.00**
Can.	**$110.00**
U.K.	**£ 45.00**
Aust.	**$120.00**

LL4
MY PONY™
(Pony)

Designer:	Diane Griffiths
Height:	7 ¼", 18.4 cm
Colour:	White pony with blue highlights in mane and tail
Issued:	1985 - 1987

U.S.	**$ 80.00**
Can.	**$110.00**
U.K.	**£ 45.00**
Aust.	**$120.00**

LL5
ON TOP OF THE WORLD™
(Elephant)

Designer:	Diane Griffiths
Height:	3 ¾", 9.5 cm
Colour:	White elephant with black eyes and gold nails
Issued:	1985 - 1987

U.S.	**$ 80.00**
Can.	**$110.00**
U.K.	**£ 45.00**
Aust.	**$120.00**

LL6
TREAT ME GENTLY™
(Fawn)

Designer:	Diane Griffiths
Height:	4 ½", 11.9 cm
Colour:	White fawn with black and brown eyes, black nose and gold hoof
Issued:	1985 - 1987

U.S.	**$ 80.00**
Can.	**$110.00**
U.K.	**£ 45.00**
Aust.	**$120.00**

LL7
OUT AT LAST™
(Duckling)

Designer:	Robert Tabbenor
Height:	3 ¼", 8.3 cm
Colour:	White duck with black and brown eyes and gold beak
Issued:	1985 - 1987

U.S.	**$ 80.00**
Can.	**$110.00**
U.K.	**£ 45.00**
Aust.	**$120.00**

LL8
CATS CHORUS™
(Cats)

Designer:	Robert Tabbenor
Height:	4 ¾", 12.1 cm
Colour:	Two white cats; black and green eyes, black nose, pink ears/mouth
Issued:	1985 - 1987

U.S.	**$ 80.00**
Can.	**$110.00**
U.K.	**£ 45.00**
Aust.	**$120.00**

LITTLE LOVABLES

HAPPY BIRTHDAY

BESWICK
B
ENGLAND
LL 1

I LOVE YOU

BESWICK
B
ENGLAND
LL 2

GOD LOVES ME

BESWICK
B
ENGLAND
LL 3

JUST FOR YOU

BESWICK
B
ENGLAND
LL 4

LL1
HAPPY BIRTHDAY™

Beswick No.:	3328
Designer:	A. Hughes-Lubeck
Height:	4 ½", 11.9 cm
Colour:	White, pink and orange (gloss)
Issued:	1992 - 1994
Varieties:	LL8; LL15; also unnamed LL22

U.S.	**$55.00**
Can.	**$70.00**
U.K.	**£30.00**
Aust.	**$75.00**

LL2
I LOVE YOU™

Beswick No.:	3320
Designer:	A. Hughes-Lubeck
Height:	4 ½", 11.9 cm
Colour:	White, green and pink (gloss)
Issued:	1992 - 1994
Varieties:	LL9, LL16; also unnamed LL23

U.S.	**$55.00**
Can.	**$70.00**
U.K.	**£30.00**
Aust.	**$75.00**

LL3
GOD LOVES ME™

Beswick No.:	3336
Designer:	A. Hughes-Lubeck
Height:	3 ¾", 9.5 cm
Colour:	White, green and turquoise (gloss)
Issued:	1992 - 1993
Varieties:	LL10, LL17; also called Please, LL33, LL34; also unnamed LL24

U.S.	**$175.00**
Can.	**$250.00**
U.K.	**£100.00**
Aust.	**$275.00**

LL4
JUST FOR YOU™

Beswick No.:	3361
Designer:	Warren Platt
Height:	4 ½", 11.9 cm
Colour:	White, pink and blue (gloss)
Issued:	1992 - 1994
Varieties:	LL11, LL18; also unnamed LL25

U.S.	**$55.00**
Can.	**$70.00**
U.K.	**£30.00**
Aust.	**$75.00**

LL 5

LL 6

LL 7

LL 8

LL5
TO MOTHER™

Beswick No.:	3331
Designer:	A. Hughes-Lubeck
Height:	4 ½", 11.9 cm
Colour:	White, blue and purple (gloss)
Issued:	1992 - 1994
Varieties:	LL12, LL19; also called To Daddy, also unnamed LL26
U.S.	**$55.00**
Can.	**$70.00**
U.K.	**£30.00**
Aust.	**$75.00**

LL6
CONGRATULATIONS™

Beswick No.:	3340
Designer:	Warren Platt
Height:	4 ½", 11.9 cm
Colour:	White, green and pink (gloss)
Issued:	1992 - 1994
Varieties:	LL13, LL20; also unnamed LL27
U.S.	**$55.00**
Can.	**$70.00**
U.K.	**£30.00**
Aust.	**$75.00**

LL7
PASSED™

Beswick No.:	3334
Designer:	A. Hughes-Lubeck
Height:	3", 7.6 cm
Colour:	White, lilac and pink (gloss)
Issued:	1992 - 1994
Varieties:	LL14, LL21; also unnamed LL28
U.S.	**$ 90.00**
Can	**$120.00**
U.K.	**£ 50.00**
Aust.	**$135.00**

LL8
HAPPY BIRTHDAY™

Beswick No.:	3328
Designer:	A. Hughes-Lubeck
Height:	4 ½", 11.9 cm
Colour:	White, yellow and green (gloss)
Issued:	1992 - 1994
Varieties:	LL1, LL15; also unnamed LL22
U.S.	**$60.00**
Can.	**$85.00**
U.K.	**£35.00**
Aust.	**$95.00**

LL 9

LL 10

LL 11

LL 12

LL9
I LOVE YOU™
Beswick No.: 3320
Designer: A. Hughes-Lubeck
Height: 4 ½", 11.9 cm
Colour: White, blue and
             orange (gloss)
Issued: 1992 - 1994
Varieties: LL2, LL16; also
             unnamed LL23

U.S.	$55.00
Can.	$70.00
U.K.	£30.00
Aust.	$75.00

LL10
GOD LOVES ME™
Beswick No.: 3336
Designer: A. Hughes-Lubeck
Height: 3 ¾", 9.5 cm
Colour: White, gold and
             blue (gloss)
Issued: 1992 - 1993
Varieties: LL3, LL17; also
             called Please, LL33,
             LL34; also unnamed
             LL24

U.S.	$135.00
Can.	$175.00
U.K.	£ 75.00
Aust.	$190.00

LL11
JUST FOR YOU™
Beswick No.: 3361
Designer: Warren Platt
Height: 4 ½", 11.9 cm
Colour: White, yellow and
             pale green (gloss)
Issued: 1992 - 1994
Varieties: LL4, LL18; also
             unnamed LL25

U.S.	$55.00
Can.	$70.00
U.K.	£30.00
Aust.	$75.00

LL12
TO MOTHER™
Beswick No.: 3331
Designer: A. Hughes-Lubeck
Height: 4 ½", 11.9 cm
Colour: White, yellow and
             pink (gloss)
Issued: 1992 - 1994
Varieties: LL5, LL19; also
             called To Daddy,
             LL29; also unnamed
             LL26

U.S.	$55.00
Can.	$70.00
U.K.	£30.00
Aust.	$75.00

LL13
CONGRATULATIONS™

Beswick No.: 3340
Designer: Warren Platt
Height: 4 ½", 11.9 cm
Colour: White, pale blue and yellow (gloss)
Issued: 1992 - 1994
Varieties: LL6, LL20; also unnamed LL27

U.S.	$55.00
Can.	$70.00
U.K.	£30.00
Aust.	$75.00

LL14
PASSED™

Beswick No.: 3334
Designer: A. Hughes-Lubeck
Height: 3", 7.6 cm
Colour: White, light blue and orange (gloss)
Issued: 1992 - 1994
Varieties: LL7, LL21; also unnamed LL28

U.S.	$ 90.00
Can.	$120.00
U.K.	£ 50.00
Aust.	$135.00

LL15
HAPPY BIRTHDAY™

Beswick No.: 3407
Designer: A. Hughes-Lubeck
Height: 4 ½", 11.9 cm
Colour: White, salmon and green (matt)
Issued: 1992 - 1993
Varieties: LL8, LL15; also unnamed LL22

U.S.	$110.00
Can.	$150.00
U.K.	£ 60.00
Aust.	$165.00

LL16
I LOVE YOU™

Beswick No.: 3406
Designer: A. Hughes-Lubeck
Height: 4 ½", 11.9 cm
Colour: White, green and yellow (matt)
Issued: 1992 - 1993
Varieties: LL2, LL9; also unnamed LL23

U.S.	$135.00
Can.	$175.00
U.K.	£ 75.00
Aust.	$200.00

LL 17

LL 18

LL 19

LL 20

LL17
GOD LOVES ME™

Beswick No.:	3410
Designer:	A. Hughes-Lubeck
Height:	3 ¾", 9.5 cm
Colour:	White, purple and yellow (matt)
Issued:	1992 - 1993
Varieties:	LL3, LL10; also called Please, LL33, LL34; also unnamed LL24

U.S.	**$135.00**
Can.	**$175.00**
U.K.	**£ 75.00**
Aust.	**$200.00**

LL18
JUST FOR YOU™

Beswick No.:	3412
Designer:	Warren Platt
Height:	4 ½", 11.9 cm
Colour:	White, yellow and dark blue (matt)
Issued:	1992 - 1993
Varieties:	LL4, LL11; also unnamed LL25

U.S.	**$135.00**
Can.	**$175.00**
U.K.	**£ 75.00**
Aust.	**$200.00**

LL19
TO MOTHER™

Beswick No.:	3408
Designer:	A. Hughes-Lubeck
Height:	4 ½", 11.9 cm
Colour:	White, green and orange (matt)
Issued:	1992 - 1993
Varieties:	LL5, LL12; also called To Daddy, LL29; also unnamed LL26

U.S.	**$135.00**
Can.	**$175.00**
U.K.	**£ 75.00**
Aust.	**$200.00**

LL20
CONGRATULATIONS™

Beswick No.:	3411
Designer:	Warren Platt
Height:	4 ½", 11.9 cm
Colour:	White, blue and red (matt)
Issued:	1992 - 1993
Varieties:	LL6, LL13; also unnamed LL27

U.S.	**$135.00**
Can.	**$175.00**
U.K.	**£ 75.00**
Aust.	**$200.00**

LL21
PASSED™
Beswick No.: 3409
Designer: A. Hughes-Lubeck
Height: 3", 7.6 cm
Colour: White, blue and orange (matt)
Issued: 1992 - 1993
Varieties: LL7, LL14; also unnamed LL28

U.S.	$135.00
Can.	$175.00
U.K.	£ 75.00
Aust.	$200.00

LL22
(No Name)
Beswick No.: 3329
Designer: A. Hughes-Lubeck
Height: 4 ½", 11.9 cm
Colour: White, pink and orange (gloss)
Issued: 1993 - 1993
Varieties: Also called Happy Birthday, LL1, LL8, LL15

U.S.	$135.00
Can.	$175.00
U.K.	£ 75.00
Aust.	$200.00

LL23
(No Name)
Beswick No.: 3320
Designer: A. Hughes-Lubeck
Height: 4 ½", 11.9 cm
Colour: White, green and pink (gloss)
Issued: 1993 - 1993
Varieties: Also called I Love You, LL2, LL9, LL16

U.S.	$135.00
Can.	$175.00
U.K.	£ 75.00
Aust.	$200.00

LL24
(No Name)
Beswick No.: 3336
Designer: A. Hughes-Lubeck
Height: 3 ¾", 9.5 cm
Colour: White, green and turquoise (gloss)
Issued: 1993 - 1993
Varieties: Also called God Loves Me, LL3. LL10, LL17; Please, LL33, LL34

U.S.	$135.00
Can.	$175.00
U.K.	£ 75.00
Aust.	$200.00

LL25
(No Name)
Beswick No.: 3361
Designer: Warren Platt
Height: 4 ½", 11.9 cm
Colour: White, pink and
             blue (gloss)
Issued: 1993 - 1993
Varieties: Also called Just For
             You, LL4, LL11,
             LL18

U.S.	**$110.00**
Can.	**$150.00**
U.K.	**£ 60.00**
Aust.	**$165.00**

LL26
(No Name)
Beswick No.: 3331
Designer: A. Hughes-Lubeck
Height: 4 ¼", 10.8 cm
Colour: White, blue and
             purple (gloss)
Issued: 1993 - 1993
Varieties: Also called To
             Mother, LL5, LL12,
             LL19;To Daddy,
             LL29

U.S.	**$110.00**
Can.	**$150.00**
U.K.	**£ 60.00**
Aust.	**$165.00**

LL27
(No Name)
Beswick No.: 3340
Designer: Warren Platt
Height: 4 ½", 11.9 cm
Colour: White, green and
             pink (gloss)
Issued: 1993 - 1993
Varieties: Also called
             Congratulations,
             LL6, LL13, LL20

U.S.	**$110.00**
Can.	**$150.00**
U.K.	**£ 60.00**
Aust	**$165.00**

LL28
(No Name)
Beswick No.: 3334
Designer: A. Hughes-Lubeck
Height: 3", 7.6 cm
Colour: White, lilac and
             pink (gloss)
Issued: 1993 - 1993
Varieties: Also called Passed,
             LL7, LL14, LL21

U.S.	**$110.00**
Can.	**$150.00**
U.K.	**£ 60.00**
Aust.	**$165.00**

LL29
TO DADDY™

Beswick No.:	3331
Designer:	A. Hughes-Lubeck
Height:	4 ½", 11.9 cm
Colour:	White, light blue and green (gloss)
Issued:	1994 - 1994
Varieties:	Also called To Mother, LL5, LL12, LL19; also unnamed LL26

U.S.	**$ 80.00**
Can.	**$110.00**
U.K.	**£ 45.00**
Aust.	**$125.00**

LL30
MERRY CHRISTMAS™

Beswick No.:	3389
Designer:	A. Hughes-Lubeck
Height:	4", 10.1 cm
Colour:	White, red and green (gloss)
Issued:	1993 - 1994

U.S.	**$ 80.00**
Can.	**$110.00**
U.K.	**£ 45.00**
Aust.	**$125.00**

LL31
GOOD LUCK™

Beswick No.:	3388
Designer:	A. Hughes-Lubeck
Height:	4 ¼", 10.8 cm
Colour:	White, pink and green (gloss)
Issued:	1993 - 1994

U.S.	**$ 80.00**
Can.	**$110.00**
U.K.	**£ 45.00**
Aust.	**$125.00**

LL32
GET WELL SOON™

Beswick No.:	3390
Designer:	A. Hughes-Lubeck
Height:	4 ¼", 10.8 cm
Colour:	White, green and purple (gloss)
Issued:	1994 - 1994

U.S.	**$ 80.00**
Can.	**$110.00**
U.K.	**£ 45.00**
Aust.	**$125.00**

LL33
PLEASE™

Beswick No.: 3336
Designer: A. Hughes-Lubeck
Height: 3 ¾", 9.5 cm
Colour: White, green and blue (gloss)
Issued: 1993 - 1994
Varieties: LL34; also called God Loves Me, LL3, LL10, LL17; also unnamed LL24

U.S.	$ 80.00
Can.	$110.00
U.K.	£ 45.00
Aust.	$125.00

LL34
PLEASE™

Beswick No.: 3336
Designer: A. Hughes-Lubeck
Height: 3 ¾", 9.5 cm
Colour: White, gold and light blue (gloss)
Issued: 1993 - 1994
Varieties: LL33; also called God Loves Me, LL3, LL10, LL17; also unnamed LL24

U.S.	$ 80.00
Can.	$110.00
U.K.	£ 45.00
Aust.	$125.00

LL35 is the prototype for "I Love Beswick." Colourway not issued.

LL36
I LOVE BESWICK™

Beswick No.: 3320
Designer: A. Hughes-Lubeck
Height: 4 ½", 11.9 cm
Colour: White, green and pink (gloss)
Issued: 1995 - 1995
Varieties: Also called I Love You, LL2, LL9, LL16; also unnamed LL23

U.S.	$135.00
Can.	$175.00
U.K.	£ 75.00
Aust.	$200.00

Note: This piece was specially commissioned for the 10th Anniversary of the Beswick Collectors Circle.

NORMAN THELWELL

EARTHENWARE SERIES 1981-1989
RESIN STUDIO SCULPTURES 1985
EARTHENWARE SERIES 2001

NORMAN THELWELL
EARTHENWARE SERIES 1981-1989

2704A	2704B	2769A	2769B
AN ANGEL ON HORSEBACK™	**AN ANGEL ON HORSEBACK™**	**KICK-START™**	**KICK-START™**
First Variation	**Second Variation**	**First Variation**	**Second Variation**
Designer: Harry Sales	Designer: Harry Sales	Designer: Harry Sales	Designer: Harry Sales
Modeller: David Lyttleton	Modeller: David Lyttleton	Modeller: David Lyttleton	Modeller: David Lyttleton
Height: 4 ½", 11.4 cm	Height: 4 ½", 11.4 cm	Height: 3 ½", 8.9 cm	Height: 3 ½", 8.9 cm
Colour: Grey horse, rider wears brown jacket, yellow jodhpurs	Colour: Bay horse, rider wears red jacket, yellow jodhpurs	Colour: Grey horse, rider wears red jacket and yellow jodhpurs	Colour: Bay horse, rider wears red jacket and yellow jodhpurs
Issued: 1981 - 1989	Issued: 1981 - 1989	Issued: 1982 - 1989	Issued: 1982 - 1989
Varieties: 2704B	Varieties: 2704A	Varieties: 2769B	Varieties: 2769B
U.S. $275.00	**U.S.** $275.00	**U.S.** $275.00	**U.S.** $275.00
Can. $350.00	**Can.** $350.00	**Can.** $350.00	**Can.** $350.00
U.K. £150.00	**U.K.** £150.00	**U.K.** £150.00	**U.K.** £150.00
Aust. $375.00	**Aust.** $375.00	**Aust.** $375.00	**Aust.** $375.00

2789A
PONY EXPRESS™
First Variation

Designer:	Harry Sales
Modeller:	David Lyttleton
Height:	4 ½", 11.4 cm
Colour:	Grey horse, rider wears green jacket and yellow jodhpurs
Issued:	1982 - 1989
Varieties:	2789B

U.S.	**$625.00**
Can.	**$850.00**
U.K.	**£350.00**
Aust.	**$900.00**

2789B
PONY EXPRESS™
Second Variation

Designer:	Harry Sales
Modeller:	David Lyttleton
Height:	4 ½", 11.4 cm
Colour:	Bay horse, rider wears red jacket and yellow jodhpurs
Issued:	1982 - 1989
Varieties:	2789A

U.S.	**$450.00**
Can.	**$600.00**
U.K.	**£250.00**
Aust.	**$650.00**

NORMAN THEWELL
RESIN STUDIO SCULPTURES 1985-1985

SS7A	SS7B	SS12A	SS12B
I FORGIVE YOU™	**I FORGIVE YOU**™	**EARLY BATH**™	**EARLY BATH**™
First Variation	Second Variation	First Variation	Second Variation

SS7A
I FORGIVE YOU™
First Variation

Designer: Harry Sales
Modeller: David Lyttleton
Height: 4", 10.1 cm
Colour: Grey horse, rider wears red jacket and yellow jodhpurs
Issued: 1985 - 1985
Series: Studio Sculptures
Varieties: SS7B

U.S.	$225.00
Can.	$300.00
U.K.	£125.00
Aust.	$325.00

SS7B
I FORGIVE YOU™
Second Variation

Designer: Harry Sales
Modeller: David Lyttleton
Height: 4", 10.1 cm
Colour: Bay horse, rider wears red jacket and yellow jodhpurs
Issued: 1985 - 1985
Series: Studio Sculptures
Varieties: SS7A

U.S.	$225.00
Can.	$300.00
U.K.	£125.00
Aust.	$325.00

SS12A
EARLY BATH™
First Variation

Designer: Harry Sales
Modeller: David Lyttleton
Height: 4 ¾", 12.1 cm
Colour: Grey horse, rider wears red jacket and yellow jodhpurs
Issued: 1985 - 1985
Series: Studio Sculptures
Varieties: SS12B

U.S.	$350.00
Can.	$475.00
U.K.	£200.00
Aust.	$525.00

SS12B
EARLY BATH™
Second Variation

Designer: Harry Sales
Modeller: David Lyttleton
Height: 4 ¾", 12.1 cm
Colour: Bay horse, rider wears red jacket and yellow jodhpurs
Issued: 1985 - 1985
Series: Studio Sculptures
Varieties: SS12A

U.S.	$325.00
Can.	$425.00
U.K.	£175.00
Aust.	$450.00

NORMAN THELWELL
EARTHENWARE SERIES 2001 to date

NT 1
LOSING HURTS™
Designer:	A. Hughes-Lubeck
Height:	5", 12.7 cm
Colour:	Palomino horse, rider wears navy jacket and hat, yellow jodhpurs
Issued:	2001 in a limited edition of 1,000

U.S.	**$225.00**
Can.	**$300.00**
U.K.	**£125.00**
Aust.	**$325.00**

NT 2
POWERFUL HINDQUARTERS ARE A DISTINCT ADVANTAGE™
Designer:	A. Hughes-Lubeck
Height:	5 ¼", 13.3 cm
Colour:	Grey horse; rider has blonde hair and wears a black cap
Issued:	2001 in a limited edition of 1,000

U.S.	**$225.00**
Can.	**$300.00**
U.K.	**£125.00**
Aust.	**$325.00**

NT 3
EXHAUSTED™
Designer:	A. Hughes-Lubeck
Height:	4 ¼", 10.8 cm
Colour:	Brown horse; rider wears red jacket, yellow jodhpurs, black hat and shoes
Issued:	2001 in a limited edition of 1,000

U.S.	**$225.00**
Can.	**$300.00**
U.K.	**£125.00**
Aust.	**$325.00**

NT 4
CHOOSING GOOD FEET™
Designer:	A. Hughes-Lubeck
Height:	4 ¼", 10.8 cm
Colour:	Chestnut horse; rider wears a burgundy jacket, white jodhpurs, black hat and shoes
Issued:	2001 in a limited edition of 1,000

U.S.	**$225.00**
Can.	**$300.00**
U.K.	**£125.00**
Aust.	**$325.00**

NT 5
EXCESSIVE PRAISE™

Designer:	A. Hughes-Lubeck
Height:	5 ¼", 13.3 cm
Colour:	Brown horse; rider wears blue jersey and pale yellow jodhpurs
Issued:	2001 in a limited edition of 1,000

U.S.	**$225.00**
Can.	**$300.00**
U.K.	**£125.00**
Aust.	**$325.00**

NT 6
SUPPLING EXERCISES™

Designer:	A. Hughes-Lubeck
Height:	4 ¾", 12.1 cm
Colour:	Black horse; rider wears red jersey, yellow jodhpurs; blonde hair
Issued:	2001 in a limited edition of 1,000

U.S.	**$225.00**
Can.	**$300.00**
U.K.	**£125.00**
Aust.	**$325.00**

NT 7
BODY BRUSH™

Designer:	Shane Ridge
Height:	5 ¼", 13.3 cm
Colour:	Grey horse; rider wears black jacket and yellow jodhpurs
Issued:	2003 to the present

U.S.	**–**
Can.	**–**
U.K.	**£40.00**
Aust.	**–**

NT 8
DETECTING AILMENTS™

Designer:	Warren Platt
Height:	5 ¼", 13.3 cm
Colour:	Chestnut horse; doctor wears white medical coat, blue tie, grey trousers
Issued:	2003 to the present

U.S.	**–**
Can.	**–**
U.K.	**£40.00**
Aust.	**–**

NT 9
ICE CREAM TREAT™

Designer:	Martyn Alcock
Height:	5", 12.7 cm
Colour:	Dun horse; rider wears black jacket and cap, white jodhpurs
Issued:	2003 to the present

U.S.	**–**
Can.	**–**
U.K.	**£40.00**
Aust.	**–**

NT 10
IDEAL PONY FOR A NERVOUS CHILD™

Designer:	Martyn Alcock
Height:	5 ¼", 13.3 cm
Colour:	Brown horse; rider wears black hat and yellow jodhpurs
Issued:	2003 to the present

U.S.	**–**
Can.	**–**
U.K.	**£40.00**
Aust.	**–**

NT 11
SO TREAT HIM LIKE A FRIEND™

Designer:	Shane Ridge
Height:	5", 12.7 cm
Colour:	Black and white horse
Issued:	2003 to the present

U.S.	**–**
Can.	**–**
U.K.	**£40.00**
Aust.	**–**

NT 12
HE'LL FIND YOU™

Designer:	Shane Ridge
Height:	4 ¼", 10.8 cm
Colour:	Grey horse; rider wears black jacket and hat, yellow jodhpurs
Issued:	2003 to the present

U.S.	**–**
Can.	**–**
U.K.	**£40.00**
Aust.	**–**

NURSERY RHYMES
COLLECTION

HUMPTY DUMPTY
DNR 1
FROM THE NURSERY RHYME COLLECTION.
PRODUCED EXCLUSIVELY FOR UK FAIRS LTD.
IN A WORLDWIDE SPECIAL EDITION OF 1,500.
© 1998 ROYAL DOULTON © UK FAIRS LTD.

1246

LITTLE MISS MUFFET
DNR 2
FROM THE NURSERY RHYME COLLECTION.
PRODUCED EXCLUSIVELY FOR UKI CERAMICS LTD.
IN A WORLDWIDE SPECIAL EDITION OF 1,500.
© 1999 ROYAL DOULTON © UKI CERAMICS LTD

151

OLD MOTHER HUBBARD
DNR 3
FROM THE NURSERY RHYME COLLECTION.
PRODUCED EXCLUSIVELY FOR UKI CERAMICS LTD.
IN A WORLDWIDE SPECIAL EDITION OF 1,500.
© 1999 ROYAL DOULTON © UKI CERAMICS LTD.

THE CAT AND THE FIDDLE
DNR 4
FROM THE NURSERY RHYME COLLECTION.
PRODUCED EXCLUSIVELY FOR UKI CERAMICS LTD.
IN A WORLDWIDE SPECIAL EDITION OF 1,500.
© 1999 ROYAL DOULTON © UKI CERAMICS LTD

DNR 1
HUMPTY DUMPTY™

Designer:	Andy Moss
Height:	5 ½", 14.0 cm
Colour:	Red, pink, orange and black
Issued:	1998 in a special edition of 1,500
U.S.	**$125.00**
Can.	**$175.00**
U.K.	**£ 75.00**
Aust.	**$200.00**

DNR 2
LITTLE MISS MUFFET™

Designer:	Andy Moss
Height:	6", 15.0 cm
Colour:	Pink, white, red and black
Issued:	1998 in a special edition of 1,500
U.S.	**$125.00**
Can.	**$175.00**
U.K.	**£ 75.00**
Aust.	**$200.00**

DNR 3
OLD MOTHER HUBBARD™

Designer:	Andy Moss
Height:	7 ½", 19.1 cm
Colour:	Red, green, blue, white and black
Issued:	1999 in a special edition of 1,500
U.S.	**$125.00**
Can.	**$175.00**
U.K.	**£ 75.00**
Aust.	**$200.00**

DNR 4
THE CAT AND THE FIDDLE™

Designer:	Andy Moss
Height:	6", 15.0 cm
Colour:	Black, white red and grey
Issued:	1999 in a special edition of 1,500
U.S.	**$125.00**
Can.	**$175.00**
U.K.	**£ 75.00**
Aust.	**$200.00**

DNR 5
OLD KING COLE™

Designer:	Andy Moss
Height:	7", 17.8 cm
Colour:	Red, white, yellow and brown
Issued:	2000 in a special edition of 1,500

OLD KING COLE
DNR 5
FROM THE NURSERY RHYME COLLECTION.
PRODUCED EXCLUSIVELY FOR UKI CERAMICS LTD.
IN A WORLDWIDE SPECIAL EDITION OF 1,500.
© 2000 ROYAL DOULTON © UKI CERAMICS LTD

46

Doulton Number	Price			
	U.S. $	Can. $	U.K. £	Aust. $
DNR5	125.00	175.00	75.00	200.00

PADDINGTON BEAR CO. LTD.

RESIN SERIES 1996-1998
CERAMIC SERIES 1999

RESIN SERIES
1996 - 1998

PB1
PADDINGTON™ "AT THE STATION"
Style One

Designer:	Zoe Annand
Height:	4 ¼", 10.8 cm
Colour:	Brown, blue and yellow
Issued:	1996 - 1998
U.S.	**$55.00**
Can.	**$70.00**
U.K.	**£30.00**
Aust.	**$75.00**

PB2
PADDINGTON™ "BAKES A CAKE"

Designer:	Zoe Annand
Height:	4 ¼", 10.8 cm
Colour:	Red, black, blue and white
Issued:	1996 - 1998
U.S.	**$55.00**
Can.	**$70.00**
U.K.	**£30.00**
Aust.	**$75.00**

PB3
PADDINGTON™ "DECORATING"

Designer:	Zoe Annand
Height:	4 ¾", 12.0 cm
Colour:	Blue, red, silver and cream
Issued:	1996 - 1998
U.S.	**$55.00**
Can.	**$70.00**
U.K.	**£30.00**
Aust.	**$75.00**

PB4
PADDINGTON™ "SURFING"

Designer:	Zoe Annand
Height:	4", 10.1 cm
Colour:	Blue, yellow , red and brown
Issued:	1996 - 1998
U.S.	**$55.00**
Can.	**$70.00**
U.K.	**£30.00**
Aust.	**$75.00**

PB5
PADDINGTON™ "GARDENING"

Designer:	Zoe Annand
Height:	4", 10.1 cm
Colour:	Blue, red, green, yellow and red
Issued:	1996 - 1998
U.S.	**$55.00**
Can.	**$70.00**
U.K.	**£30.00**
Aust.	**$75.00**

PB6
PADDINGTON™ "BATHTIME"

Designer:	Zoe Annand
Height:	3 ¼", 8.5 cm
Colour:	Blue, yellow, brown and pink
Issued:	1996 - 1998
U.S.	**$55.00**
Can.	**$70.00**
U.K.	**£30.00**
Aust.	**$75.00**

PB7
PADDINGTON™ "THE GOLFER"

Designer:	Zoe Annand
Height:	3 ¾", 9.5 cm
Colour:	White, red, yellow and green
Issued:	1996 - 1998
U.S.	**$55.00**
Can.	**$70.00**
U.K.	**£30.00**
Aust.	**$75.00**

PB8
PADDINGTON™ "THE MUSICIAN"

Designer:	Zoe Annand
Height:	3 ¾", 9.5 cm
Colour:	Black, red, brown and brass
Issued:	1996 - 1998
U.S.	**$55.00**
Can.	**$70.00**
U.K.	**£30.00**
Aust.	**$75.00**

PB9
PADDINGTON™ "AT CHRISTMAS TIME"
Designer: Zoe Annand
Height: 3 ½", 8.9 cm
Colour: Red coat, blue boots, yellow sleigh
Issued: 1996 - 1998
U.S. **$55.00**
Can. **$70.00**
U.K. **£30.00**
Aust. **$75.00**

PB10
PADDINGTON™ "MARMALADE SANDWICH"
Designer: Zoe Annand
Height: 3 ½", 8.9 cm
Colour: Dark blue coat, yellow hat, green book, orange and white sandwiches
Issued: 1997 - 1998
U.S. **$55.00**
Can. **$70.00**
U.K. **£30.00**
Aust. **$75.00**

PB11
PADDINGTON™ "GOING TO BED"
Designer: Zoe Annand
Height: 3 ¾", 9.5 cm
Colour: Turquoise, red and yellow pyjamas, red hat
Issued: 1997 - 1998
U.S. **$55.00**
Can. **$70.00**
U.K. **£30.00**
Aust. **$75.00**

PB12
PADDINGTON™ "THE FISHERMAN"
Designer: Zoe Annand
Height: 3 ½", 8.9 cm
Colour: Red jacket with yellow buttons; dark blue hat and wellingtons
Issued: 1997 - 1998
U.S. **$55.00**
Can. **$70.00**
U.K. **£30.00**
Aust. **$75.00**

CERAMIC SERIES
1999

PADDINGTON™ "AT THE STATION"
Style Two

Modeller:	Warren Platt
Height:	3 ¼", 8.5 cm
Colour:	Brown, blue, red, grey and gold
Issued:	1999 in a special edition of 2,000
Series:	Gold edition
U.S.	**$ 90.00**
Can.	**$120.00**
U.K.	**£ 50.00**
Aust.	**$130.00**

Note: Commissioned by Paddington and Friends.

THE PIG PROMENADE

JOHN
PP 1

MATTHEW
PP 2

DAVID
PP 3

ANDREW
PP 4

PP 1
JOHN THE CONDUCTOR™
(Vietnamese Pot Bellied Pig)

Designer:	Martyn Alcock
Height:	4 ¾", 12.1 cm
Colour:	Black jacket and bowtie
Issued:	1993 - 1996

U.S.	**$ 80.00**
Can.	**$110.00**
U.K.	**£ 45.00**
Aust.	**$120.00**

PP 2
MATTHEW THE TRUMPET PLAYER™
(Large White Pig)

Designer:	A. Hughes-Lubeck
Height:	5", 12.7 cm
Colour:	Light red waistcoat, black bowtie
Issued:	1993 - 1996

U.S.	**$ 80.00**
Can.	**$110.00**
U.K.	**£ 45.00**
Aust.	**$120.00**

PP 3
DAVID THE FLUTE PLAYER™
(Tamworth Pig)

Designer:	A. Hughes-Lubeck
Height:	5 ¼", 13.3 cm
Colour:	Dark green waistcoat, black bowtie
Issued:	1993 - 1996

U.S.	**$ 80.00**
Can.	**$110.00**
U.K.	**£ 45.00**
Aust.	**$120.00**

PP 4
ANDREW THE CYMBAL PLAYER™
(Gloucester Old Spotted Pig)

Designer:	Martyn Alcock
Height:	4 ¾", 12.1 cm
Colour:	Blue waistcoat, yellow cymbals, black bowtie
Issued:	1993 - 1996
Varieties:	Also called George, PP10

U.S.	**$ 80.00**
Can.	**$110.00**
U.K.	**£ 45.00**
Aust.	**$120.00**

Beswick Ware
DANIEL
PP 5

Beswick Ware
MICHAEL
PP 6

BESWICK
B
ENGLAND
PP 7
JAMES

BESWICK
B
ENGLAND
PP 8
RICHARD

PP 5
DANIEL THE VIOLINIST™
(Saddleback Pig)

Designer:	A. Hughes-Lubeck
Height:	5 ¼", 13.3 cm
Colour:	Pale blue waistcoat, brown violin
Issued:	1993 - 1996

U.S.	**$ 80.00**
Can.	**$110.00**
U.K.	**£ 45.00**
Aust.	**$120.00**

PP 6
MICHAEL THE BASS DRUM PLAYER™ (Large Black Pig)

Designer:	Martyn Alcock
Height:	4 ¾", 12.1 cm
Colour:	Yellow waistcoat, red and white drum
Issued:	1993 - 1996

U.S.	**$ 80.00**
Can.	**$110.00**
U.K.	**£ 45.00**
Aust.	**$120.00**

PP 7
JAMES THE TRIANGLE PLAYER™
(Tamworth Piglet)

Designer:	Warren Platt
Height:	4", 10.1 cm
Colour:	Purple waistcoat, black bowtie
Issued:	1995 - 1996

U.S.	**$ 80.00**
Can.	**$110.00**
U.K.	**£ 45.00**
Aust.	**$120.00**

PP 8
RICHARD THE FRENCH HORN PLAYER™

Designer:	Shane Ridge
Height:	5", 12.7 cm
Colour:	Pale pink with dark grey spots, tan and beige waistcoat
Issued:	1996 - 1996
Varieties:	Also called Benjamin, PP12

U.S.	**$ 80.00**
Can.	**$110.00**
U.K.	**£ 45.00**
Aust.	**$120.00**

PP 9
CHRISTOPHER THE GUITAR PLAYER™

Designer:	Warren Platt
Height:	5 ½", 13.3 cm
Colour:	Dark grey, yellow and cream waistcoat, black bowtie
Issued:	1996 - 1996
Varieties:	Also called Thomas, PP11

U.S.	**$ 80.00**
Can.	**$110.00**
U.K.	**£ 45.00**
Aust.	**$120.00**

PP 10
GEORGE™

Designer:	Martyn Alcock
Height:	4 ¾", 12.1 cm
Colour:	Dark green waistcoat, yellow cymbals, black bowtie
Issued:	1996 in a limited edition of 2,000
Varieties:	Also called Andrew, PP4

U.S.	**$110.00**
Can.	**$150.00**
U.K.	**£ 60.00**
Aust.	**$165.00**

PP 11
THOMAS™

Designer:	Warren Platt
Height:	5", 12.7 cm
Colour:	Black pig with green waistcoat, yellow bowtie, white guitar
Issued:	1997 in a special edition of 2,000
Varieties:	Also called Christopher the Guitar Player, PP9

U.S.	**$110.00**
Can.	**$150.00**
U.K.	**£ 60.00**
Aust.	**$165.00**

PP 12
BENJAMIN™

Designer:	Shane Ridge
Height:	5", 12.7 cm
Colour:	White and black pig, orange bowtie, gold french horn
Issued:	1997 in a special edition of 2,000
Varieties:	Also called Richard the French Horn Player, PP8

U.S.	**$110.00**
Can.	**$150.00**
U.K.	**£ 60.00**
Aust.	**$165.00**

PUNCH AND JUDY

JUDY™

Modeller:	Shane Ridge
Height:	5 ¼", 13.3 cm
Colour:	Blue and white striped dress, white apron and mob cap, brown hair and rolling pin
Issued:	2001 in a limited edition of 2,500
Comm. by:	Doulton-Direct

Beswick Number		Price			
		U.S. $	Can. $	U.K. £	Aust. $
—		115.00	155.00	65.00	170.00

PUNCH™

Modeller:	Shane Ridge
Height:	5 ½", 14.0 cm
Colour:	Red and yellow tunic and hat, red and white striped stockings, brown shoes, green crocodile
Issued:	2001 in a limited edition of 2,500
Comm. by:	Doulton-Direct

Beswick Number		Price			
		U.S. $	Can. $	U.K. £	Aust. $
—		115.00	155.00	65.00	170.00

ST. TIGGYWINKLES

Royal Doulton
St. Tiggywinkles®
Henry Hedgehog
TW1/ 1979
© St.Tiggywinkles 1996
Made in Thailand

Royal Doulton
St. Tiggywinkles®
Harry Hedgehog
TW2/ 1269
© St.Tiggywinkles 1996
Made in Thailand

Royal Doulton
St. Tiggywinkles®
Fred Fox
TW3/ 1094
© St.Tiggywinkles 1996
Made in Thailand

Royal Doulton
St. Tiggywinkles®
Bob Badger
TW4/ 1698
© St.Tiggywinkles 1996
Made in Thailand

TW1
HENRY HEDGEHOG™
(Standing)

Modeller:	A. Hughes-Lubeck
Height:	3 ½", 8.5 cm
Colour:	Light and dark brown hedgehog wearing a purple sweater
Issued:	1997 - 1999
Series:	Wildlife Hospital Trust
U.S.	**$35.00**
Can.	**$50.00**
U.K.	**£20.00**
Aust.	**$55.00**

TW2
HARRY HEDGEHOG™
(Sitting)

Modeller:	A. Hughes-Lubeck
Height:	3 ½", 8.9 cm
Colour:	Light and dark brown hedgehog wearing a purple sweater, red cap
Issued:	1997 - 1999
Series:	Wildlife Hospital Trust
U.S.	**$35.00**
Can.	**$50.00**
U.K.	**£20.00**
Aust.	**$55.00**

TW3
FRED FOX™

Modeller:	Warren Platt
Height:	4", 10.1 cm
Colour:	Light brown fox wearing light blue overalls, pink shirt, white bandage around his head and tail
Issued:	1997 - 1998
Series:	Wildlife Hospital Trust
U.S.	**$35.00**
Can.	**$50.00**
U.K.	**£20.00**
Aust.	**$55.00**

TW4
BOB BADGER™

Modeller:	A. Hughes-Lubeck
Height:	3 ¾", 9.5 cm
Colour:	Brown, black and white badger wearing a yellow jumper and brown scarf; beige crutch
Issued:	1997 - 1999
Series:	Wildlife Hospital Trust
U.S.	**$35.00**
Can.	**$50.00**
U.K.	**£20.00**
Aust.	**$55.00**

Royal Doulton
St. Tiggywinkles
Rosie Rabbit
TW5/ 1456
© St.Tiggywinkles 1996
Made in Thailand

Royal Doulton
St. Tiggywinkles
Sarah Squirrel
TW6/ 0123
© St.Tiggywinkles 1996
Made in Thailand

Royal Doulton
St. Tiggywinkles
Daniel Duck
TW7/ 1925
© St.Tiggywinkles 1996
Made in Thailand

Royal Doulton
St. Tiggywinkles
Oliver Owl
TW8/ 1703
© St.Tiggywinkles 1996
Made in Thailand

TW5
ROSIE RABBIT™

Modeller:	A. Hughes-Lubeck
Height:	3 ½", 8.9 cm
Colour:	Grey rabbit wearing a light blue dress and rose pinafore
Issued:	1997 - 1999
Series:	Wildlife Hospital Trust

U.S.	**$35.00**
Can.	**$50.00**
U.K.	**£20.00**
Aust.	**$55.00**

TW6
SARAH SQUIRREL™

Modeller:	A. Hughes-Lubeck
Height:	3 ¼", 8.3 cm
Colour:	Brown squirrel wearing a pink and white dress
Issued:	1997 - 1998
Series:	Wildlife Hospital Trust

U.S.	**$35.00**
Can.	**$50.00**
U.K.	**£20.00**
Aust.	**$55.00**

TW7
DANIEL DUCK™

Modeller:	Shane Ridge
Height:	3 ½", 8.5 cm
Colour:	Yellow duck, white and red bandage, brown satchel
Issued:	1997 - 1999
Series:	Wildlife Hospital Trust

U.S.	**$35.00**
Can.	**$50.00**
U.K.	**£20.00**
Aust.	**$55.00**

TW8
OLIVER OWL™

Modeller:	Warren Platt
Height:	4", 10.1 cm
Colour:	Dark and light brown owl, white arm sling, red book
Issued:	1997 - 1999
Series:	Wildlife Hospital Trust

U.S.	**$35.00**
Can.	**$50.00**
U.K.	**£20.00**
Aust.	**$55.00**

Royal Doulton
St. Tiggywinkles®
Friends
TW9/ *1430*
© St. Tiggywinkles 1996
Made in Thailand

Royal Doulton
St. Tiggywinkles®
A Helping Hand
TW10/ *0303*
© St. Tiggywinkles 1996
Made in Thailand

Royal Doulton
St. Tiggywinkles®
Deborah Dormouse
TW11/ *458*
© St. Tiggywinkles 1998
Made in Thailand

Royal Doulton
St. Tiggywinkles®
Monty Mole
TW12/ *549*
© St. Tiggywinkles 1998
Made in Thailand

TW9
FRIENDS™

Modeller:	A. Hughes-Lubeck
Height:	4", 10.1 cm
Colour:	Light /dark brown hedgehog, green and yellow jacket, maroon hat; yellow ducklings, white bandages
Issued:	1997 - 1999
Series:	Wildlife Hospital Trust
U.S.	**$35.00**
Can.	**$50.00**
U.K.	**£20.00**
Aust.	**$55.00**

TW10
A HELPING HAND™

Modeller:	A. Hughes-Lubeck
Height:	4", 10.1 cm
Colour:	Light and dark brown hedgehog, white and grey rabbits, blue, pink and yellow clothing
Issued:	1997 - 1999
Series:	Wildlife Hospital Trust
U.S.	**$35.00**
Can.	**$50.00**
U.K.	**£20.00**
Aust.	**$55.00**

TW11
DEBORAH DORMOUSE™

Modeller:	Rob Simpson
Height:	3 ¼", 8.3 cm
Colour:	Brown dormouse, pink dress, white apron, brown basket
Issued:	1998 - 1999
Series:	Wildlife Hospital Trust
U.S.	**$35.00**
Can.	**$50.00**
U.K.	**£20.00**
Aust.	**$55.00**

TW12
MONTY MOLE™

Modeller:	Rob Simpson
Height:	3 ½", 8.5 cm
Colour:	Dark brown mole wearing a blue jacket, yellow hat, white arm sling
Issued:	1998 - 1999
Series:	Wildlife Hospital Trust
U.S.	**$35.00**
Can.	**$50.00**
U.K.	**£20.00**
Aust.	**$55.00**

TW13
FRANCHESCA FAWN™

Modeller:	Rob Simpson
Height:	3", 7.6 cm
Colour:	Pale brown fawn; white bandages
Issued:	1998 - 1999
Series:	Wildlife Hospital Trust

Royal Doulton
St. Tiggywinkles®
Franchesca Fawn
TW13/ *48*
© St. Tiggywinkles 1998
Made in Thailand

Doulton Number	Price			
	U.S. $	Can. $	U.K. £	Aust. $
TW13	35.00	50.00	20.00	55.00

THE SNOWMAN
GIFT COLLECTION

Royal Doulton®
THE SNOWMAN™
GIFT COLLECTION
JAMES
DS 1
© 1985 ROYAL DOULTON (UK)
© S ENT 1985

Royal Doulton®
THE SNOWMAN™
GIFT COLLECTION
THE SNOWMAN
DS 2
© 1985 ROYAL DOULTON (UK)
© S ENT 1985

Royal Doulton®
THE SNOWMAN™
GIFT COLLECTION
STYLISH SNOWMAN
DS 3
© 1985 ROYAL DOULTON (UK)
© S ENT 1985

Royal Doulton®
THE SNOWMAN™
GIFT COLLECTION
THANK YOU SNOWMAN
DS 4
© 1985 ROYAL DOULTON (UK)
© S ENT 1985

DS 1 **JAMES™** **Style One**		**DS 2** **THE SNOWMAN™** **Style One**		**DS 3** **STYLISH SNOWMAN™**		**DS 4** **THANK YOU SNOWMAN™**	
Designer:	Harry Sales	Designer:	Harry Sales	Designer:	Harry Sales	Designer:	Harry Sales
Modeller:	David Lyttleton	Modeller:	David Lyttleton	Modeller:	David Lyttleton	Modeller:	David Lyttleton
Height:	3 ¾", 9.5 cm	Height:	5", 12.7 cm	Height:	5", 12.7 cm	Height:	5", 12.7 cm
Colour:	Brown dressing-gown, blue and white striped pyjamas,	Colour:	White snowman wearing a green hat and scarf	Colour:	White snowman wearing blue trousers, lilac braces, grey hat, yellow tie with red stripes	Colour:	Snowman - green hat and scarf James - brown dressing-gown
Issued:	1985 - 1993	Issued:	1985 - 1994			Issued:	1985 - 1994
U.S.	**$200.00**	**U.S.**	**$150.00**	Issued:	1985 - 1993	**U.S.**	**$135.00**
Can.	**$265.00**	**Can.**	**$200.00**	**U.S.**	**$175.00**	**Can.**	**$175.00**
U.K.	**£110.00**	**U.K.**	**£ 85.00**	**Can.**	**$250.00**	**U.K.**	**£ 75.00**
Aust.	**$280.00**	**Aust.**	**$225.00**	**U.K.**	**£100.00**	**Aust.**	**$190.00**
				Aust.	**$275.00**		

Backstamp not
available
at press time

Royal Doulton ®
THE SNOWMAN ™
GIFT COLLECTION
COWBOY SNOWMAN
DS 6
© 1985 ROYAL DOULTON (UK)
© S ENT 1985

Royal Doulton ®
THE SNOWMAN ™
GIFT COLLECTION
HIGHLAND SNOWMAN
DS 7
© 1985 ROYAL DOULTON (UK)
© S ENT 1985

Royal Doulton ®
THE SNOWMAN ™
GIFT COLLECTION
LADY SNOWMAN
DS 8
© 1985 ROYAL DOULTON (UK)
© S ENT 1985

DS 5
SNOWMAN MAGIC MUSIC BOX™

Designer:	Harry Sales
Modeller:	David Lyttleton
Height:	8", 20.3 cm
Colour:	White snowman wearing a green hat and scarf, cream music box with blue, green and pink balloon design
Issued:	1985 - 1994
Tune:	Walking in the Air

U.S.	**$275.00**
Can.	**$350.00**
U.K.	**£150.00**
Aust.	**$375.00**

DS 6
COWBOY SNOWMAN™

Designer:	Harry Sales
Modeller:	David Lyttleton
Height:	5", 12.7 cm
Colour:	White snowman wearing a brown hat and holster belt
Issued:	1986 - 1992

U.S.	**$275.00**
Can.	**$350.00**
U.K.	**£150.00**
Aust.	**$375.00**

DS 7
HIGHLAND SNOWMAN™

Designer:	Harry Sales
Modeller:	David Lyttleton
Height:	5 ¼", 13.3 cm
Colour:	White snowman wearing a red, blue and white kilt
Issued:	1987 - 1993

U.S.	**$275.00**
Can.	**$350.00**
U.K.	**£150.00**
Aust.	**$375.00**

DS 8
LADY SNOWMAN™

Designer:	Harry Sales
Modeller:	David Lyttleton
Height:	5", 12.7 cm
Colour:	White snowman wearing a pink apron and blue hat
Issued:	1987 - 1992

U.S.	**$550.00**
Can.	**$725.00**
U.K.	**£300.00**
Aust.	**$775.00**

Royal Doulton®
THE SNOWMAN ™
GIFT COLLECTION
BASS DRUMMER SNOWMAN
DS 9
© 1987 ROYAL DOULTON
© S ENT 1987

Royal Doulton®
THE SNOWMAN ™
GIFT COLLECTION
FLAUTIST SNOWMAN
DS 10
© 1987 ROYAL DOULTON
© S ENT 1987

Royal Doulton®
THE SNOWMAN ™
GIFT COLLECTION
VIOLINIST SNOWMAN
DS 11
© 1987 ROYAL DOULTON
© S ENT 1987

Royal Doulton®
THE SNOWMAN ™
GIFT COLLECTION
PIANIST SNOWMAN
DS 12
© 1987 ROYAL DOULTON
© S ENT 1987

DS 9
BASS DRUMMER SNOWMAN™

Designer:	Graham Tongue
Modeller:	Warren Platt
Height:	5 ¼", 13.3 cm
Colour:	White snowman wearing a pale blue hat; pink and yellow drum, pale brown straps
Issued:	1987 - 1993
U.S.	**$325.00**
Can.	**$425.00**
U.K.	**£175.00**
Aust.	**$450.00**

DS 10
FLAUTIST SNOWMAN™

Designer:	Graham Tongue
Modeller:	Warren Platt
Height:	5 ½", 14.0 cm
Colour:	White snowman wearing a yellow and red hat and a brown tie
Issued:	1987 - 1993
U.S.	**$245.00**
Can.	**$325.00**
U.K.	**£135.00**
Aust.	**$350.00**

DS 11
VIOLINIST SNOWMAN™

Designer:	Graham Tongue
Modeller:	Warren Platt
Height:	5 ¼", 13.3 cm
Colour:	White snowman wearing a green waistcoat with yellow collar, blue bowtie, brown hat, playing a violin
Issued:	1987 - 1994
U.S.	**$160.00**
Can.	**$215.00**
U.K.	**£ 90.00**
Aust.	**$230.00**

DS 12
PIANIST SNOWMAN™

Designer:	Graham Tongue
Modeller:	Warren Platt
Height:	5", 12.7 cm
Colour:	White snowman wearing a blue crown / orange tie
Issued:	1987 - 1994
U.S.	**$135.00**
Can.	**$175.00**
U.K.	**£ 75.00**
Aust.	**$200.00**

Royal Doulton®
THE SNOWMAN™
GIFT COLLECTION
SNOWMAN'S PIANO
DS 13
© 1987 ROYAL DOULTON
© S. ENT 1987

Royal Doulton®
THE SNOWMAN™
GIFT COLLECTION
CYMBAL PLAYER SNOWMAN
DS 14
© 1988 ROYAL DOULTON
© S ENT 1988

Royal Doulton®
THE SNOWMAN™
GIFT COLLECTION
DRUMMER SNOWMAN
DS 15
© 1988 ROYAL DOULTON
© S ENT 1988

Royal Doulton®
THE SNOWMAN™
GIFT COLLECTION
TRUMPETER SNOWMAN
DS 16
© 1988 ROYAL DOULTON
© S ENT 1988

DS 13
SNOWMAN'S PIANO™

Designer:	Graham Tongue
Modeller:	Warren Platt
Height:	5 ¼", 13.3 cm
Colour:	White piano
Issued:	1987 - 1994
U.S.	**$ 90.00**
Can.	**$125.00**
U.K.	**£ 50.00**
Aust.	**$135.00**

DS 14
CYMBAL PLAYER SNOWMAN™

Designer:	Graham Tongue
Modeller:	Warren Platt
Height:	5 ¼", 13.3 cm
Colour:	White snowman wearing a brown waistcoat, green hat and bowtie, playing yellow cymbals
Issued:	1988 - 1993
U.S.	**$500.00**
Can.	**$650.00**
U.K.	**£275.00**
Aust.	**$675.00**

DS 15
DRUMMER SNOWMAN™

Designer:	Graham Tongue
Modeller:	Warren Platt
Height:	5 ¾", 14.6 cm
Colour:	White snowman wearing a red and black hat, purple bowtie, playing pink and yellow drum
Issued:	1988 - 1994
U.S.	**$175.00**
Can.	**$250.00**
U.K.	**£100.00**
Aust.	**$275.00**

DS 16
TRUMPETER SNOWMAN™

Designer:	Graham Tongue
Modeller:	Warren Platt
Height:	5", 12.7 cm
Colour:	White snowman wearing a pink hat playing a yellow trumpet
Issued:	1988 - 1993
U.S.	**$550.00**
Can.	**$725.00**
U.K.	**£300.00**
Aust.	**$775.00**

Royal Doulton®
THE SNOWMAN™
GIFT COLLECTION
CELLIST SNOWMAN
DS 17
© 1988 ROYAL DOULTON
© S ENT 1988

Backstamp not
available
at press time

Royal Doulton®
THE SNOWMAN™
GIFT COLLECTION
THE SNOWMAN
MONEY BOX
DS 19
© 1990 ROYAL DOULTON
© S ENT 1990

Royal Doulton®
THE SNOWMAN™
GIFT COLLECTION
THE SNOWMAN
TOBOGGANING
DS 20
© 1990 ROYAL DOULTON
© S ENT 1990

DS 17
CELLIST SNOWMAN™

Designer:	Graham Tongue
Modeller:	Warren Platt
Height:	5 ¼", 13.3 cm
Colour:	White snowman wearing a green waistcoat with yellow collar, blue bowtie, playing a brown cello
Issued:	1988 - 1993
U.S.	**$175.00**
Can.	**$250.00**
U.K.	**£100.00**
Aust.	**$275.00**

DS 18
SNOWMAN MUSICAL BOX™

Designer:	Unknown
Height:	8", 22.5 cm
Colour:	White snowman wearing a red, blue and white kilt, green, pink and blue balloons on box
Issued:	1988 - 1990
Tune:	Blue Bells of Scotland
U.S.	**$550.00**
Can.	**$725.00**
U.K.	**£300.00**
Aust.	**$775.00**

DS 19
SNOWMAN MONEY BOX™

Designer:	Graham Tongue
Modeller:	Warren Platt
Height:	8 ½", 21.6 cm
Colour:	White snowman wearing a green hat with grey band and green scarf
Issued:	1990 - 1994
U.S.	**$225.00**
Can.	**$300.00**
U.K.	**£125.00**
Aust.	**$325.00**

DS 20
THE SNOWMAN TOBOGGANING™

Designer:	Graham Tongue
Modeller:	Warren Platt
Height:	5", 12.7 cm
Colour:	White snowman wearing a green hat and scarf, rose-pink toboggan
Issued:	1990 - 1994
U.S.	**$225.00**
Can.	**$300.00**
U.K.	**£125.00**
Aust.	**$325.00**

Royal Doulton®
THE SNOWMAN™
GIFT COLLECTION
THE SNOWMAN
SKIING
DS 21
© 1990 ROYAL DOULTON
© S. ENT 1990

Royal Doulton®
THE SNOWMAN™
GIFT COLLECTION
THE SNOWMAN
SNOWBALLING
DS 22
© 1990 ROYAL DOULTON
© S. ENT 1990

Royal Doulton®
THE SNOWMAN™
GIFT COLLECTION
BUILDING THE
SNOWMAN
DS 23
© 1990 ROYAL DOULTON
© S. ENT 1990

Backstamp not
available
at press time

DS 21
THE SNOWMAN SKIING™

Designer:	Graham Tongue
Modeller:	Warren Platt
Height:	5", 12.7 cm
Colour:	White snowman wearing a green hat and scarf, yellow and black goggles
Issued:	1990 - 1992
U.S.	**$ 900.00**
Can.	**$1,200.00**
U.K.	**£ 500.00**
Aust.	**$1,300.00**

DS 22
THE SNOWMAN SNOWBALLING™

Designer:	Graham Tongue
Modeller:	Warren Platt
Height:	5", 12.7 cm
Colour:	White snowman wearing a green hat and scarf, brown tree stump
Issued:	1990 - 1994
U.S.	**$275.00**
Can.	**$350.00**
U.K.	**£150.00**
Aust.	**$375.00**

DS 23
BUILDING THE SNOWMAN™

Designer:	Graham Tongue
Modeller:	Warren Platt
Height:	4", 10.1 cm
Colour:	White snowman wearing a green hat and scarf
Issued:	1990 - 1994
U.S.	**$275.00**
Can.	**$350.00**
U.K.	**£150.00**
Aust.	**$375.00**

DANCING IN THE SNOW™

Designer.:	Shane Ridge
Modeller:	Shane Ridge
Height:	5 ¾", 14.6 cm
Colour:	White, green, brown and blue
Issued:	1999 ltd. ed. 2,500
Series:	Tableau
Comm. by:	Doulton-Direct
U.S.	**$450.00**
Can.	**$600.00**
U.K.	**£250.00**
Aust.	**$650.00**

Note: Issued to commemorate the 21st Anniversary of Raymond Briggs' Tale.

JAMES™
Style Two

Designer:	Shane Ridge
Modeller:	Shane Ridge
Height:	4 ¼", 10.8 cm
Colour:	Brown, white and blue
Issued:	1999 in a limited edition of 2,500

U.S.	**$135.00**
Can.	**$175.00**
U.K.	**£ 75.00**
Aust.	**$200.00**

Note: Issued as a pair with The Snowman (Style Two).

THE SNOWMAN™
Style Two

Designer:	Shane Ridge
Modeller:	Shane Ridge
Height:	5 ¾", 14.6 cm
Colour:	White and green
Issued:	1999 in a limited edition of 2,500

U.S.	**$135.00**
Can.	**$175.00**
U.K.	**£ 75.00**
Aust.	**$200.00**

Note: Issued as a pair with James (Style Two).

JAMES™
Style Three
(James Builds a Snowman)

Designer:	Shane Ridge
Height:	4", 10.1 cm
Colour:	Maroon/blue/black
Issued:	2000 ltd. ed. 2,500
Comm. by:	Doulton-Direct

U.S.	**$135.00**
Can.	**$175.00**
U.K.	**£ 75.00**
Aust.	**$200.00**

Note: Issued, numbered and sold as a pair with The Snowman (Style Three).

THE SNOWMAN™
Style Three
(James Builds a Snowman)

Designer:	Shane Ridge
Modeller:	Shane Ridge
Height:	6", 15.0 cm
Colour:	White and green
Issued:	2000 ltd. ed. 2,500
Comm. by:	Doulton-DIrect

U.S.	**$135.00**
Can.	**$175.00**
U.K.	**£ 75.00**
Aust.	**$200.00**

Note: Issued, numbered and sold as a pair with James (Style Three).

SNOWMAN AND JAMES
THE ADVENTURE BEGINS™

Designer:	Shane Ridge
Height:	6", 15.0 cm
Colour:	White, green, brown and blue
Issued:	2000 in a limited edition of 2,500
Series:	Tableau
Comm. by:	Doulton-Direct

U.S.	**$350.00**
Can.	**$475.00**
U.K.	**£200.00**
Aust.	**$500.00**

WALKING IN THE AIR™
Wall Plaque

Designer:	Shane Ridge
Modeller:	Shane Ridge
Height:	8" x 13 ½"
Colour:	Blue, white, tan, brown, green
Issued:	2001 ltd. ed. 2,500
Comm. by:	Doulton-Direct

U.S.	**$175.00**
Can.	**$250.00**
U.K.	**£100.00**
Aust.	**$275.00**

DRESSING THE SNOWMAN™

Designer:	Shane Ridge
Modeller:	Shane Ridge
Height:	6". 15.0 cm
Colour:	White, green, red, blue, black
Issued:	2002 in a limited edition of 2,500
Comm. by:	Doulton-Direct

U.S.	**$550.00**
Can.	**$725.00**
U.K.	**£300.00**
Aust.	**$775.00**

THE JOURNEY ENDS™

Designer:	Shane Ridge
Modeller:	Shane Ridge
Height:	4", 10.0 cm
Colour:	Blue, white, tan, brown, green
Issued:	2002 in a limited edition of 2,500
Comm. by:	Doulton-Direct

U.S.	**$ 725.00**
Can.	**$ 950.00**
U.K.	**£ 400.00**
Aust.	**$1,000.00**

SPORTING
CHARACTERS

SC1
FLY FISHING

Designer:	Andy Moss
Height:	3 ¼", 8.3 cm
Colour:	Green, slate blue, and black
Issued:	1998 in a special edition of 1,500

U.S.	**$ 80.00**
Can.	**$100.00**
U.K.	**£ 45.00**
Aust.	**$110.00**

SC2
LAST LION OF DEFENCE

Designer:	Andy Moss
Height:	4 ¼", 10.8 cm
Colour:	Red and white
Issued:	1998 in a special edition of 1,500

U.S.	**$ 70.00**
Can.	**$ 95.00**
U.K.	**£ 40.00**
Aust.	**$100.00**

SC3
IT'S A KNOCKOUT

Designer:	Andy Moss
Height:	4 ¼", 10.8 cm
Colour:	Red, white and black
Issued:	1998 in a special edition of 1,500

U.S.	**$ 70.00**
Can.	**$ 95.00**
U.K.	**£ 40.00**
Aust.	**$100.00**

SC4
SLOPING OFF

Designer:	Andy Moss
Height:	5 ¼", 13.3 cm
Colour:	White, black and yellow
Issued:	1999 in a special edition of 1,500

U.S.	**$ 90.00**
Can.	**$125.00**
U.K.	**£ 50.00**
Aust.	**$135.00**

SC5
A ROUND WITH FOXY

Designer:	Andy Moss
Height:	6", 15.0 cm
Colour:	Green, yellow and brown
Issued:	2000 in a special edition of 1,500

U.S.	**$ 80.00**
Can.	**$100.00**
U.K.	**£ 45.00**
Aust.	**$110.00**

SC6
OUT FOR A DUCK

Designer:	Andy Moss
Height:	5 ½", 14.0 cm
Colour:	Cream
Issued:	2000 in a special edition of 1,500

U.S.	**$ 90.00**
Can.	**$125.00**
U.K.	**£ 50.00**
Aust.	**$135.00**

BRAMBLY HEDGE

(DBH1)   POPPY EYEBRIGHT
Style One

(DBH2)   MR. APPLE
Style One

(DBH3)   MRS. APPLE
Style One

(DBH4)   LORD WOODMOUSE
Style One

(DBH5)   LADY WOODMOUSE
Style One

(DBH6)   DUSTY DOGWOOD
Style One

(DBH7)   WILFRED TOADFLAX
Style One

(DBH8)   PRIMROSE WOODMOUSE

(DBH9)   OLD MRS. EYEBRIGHT

BRAMBLY HEDGE

(DBH10A)   MR. TOADFLAX
Tail At Front, With Cushion

(DBH10B)   MR. TOADFLAX
Style One, Tail At Back, Without Cushion

(DBH10B)   MR. TOADFLAX
Tail At Back, With Cushion

(DBH11)   MRS. TOADFLAX

(DBH12)   CATKIN

(DBH13)   OLD VOLE

(DBH14)   BASIL
Style One

(DBH15)   MRS. CRUSTYBREAD

(DBH16)   CLOVER

BRAMBLY HEDGE

(DBH17) TEASEL

(DBH18) STORE STUMP
MONEY BOX

(DBH19) LILY WEAVER
Style One

(DBH20) FLAX WEAVER
Style One

(DBH21) CONKER

(DBH22) PRIMROSE ENTERTAINS

(DBH23) WILFRED ENTERTAINS

(DBH24) MR. SALTAPPLE
Style One

(DBH25) MRS. SALTAPPLE
Style One

BRAMBLY HEDGE

(DBH26)   DUSTY AND BABY

(DBH30)   THE ICE BALL

(DBH31)   LORD WOODMOUSE
           Style Two

(DBH32)   LADY WOODMOUSE
           Style Two

(DBH33)   PRIMROSE PICKING
                    BERRIES

(DBH34)   WILFRED CARRIES
           THE PICNIC

(DBH35)   WILFRED AND THE TOY CHEST MONEY BOX

BRAMBLY HEDGE

(DBH36)   POPPY EYEBRIGHT
Style Two

(DBH37)   DUSTY DOGWOOD
Style Two

(DBH38)   BASIL
Style Two

(DBH39)   MR. SALTAPPLE
Style Two

(DBH40)   MRS. SALTAPPLE
Style Two

(DBH41)   PEBBLE

(DBH42)   SHELL

(DBH43)   SHRIMP

(DBH44)   THE BRIDE
AND THE GROOM

BRAMBLY HEDGE

(DBH45)   HAPPY BIRTHDAY WILFRED

(DBH46)   MR. TOADFLAX
Style Two

(DBH47)   MRS. APPLE
Style Two

(DBH48)   HEADING HOME

(DBH49)   WILFRED'S
BIRTHDAY CAKE

(DBH50)   WHERE ARE BASIL'S
TROUSERS?

(DBH51)   DUSTY'S BUNS

BRAMBLY HEDGE

(DBH52) MRS. TOADFLAX
DECORATES CAKE

MR. APPLE
Style Two

(DBH54) LILY WEAVER
Style Two

(DBH55) FLAX WEAVER
Style Two

(DBH56) WILFRED TOADFLAX
Style Two

(DBH57) ON THE LEDGE

(DBH58) LILY WEAVER SPINNING

(DBH59) TEA AT
HORNBEAM TREE

(DBH60) A CHEERFUL
BLAZE

BRAMBLY HEDGE

(DBH61)   SHOOTING THE RAPIDS

(DBH62)   OLD MRS. EYEBRIGHT

(DBH63)   YOU'RE SAFE

(DBH64)   IN THE WOODS

(DBH65)   IN THE BRAMBLES

(DBH66)   OFF TO PICK MUSHROOMS

(DBH67)   LET'S MAKE A SNOWMOUSE

(DBH68)   HOT BUTTERED TOAST FOR
BREAKFAST

(DBH69)   HOME FOR SUPPER

TEDDY BEARS

4130
HENRY

Designer:	Robert Tabbenor
Height:	5 ½", 14.0 cm
Colour:	Light brown
Issued:	2001 in a limited edition of 2,500
Comm. by:	Doulton-Direct

U.S.	**$100.00**
Can.	**$150.00**
U.K.	**£ 60.00**
Aust.	**$175.00**

4131
EDWARD

Designer:	Robert Tabbenor
Height:	6", 15.0 cm
Colour:	Dark brown
Issued:	2001 in a limited edition of 2,500
Comm. by:	Doulton-Direct

U.S.	**$100.00**
Can.	**$150.00**
U.K.	**£ 60.00**
Aust.	**$175.00**

4132
GEORGE

Designer:	Robert Tabbenor
Height:	6", 15.0 cm
Colour:	Golden Brown
Issued:	2001 in a limited edition of 2,500
Comm. by:	Doulton-Direct

U.S.	**$100.00**
Can.	**$150.00**
U.K.	**£ 60.00**
Aust.	**$175.00**

4133
WILLIAM

Designer:	Robert Tabbenor
Height:	6", 15.0 cm
Colour:	Light brown
Issued:	2001 in a limited edition of 2,500
Comm. by:	Doulton-Direct

U.S.	**$100.00**
Can.	**$150.00**
U.K.	**£ 60.00**
Aust.	**$175.00**

THUNDERBIRDS

3337
LADY PENELOPE™

Beswick:	3337
Designer:	William K. Harper
Height:	4", 10.1 cm
Colour:	Pink hat and coat, blonde hair
Issued:	1992 in a limited edition of 2,500
U.S.	**$200.00**
Can.	**$275.00**
U.K.	**£125.00**
Aust.	**$300.00**

3339
BRAINS™

Beswick:	3339
Designer:	William K. Harper
Height:	4", 10.1 cm
Colour:	Black and blue uniform, blue glasses, black hair
Issued:	1992 in a limited edition of 2,500
U.S.	**$185.00**
Can.	**$250.00**
U.K.	**£115.00**
Aust.	**$275.00**

3344
SCOTT TRACY™

Beswick:	3344
Designer:	William K. Harper
Height:	4", 10.1 cm
Colour:	Blue uniform, light blue band
Issued:	1992 in a limited edition of 2,500
U.S.	**$200.00**
Can.	**$275.00**
U.K.	**£125.00**
Aust.	**$300.00**

3345
VIRGIL TRACY™

Beswick:	3345
Designer:	William K. Harper
Height:	4", 10.1 cm
Colour:	Blue uniform, yellow band
Issued:	1992 in a limited edition of 2,500
U.S.	**$185.00**
Can.	**$250.00**
U.K.	**£115.00**
Aust.	**$275.00**

3346
PARKER™

Beswick:	3346
Designer:	William K. Harper
Height:	4", 10.1 cm
Colour:	Blue-grey uniform
Issued:	1992 in a limited edition of 2,500
U.S.	**$165.00**
Can.	**$225.00**
U.K.	**£100.00**
Aust.	**$250.00**

3348
THE HOOD™

Beswick:	3348
Designer:	William K. Harper
Height:	4", 10.1 cm
Colour:	Browns
Issued:	1992 in a limited edition of 2,500
U.S.	**$165.00**
Can.	**$225.00**
U.K.	**£100.00**
Aust.	**$250.00**

TRUMPTONSHIRE

4054
PC MCGARRY™

Designer:	Gordon Murray
Modeller:	Robert Simpson
Height:	5 ¾", 14.6 cm
Colour:	Navy and white
Issued:	2001 in a limited edition of 2,500
Comm. by:	Doulton-Direct

U.S.	**$225.00**
Can.	**$300.00**
U.K.	**£125.00**
Aust.	**$325.00**

4055
WINDY MILLER™

Designer:	Gordon Murray
Modeller:	Robert Simpson
Height:	5 ½", 14.0 cm
Colour:	Blue, red and black
Issued:	2001 in a limited edition of 2,500
Comm. by:	Doutlon-Direct

U.S.	**$115.00**
Can.	**$150.00**
U.K.	**£ 65.00**
Aust.	**$175.00**

4063
CAPTAIN FLACK™

Designer:	Gordon Murray
Modeller:	Robert Simpson
Height:	6", 15.0 cm
Colour:	Navy, gold, yellow and black
Issued:	2001 in a limited edition of 2,500
Comm. by:	Doulton-Direct

U.S.	**$115.00**
Can.	**$150.00**
U.K.	**£ 65.00**
Aust.	**$175.00**

4065
DR. MOPP™

Designer:	Gordon Murray
Modeller:	Robert Simpson
Height:	5 ¾", 14.6 cm
Colour:	Purple, blue, white, yellow and black
Issued:	2001 in a limited edition of 2,500
Comm. by:	Doulton-Direct

U.S.	**$ 80.00**
Can.	**$100.00**
U.K.	**£ 45.00**
Aust.	**$110.00**

4066
THE MAYOR™

Designer:	Gordon Murray
Modeller:	Robert Simpson
Height:	5 ½", 14.0 cm
Colour:	Black, red, blue and gold
Issued:	2001 in a limited edition of 2,500
Comm. by:	Doulton-Direct

U.S.	**$ 80.00**
Can.	**$100.00**
U.K.	**£ 45.00**
Aust.	**$110.00**

4067
MRS. HONEYMAN™

Designer:	Gordon Murray
Modeller:	Robert Simpson
Height:	5 ½", 14.0 cm
Colour:	Pink, black, white, yellow and purple
Issued:	2001 in a limited edition of 2,500
Comm. by:	Doulton-Direct

U.S.	**$100.00**
Can.	**$125.00**
U.K.	**£ 55.00**
Aust.	**$135.00**

4184
MRS. DINGLE™

Designer:	Gordon Murray
Modeller:	Robert Simpson
Height:	5 ¼", 13.3 cm
Colour:	Blue, red and white
Issued:	2001 in a limited edition of 2,500
Comm. by:	Doulton-Direct

U.S.	**$250.00**
Can.	**$325.00**
U.K.	**£135.00**
Aust.	**$350.00**

4185
JONATHAN BELL™

Designer:	Gordon Murray
Modeller:	Robert Simpson
Height:	5 ¼", 13.3 cm
Colour:	Brown, yellow, green and black
Issued:	2001 in a limited edition of 2,500
Comm. by:	Doulton-Direct

U.S.	**$175.00**
Can.	**$250.00**
U.K.	**£100.00**
Aust.	**$275.00**

4186
MICKEY MURPHY™

Designer:	Gordon Murray
Modeller:	Robert Simpson
Height:	5 ½", 14.0 cm
Colour:	White, blue and yellow
Issued:	2001 in a limited edition of 2,500
Comm. by:	Doulton-Direct

U.S.	**$350.00**
Can.	**$450.00**
U.K.	**£200.00**
Aust.	**$500.00**

4187
MRS COBBIT™

Designer:	Gordon Murray
Modeller:	Robert Simpson
Height:	5 ¼", 13.3 cm
Colour:	Yellow, navy and light blue
Issued:	2001 in a limited edition of 2,500
Comm. by:	Doulton-Direct

U.S.	**$350.00**
Can.	**$450.00**
U.K.	**£200.00**
Aust.	**$500.00**

P. C. McGarry, Jonathan Bell, Dr. Mopp

TURNER ENTERTAINMENT

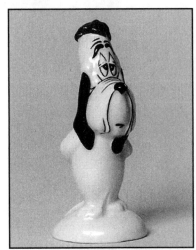

3547
DROOPY™

Designer:	Simon Ward
Height:	4 ½", 11.4 cm
Colour:	White dog with black ears, red cap
Issued:	1995 in a special edition of 2,000

Beswick		Price		
Number	U.S. $	Can. $	U.K. £	Aust. $
3547	115.00	150.00	65.00	175.00

3549
JERRY™

Designer:	Simon Ward
Height:	3", 7.6 cm
Colour	Red-brown and cream mouse, white base
Issued:	1995 in special edition of 2,000
Series:	Tom and Jerry

Beswick		Price		
Number	U.S. $	Can. $	U.K. £	Aust. $
3549	115.00	150.00	65.00	175.00

3552
TOM™

Designer:	Simon Ward
Height:	4 ½", 11.4 cm
Colour:	Grey-blue and pink cat, white base
Issued:	1995 in a special edition of 2,000
Series:	Tom and Jerry

Beswick		Price		
Number	U.S. $	Can. $	U.K. £	Aust. $
3552	115.00	150.00	65.00	175.00

THE WIZARD OF OZ™

3709
SCARECROW™

Designer:	Andy Moss
Height:	6 ½", 16.5 cm
Colour:	Black hat and shirt, brown pants and shoes
Issued:	1998 in a special edition of 1,500
Series:	The Wizard of Oz

Doulton Number	Price			
	U.S. $	Can. $	U.K. £	Aust. $
3709	175.00	225.00	100.00	250.00

3731
LION™

Designer:	Andy Moss
Height:	6", 15.0 cm
Colour:	Light and dark brown
Issued:	1998 in a special edition of 1,500
Series:	The Wizard of Oz

Doulton Number	Price			
	U.S. $	Can. $	U.K. £	Aust. $
3731	175.00	225.00	100.00	250.00

3732
DOROTHY™

Designer:	Andy Moss
Height:	5", 12.7 cm
Colour:	Blue and white dress, red shoes, black dog
Issued:	1998 in a special edition of 1,500
Series:	The Wizard of Oz

Doulton Number	Price			
	U.S. $	Can. $	U.K. £	Aust. $
3732	175.00	225.00	100.00	250.00

3738
TINMAN™

Designer:	Andy Moss
Height:	7", 17.8 cm
Colour:	Grey
Issued:	1998 in a special edition of 1,500
Series:	The Wizard of Oz

Doulton Number	Price			
	U.S. $	Can. $	U.K. £	Aust. $
3738	175.00	225.00	100.00	250.00

20TH CENTURY ADVERTISING CLASSICS

AC 1
GOLLY™

Modeller:	William K. Harper
Height:	5 ¾", 14.6 cm
Colour:	Blue, red, orange and white
Issued:	1999 in a limited edition of 2,000
Slogan:	Golly it's Good!
U.S.	**$350.00**
Can.	**$450.00**
U.K.	**£200.00**
Aust.	**$500.00**

AC 2
FATHER WILLIAM™

Modeller:	William K. Harper
Height:	6 ¼", 15.9 cm
Colour:	Black, yellow, red and grey
Issued:	1999 in a limited edition of 2,000
Slogan:	Get YOUNGER every day
U.S.	**$225.00**
Can.	**$300.00**
U.K.	**£125.00**
Aust.	**$350.00**

AC 3
SIR KREEMY KNUT™
(Sharps Toffee-Trebor Bassett Ltd)

Modeller:	William K. Harper
Height:	6 ¼", 15.9 cm
Colour:	Blue, white, red black and brown
Issued:	1999 in a limited edition of 2,000
Slogan:	Sharps the word for Toffee!
U.S.	**$225.00**
Can.	**$300.00**
U.K.	**£125.00**
Aust.	**$350.00**

AC 4
FOX'S POLAR BEAR™
(Fox's Glacier Mints - Nestlé)

Modeller:	William K. Harper
Height:	4", 10.1 cm
Colour:	White
Issued:	1999 in a limited edition of 2,000
Slogan:	FOX
U.S.	**$275.00**
Can.	**$350.00**
U.K.	**£150.00**
Aust.	**$400.00**

AC 5
PLAYER'S 'HERO' SAILOR™
(John Player & Sons Ltd - Imperial Tobacco Ltd)

Modeller:	William K. Harper
Height:	6", 15.0 cm
Colour:	Navy and white
Issued:	1999 in a limited edition of 2,000
Slogan:	Player's / Please
U.S.	**$225.00**
Can.	**$300.00**
U.K.	**£125.00**
Aust.	**$350.00**

AC 6
JOHN GINGER™
(Huntley & Palmers - Jacobs Bakery Ltd)

Modeller:	William K. Harper
Height:	6", 15.0 cm
Colour:	Dark green, white
Issued:	2000 ltd. ed. 2,000
Slogan:	There are no ifs, nor ands, not buts, they are the finest Ginger Nuts!
U.S.	**$225.00**
Can.	**$300.00**
U.K.	**£125.00**
Aust.	**$350.00**

AC 7
THE MILKY BAR KID™
(Nestlé)

Modeller:	William K. Harper David Biggs
Height:	5 ¾", 14.6 cm
Colour:	Blue, red, brown
Issued:	2000 ltd. ed. 2,000
Slogan:	The Milkybars are on me!
U.S.	**$225.00**
Can.	**$300.00**
U.K.	**£125.00**
Aust.	**$325.00**

AC 8
GUINNESS TOUCAN™
(©Guinness Ltd)

Modeller:	William K. Harper
Height:	5", 12.7 cm
Colour:	Black, white, blue and orange
Issued:	2000 in a limited edition of 2,000
Slogan:	Lovely day for a / GUINNESS
U.S.	**$1,250.00**
Can.	**$1,700.00**
U.K.	**£ 700.00**
Aust.	**$1,850.00**

MCL 1
PENFOLD GOLFER™
Modeller:	David Biggs
Height:	5 ¾", 14.6 cm
Colour:	Grey, white, tan, black and green
Issued:	2001 ltd. ed. 2,000
Slogan:	He Played A Penfold
Comm. by:	Millennium Collectables Ltd.

U.S.	**$175.00**
Can.	**$250.00**
U.K.	**£100.00**
Aust.	**$275.00**

MCL 2
DUNLOP CADDIE™
Modeller:	David Biggs
Height:	5 ¼", 13.3 cm
Colour:	Blue, red, white, black and green
Issued:	2001 ltd. ed. 2,000
Slogan:	We Plan Dunlop 65
Comm. by:	Millennium Collectables Ltd.

U.S.	**$175.00**
Can.	**$250.00**
U.K.	**£100.00**
Aust.	**$275.00**

MCL 3
BIG CHIEF TOUCAN™
Modeller:	Shane Ridge
Height:	6", 15.0 cm
Colour:	Black, white, yellow, red and blue
Issued:	2001 ltd. ed. 2,000
Slogan:	Guinness – Him Strong
Comm. by:	Millennium Collectables Ltd.

U.S.	**$350.00**
Can.	**$475.00**
U.K.	**£200.00**
Aust.	**$500.00**

MCL 4
BISTO KIDS™
Modeller:	Rob Donaldson
Height:	4 ½", 11.9 cm
Colour:	Black, red, green, blue, brown, yellow
Issued:	2002 in a limited edition of 1,000
Comm. by:	Millennium Collectables Ltd.

U.S.	**$450.00**
Can.	**$600.00**
U.K.	**£250.00**
Aust.	**$650.00**

MCL 5
P..P..P..PICK UP A..PENGUIN™
Modeller:	Martyn Alcock
Height:	4 ½", 11.9 cm
Colour:	Black, white, yellow
Issued:	2002 in a limited edition of 1,500
Slogan:	P... P... P... PICK UP A ...PENGUIN
Comm. by:	Millennium Collectables Ltd.

U.S.	**$175.00**
Can.	**$250.00**
U.K.	**£100.00**
Aust.	**$275.00**

MCL 6
CHRISTMAS TOUCAN™
Modeller:	Shane Ridge
Height:	5 ¾", 14.6 cm
Colour:	Black, white, red, orange, green, blue
Issued:	2002 ltd. ed. 2,000
Slogan:	GUINNESS / is good for yule
Comm. by:	Millennium Collectables Ltd.

U.S.	**$300.00**
Can.	**$400.00**
U.K.	**£175.00**
Aust.	**$450.00**

MCL 7
SEASIDE TOUCAN™
Modeller:	Martyn Alcock
Height:	6", 15.0 cm
Colour:	Black, white, yellow, red and beige
Issued:	2003 ltd. ed. 2,000
Slogan:	GUINNESS / Goodness-on-sea
Comm. by:	Millennium Collectables Ltd.

U.S.	**$300.00**
Can.	**$400.00**
U.K.	**£175.00**
Aust.	**$450.00**

MCL 8
TONY THE TIGER™
Modeller:	Martyn Alcock
Height:	5 ½", 14.0 cm
Colour:	Orange and black
Issued:	2003 ltd. ed. 1,500
Slogan:	"THEY'RE GR-R-REAT!"
Comm. by:	Millennium Collectables Ltd.

U.S.	**$175.00**
Can.	**$250.00**
U.K.	**£100.00**
Aust.	**$275.00**

MCL 9
BIBENDUM THE MICHELIN MAN

Designer:	Martyn Alcock
Height:	5 ½", 14.0 cm
Colour:	White, dark red and black
Issued:	2003 in a limited edition of 2,000
Comm. by:	Millennium Collectables Ltd.
Slogan:	Switch to Michelin
U.S.	−
Can.	−
U.K.	**£89.00**
Aust.	−

MCL 10
MINER TOUCAN

Modeller:	Martyn Alcock
Height:	5 ¼", 13.3 cm
Colour:	Black, white, yellow and blue
Issued:	2004 in a limited edition of 2,000
Slogan:	Mine's a GUINNESS
U.S.	−
Can.	−
U.K.	**£89.00**
Aust.	−

MCL 11
NEWSVENDOR NAMESTAND

Height:	3", 7.6 cm
Colour:	Black, yellow and blue
Issued:	2004 in a limited edition of 2,000
Slogan:	Royal Doulton Guinness Toucans 2000-2004
U.S.	−
Can.	−
U.K.	**£29.00**
Aust.	−

HIS MASTER'S VOICE 'NIPPER'™

Modeller:	David Biggs
Size:	6 ¼" x 12", 15.9 X 30.5 CM
Colour:	White dog with brown ears; brown and copper phonograph
Issued:	2000 in a limited edition of 2,000
Comm. by:	Millennium Collectables Ltd.
U.S.	$ 725.00
Can.	$ 950.00
U.K.	£ 400.00
Aust.	$1,000.00

Note: 1. Issued to commemorate the 100th anniversary of the use of the dog "Nipper" in the advertising of EMI's products (EMI REcords Ltd.)
2. Only 1,000 pieces were produced due to breakages in shipping.

DISNEY FIGURINES

101 DALMATIANS
DISNEY CHARACTERS
DISNEY PRINCESS COLLECTION
DISNEY SHOWCASE COLLECTION
DISNEY VILLAINS COLLECTION
FANTASIA 2000
FILM CLASSICS COLLECTION
MICKEY MOUSE COLLECTION
PETER PAN
SNOW WHITE AND THE SEVEN DWARFS
WINNIE THE POOH

101 DALMATIANS
1997 to the present

DM 1
CRUELLA DE VIL™
Style One

Designer:	Martyn Alcock
Modeller:	Martyn Alcock
Height:	6 ¼", 15.9 cm
Colour:	Black dress, pale yellow coat with red lining, red gloves
Issued:	1997 - 2001
Series:	101 Dalmatians Collection

Doulton		Price		
Number	U.S. $	Can. $	U.K. £	Aust. $
DM 1	175.00	225.00	95.00	250.00

DM 2
PENNY™

Designer:	Shane Ridge
Modeller:	Shane Ridge
Height:	2 ¾", 7.0 cm
Colour:	White and black dalmatian, red collar
Issued:	1997 - 2001
Series:	101 Dalmatians Collection

Doulton		Price		
Number	U.S. $	Can. $	U.K. £	Aust. $
DM 2	45.00	60.00	25.00	65.00

DM 3
PENNY™ AND FRECKLES™

Designer:	Martyn Alcock
Modeller:	Martyn Alcock
Height:	2 ¼", 5.5 cm
Colour:	Two white and black dalmatians with red collars
Issued:	1997 - 2001
Series:	101 Dalmatians Collection

Doulton		Price		
Number	U.S. $	Can. $	U.K. £	Aust. $
DM 3	55.00	70.00	30.00	80.00

DM 4
ROLLY™

Designer:	Shane Ridge
Modeller:	Shane Ridge
Height:	2 ¾", 7.0 cm
Colour:	White and black dalmatian, red collar, black base
Issued:	1997 - 1999
Series:	101 Dalmatians Collection

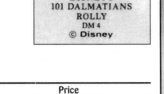

Doulton Number	Price			
	U.S. $	Can. $	U.K. £	Aust. $
DM 4	45.00	60.00	25.00	65.00

DM 5
PATCH™, ROLLY™ AND FRECKLES™

Designer:	Shane Ridge
Modeller:	Shane Ridge
Height:	3 ¾", 9.5 cm
Length:	7 ½", 19.0 cm
Colour:	Three white and black dalmatians wearing red collars
Issued:	1997 in a limited edition of 3,500
Series:	1. 101 Dalmatians Collection
	2. Tableau

Doulton Number	Price			
	U.S. $	Can. $	U.K. £	Aust. $
DM 5	225.00	300.00	125.00	325.00

DM 6
PONGO™

Designer:	Martyn Alcock
Modeller:	Martyn Alcock
Height:	4 ½", 11.9 cm
Colour:	White and black dalmatian, red collar
Issued:	1997 - 1998
Series:	101 Dalmatians Collection

Doulton Number	Price			
	U.S. $	Can. $	U.K. £	Aust. $
DM 6	60.00	85.00	35.00	95.00

DM 7
PERDITA™

Designer:	Martyn Alcock
Modeller:	Martyn Alcock
Height:	2 ½", 6.4 cm
Colour:	White and black dalmatian, dark turquoise collar and blanket
Issued:	1997 - 2001
Series:	101 Dalmatians Collection

Doulton Number	Price			
	U.S. $	Can. $	U.K. £	Aust. $
DM 7	55.00	70.00	30.00	75.00

DM 8
LUCKY™

Designer:	Martyn Alcock
Modeller:	Martyn Alcock
Height:	2 ¾", 7.0 cm
Colour:	White and black dalmatian, red collar
Issued:	1997 - 2001
Series:	101 Dalmatians Collection

Doulton Number	Price			
	U.S. $	Can. $	U.K. £	Aust. $
DM 8	55.00	70.00	30.00	75.00

DM 9
PATCH™ IN BASKET

Designer:	Graham Tongue
Modeller:	Graham Tongue
Height:	2 ¼", 5.7 cm
Colour:	White and black dalmatian, beige basket
Issued:	1998 - 2001
Series:	101 Dalmatians Collection

Doulton Number	Price			
	U.S. $	Can. $	U.K. £	Aust. $
DM 9	55.00	70.00	30.00	75.00

DM 10
LUCKY™ AND FRECKLES™ ON ICE

Designer: Warren Platt
Modeller: Warren Platt
Height: 2 ½", 6.4 cm
Colour: White and black dalmatians
Issued: 1998 - 1999
Series: 101 Dalmatians Collection

Doulton Number	Price			
	U.S. $	Can. $	U.K. £	Aust. $
DM 10	115.00	155.00	65.00	170.00

DM 11
PUPS IN THE CHAIR™

Designer: Martyn Alcock
Modeller: Martyn Alcock
Height: 4", 10.1 cm
Colour: White and black dalmatians, yellow chair
Issued: February 1st to May 12th, 1999 (101 days)
Series: 101 Dalmatians Collection

Doulton Number	Price			
	U.S. $	Can. $	U.K. £	Aust. $
DM 11	175.00	250.00	100.00	275.00

DISNEY CHARACTERS

1952-1965

1278
MICKEY MOUSE™
Style One

Designer:	Jan Granoska
Height:	4", 10.1 cm
Colour:	Black, white and red
Issued:	1952 - 1965

Back Stamp	Beswick Number	Price			
		U.S. $	Can. $	U.K. £	Aust. $
Beswick Gold	1278	725.00	950.00	400.00	1,000.00

1279
JIMINY CRICKET™
Style One

Designer:	Jan Granoska
Height:	4", 10.1 cm
Colour:	Black, white, beige and blue
Issued:	1952 - 1965

Back Stamp	Beswick Number	Price			
		U.S. $	Can. $	U.K. £	Aust. $
Beswick Gold	1279	575.00	775.00	325.00	825.00

1280
PLUTO™
Style One

Designer:	Jan Granoska
Height:	3 ½", 8.9 cm
Colour:	Brown dog with red collar
Issued:	1953 - 1965

Back Stamp	Beswick Number	Price			
		U.S. $	Can. $	U.K. £	Aust. $
Beswick Gold	1280	625.00	850.00	350.00	900.00

1281
GOOFY™
Style One

Designer:	Jan Granoska
Height:	4 ¼", 10.8 cm
Colour:	Red jersey, blue trousers, black suspenders,
	white gloves, brown and black hat, brown boots
Issued:	1953 - 1965

Back Stamp	Beswick Number	Price			
		U.S. $	Can. $	U.K. £	Aust. $
Beswick Gold	1281	575.00	775.00	325.00	825.00

1282
PINOCCHIO™
Style One

Designer:	Jan Granoska
Height:	4", 10.1 cm
Colour:	White and yellow jacket, red trousers,
	blue bowtie and shoes, brown cap
Issued:	1953 - 1965

Back Stamp	Beswick Number	Price			
		U.S. $	Can. $	U.K. £	Aust. $
Beswick Gold	1282	725.00	950.00	400.00	1,000.00

1283
DONALD DUCK™
Style One

Designer:	Jan Granoska
Height:	4", 10.1 cm
Colour:	White duck, blue sailors jacket,
	red bow, blue and black hat
Issued:	1953 - 1965

Back Stamp	Beswick Number	Price			
		U.S. $	Can. $	U.K. £	Aust. $
Beswick Gold	1283	675.00	900.00	375.00	950.00

1289
MINNIE MOUSE™
Style One

Designer:	Jan Granoska
Height:	4", 10.1 cm
Colour:	Black and white mouse wearing a yellow top and red skirt with white spots, white gloves and hair bow, brown shoes
Issued:	1953 - 1965

Back Stamp	Beswick Number	Price U.S. $	Can. $	U.K. £	Aust. $
Beswick Gold	1289	675.00	900.00	375.00	950.00

1291
THUMPER™
Style One

Designer:	Jan Granoska
Height:	3 ¾", 9.5 cm
Colour:	Grey and white rabbit, yellow, red and pink flowers on brown base
Issued:	1953 - 1965

Back Stamp	Beswick Number	Price U.S. $	Can. $	U.K. £	Aust. $
Beswick Gold	1291	400.00	550.00	225.00	600.00

THE DISNEY PRINCESS COLLECTION
1995-1996

HN 3677
CINDERELLA™

Designer:	Pauline Parsons
Height:	8", 20.3 cm
Colour:	Blue and white dress, yellow hair
Issued:	1995 in a limited edition of 2,000
Series:	The Disney Princess Collection

Back Stamp	Doulton Number	Price			
		U.S. $	Can. $	U.K. £	Aust. $
Doulton	HN 3677	425.00	600.00	275.00	650.00

HN 3678
SNOW WHITE™
Style Two

Designer:	Pauline Parsons
Height:	8 ¼", 21.0 cm
Colour:	Yellow, blue and white dress, royal blue and red cape, black hair
Issued:	1995 in a limited edition of 2,000
Series:	The Disney Princess Collection

Back Stamp	Doulton Number	Price			
		U.S. $	Can. $	U.K. £	Aust. $
Doulton	HN 3678	500.00	700.00	325.00	750.00

HN 3830
BELLE™

Designer:	Pauline Parsons
Height:	8", 20.3 cm
Colour:	Yellow dress and gloves, brown hair
Issued:	1996 in a limited edition of 2,000
Series:	The Disney Princess Collection

Back Stamp	Doulton Number	Price			
		U.S. $	Can. $	U.K. £	Aust. $
Doulton	HN 3830	400.00	600.00	250.00	650.00

HN 3831
ARIEL™
Style One

Designer:	Pauline Parsons
Height:	8 ¼", 21.0 cm
Colour:	White dress and veil, red hair
Issued:	1996 in a limited edition of 2,000
Series:	The Disney Princess Collection

Back Stamp	Doulton Number	Price			
		U.S. $	Can. $	U.K. £	Aust. $
Doulton	HN 3831	400.00	600.00	250.00	650.00

HN 3832
JASMINE™

Designer:	Pauline Parsons
Height:	7 ½", 19.1 cm
Colour:	Lilac dress
Issued:	1996 in a limited edition of 2,000
Series:	The Disney Princess Collection

Back Stamp	Doulton Number	Price			
		U.S. $	Can. $	U.K. £	Aust. $
Doulton	HN 3832	400.00	600.00	250.00	650.00

HN 3833
AURORA™

Designer:	Pauline Parsons
Height:	7 ½", 19.1 cm
Colour:	Light and dark blue dress with white trim
Issued:	1996 in a limited edition of 2,000
Series:	The Disney Princess Collection

Back Stamp	Doulton Number	Price			
		U.S. $	Can. $	U.K. £	Aust. $
Doulton	HN 3833	250.00	375.00	150.00	425.00

DISNEY SHOWCASE COLLECTION
ALICE IN WONDERLAND

AW1
ALICE™
Style Four

Designer:	Shane Ridge
Modeller:	Shane Ridge
Height:	4 ¾", 12.1 cm
Colour:	Blue dress, white apron; red with white polka-dot mushroom
Issued:	2001 in a limited edition of 2,000
Series:	Alice In Wonderland

Doulton	Price			
Number	U.S. $	Can. $	U.K. £	Aust. $
AW1	100.00	125.00	55.00	135.00

AW2
MAD HATTER™
Style Three

Designer:	Martyn Alcock
Modeller:	Martyn Alcock
Height:	4 ¾", 12.1 cm
Colour:	Yellow coat, black shirt and shoes, green trousers and bowtie, black and green top hat with black band
Issued:	2001 in a limited edition of 2,000
Series:	Alice In Wonderland

Doulton	Price			
Number	U.S. $	Can. $	U.K. £	Aust. $
AW2	125.00	175.00	70.00	200.00

AW3
MARCH HARE™

Designer:	Martyn C. R. Alcock
Modeller:	Martyn C. R. Alcock
Height:	2 ½", 6.4 cm
Colour:	Yellow rabbit; red coat, black leggings, white and red tea pot and cup
Issued:	2001 in a limited edition of 2,000
Series:	Alice In Wonderland

Doulton	Price			
Number	U.S. $	Can. $	U.K. £	Aust. $
AW3	100.00	125.00	55.00	135.00

AW4
WHITE RABBIT™
Style Three

Designer:	Shane Ridge
Modeller:	Shane Ridge
Height:	2 ¾", 7.0 cm
Colour:	Red coat, yellow shirt, black bowtie, grey trousers; yellow and white clock
Issued:	2001 in a limited edition of 2,000
Series:	Alice In Wonderland

Doulton Number	Price			
	U.S. $	Can. $	U.K. £	Aust. $
AW4	125.00	150.00	65.00	175.00

AW5
CHESHIRE CAT™
Style Four

Designer:	Shane Ridge
Modeller:	Shane Ridge
Height:	2 ¾", 7.0 cm
Colour:	Pink and white striped cat
Issued:	2001 in a limited edition of 2,000
Series:	Alice In Wonderland

Doulton Number	Price			
	U.S. $	Can. $	U.K. £	Aust. $
AW5	125.00	150.00	65.00	175.00

DISNEY SHOWCASE COLLECTION
THE JUNGLE BOOK

JB 1
MOWGLI™

Designer:	Shane Ridge
Modeller:	Shane Ridge
Height:	2 ½", 6.4 cm
Colour:	Fleshtones, black and red
Issued:	2000 - 2001
Series:	Jungle Book

Doulton Number	Price			
	U.S. $	Can. $	U.K. £	Aust. $
JB 1	100.00	150.00	60.00	175.00

JB 2
BABY ELEPHANT™

Designer:	Martyn Alcock
Modeller:	Martyn Alcock
Height:	3 ¼", 8.3 cm
Colour:	Tan
Issued:	2000 - 2001
Series:	Jungle Book

Doulton Number	Price			
	U.S. $	Can. $	U.K. £	Aust. $
JB 2	70.00	95.00	40.00	100.00

JB 3
BALOO™

Designer:	Shane Ridge
Modeller:	Shane Ridge
Height:	5 ¼", 13.3 cm
Colour:	Grey and white
Issued:	2000 - 2001
Series:	Jungle Book

Doulton Number	Price			
	U.S. $	Can. $	U.K. £	Aust. $
JB 3	100.00	150.00	60.00	175.00

JB 4
BAGHEERA™

Designer:	Shane Ridge
Modeller:	Shane Ridge
Height:	4 ¾", 12.1 cm
Colour:	Black
Issued:	2000 - 2001
Series:	Jungle Book

Doulton Number	Price			
	U.S. $	Can. $	U.K. £	Aust. $
JB 4	100.00	150.00	60.00	175.00

JB 5
SHERE KHAN™

Designer:	Martyn Alcock
Modeller:	Martyn Alcock
Height:	3 ¼", 8.3 cm
Colour:	Yellow with dark brown stripes
Issued:	2000 - 2001
Series:	Jungle Book

Doulton Number	Price			
	U.S. $	Can. $	U.K. £	Aust. $
JB 5	125.00	175.00	70.00	200.00

JB 6
FLOATING ALONG™

Designer:	Martyn Alcock
Modeller:	Martyn Alcock
Height:	2 ¾", 7.0 cm
Colour:	White and grey bear; fleshtones, black and red
Issued:	2001 in a limited edition of 3,500
Series:	1. Jungle Book
	2. Tableau

Doulton Number	Price			
	U.S. $	Can. $	U.K. £	Aust. $
JB 6	150.00	200.00	80.00	225.00

JB 7
KING LOUIE™

Designer:	Warren Platt
Modeller:	Warren Platt
Height:	4", 10.1 cm
Colour:	Orange
Issued:	2001 - 2003
Series:	Jungle Book

Doulton Number	Price			
	U.S. $	Can. $	U.K. £	Aust. $
JB 7	150.00	200.00	80.00	225.00

DISNEY SHOWCASE COLLECTION
THE LITTLE MERMAID

LM 1
ARIEL™
Style Two

Height:	4 ½", 11.9 cm
Colour:	Green, purple, red and yellow
Issued:	2002 - 2003
Series:	The Little Mermaid

Doulton Number	Price			
	U.S. $	Can. $	U.K. £	Aust. $
LM 1	65.00	85.00	35.00	90.00

LM 2
FLOUNDER™

Height:	2 ½", 6.4 cm
Colour:	Yellow fish with blue striped fins
Issued:	2002 - 2003
Series:	The Little Mermaid

Doulton Number	Price			
	U.S. $	Can. $	U.K. £	Aust. $
LM 2	45.00	60.00	25.00	65.00

LM 3
SEBASTIAN™

Height:	2 ¼", 5.5 cm
Colour:	Yellow, red, coral
Issued:	2002 - 2003
Series:	The Little Mermaid

Doulton Number	Price			
	U.S. $	Can. $	U.K. £	Aust. $
LM 3	45.00	60.00	25.00	65.00

LM 4
URSULA™

Height:	4 ¼", 10.8 cm
Colour:	Purple, black and green
Issued:	2002 - 2003
Series:	The Little Mermaid

Doulton Number	Price			
	U.S. $	Can. $	U.K. £	Aust. $
LM 4	80.00	100.00	45.00	110.00

LM 5
SCUTTLE™

Height:	3", 7.6 cm
Colour:	White, purple, black and orange
Issued:	2002 - 2003
Series:	The Little Mermaid

Doulton Number	Price			
	U.S. $	Can. $	U.K. £	Aust. $
LM 5	45.00	60.00	25.00	65.00

DISNEY SHOWCASE COLLECTION
PETER PAN SERIES 2002 to date

PAN 1
PETER PAN™
Style Two

Height:	5 ½", 14.0 cm
Colour:	Light green tunic, darker green tights and cap, brown shoes
Issued:	2002 to the present
Series:	Peter Pan (Series Two)

Doulton Number	Price			
	U.S. $	Can. $	U.K. £	Aust. $
PAN 1	70.00	95.00	40.00	100.00

PAN 2
TINKER BELL™
Style Two

Height:	6", 15.0 cm
Colour:	Green dress and slippers, lilac and white wings
Issued:	2002 to the present
Series:	Peter Pan (Series Two)

Doulton Number	Price			
	U.S. $	Can. $	U.K. £	Aust. $
PAN 2	70.00	95.00	40.00	100.00

PAN 3
THE DUEL™

Height: 6 ¼", 15.9 cm
Colour: Peter Pan: Green tunic and cap,
darker green tights; brown belt
Captain: Red and gold coat, pink
and lilac hat, white neckerchief and
stockings, black shoes
Issued: 2002 in a limited edition of 3,000
Series: Peter Pan (Series Two)

Doulton Number	Price			
	U.S. $	Can. $	U.K. £	Aust. $
PAN 3	150.00	200.00	85.00	225.00

PAN 4
CAPTAIN HOOK™

Height: 7", 17.8 cm
Colour: Red and gold coat, pink and lilac hat, white
neckerchief and stockings, black shoes
Issued: 2002 to the present
Series: Peter Pan (Series Two)

Doulton Number	Price			
	U.S. $	Can. $	U.K. £	Aust. $
PAN 4	80.00	100.00	45.00	110.00

PAN 5
WENDY™

Height: 5", 12.7 cm
Colour: Blue dress, blonde hair, yellow block
Issued: 2002 to the present
Series: Peter Pan (Series Two)

Doulton Number	Price			
	U.S. $	Can. $	U.K. £	Aust. $
PAN 5	65.00	85.00	35.00	90.00

PAN 6
TIC TOC CROCODILE™

Height:	5 ½", 14.0 cm
Colour:	Green, grey, red, blue and white
Issued:	2002 to the present
Series:	Peter Pan (Series Two)

Doulton Number	Price			
	U.S. $	Can. $	U.K. £	Aust. $
PAN 6	70.00	95.00	40.00	100.00

PAN 7
HEADING FOR SKULL ROCK

Height:	6", 15.0 cm
Colour:	Captain Hook: Red and gold coat; pink and lilac hat
	Princess Tiger Lily: Brown, red and orange dress
	Smee: Blue and white striped shirt, blue shorts, red cap
Issued:	2002 in a limited edition of 3,000
Series:	Peter Pan (Series Two)

Doulton Number	Price			
	U.S. $	Can. $	U.K. £	Aust. $
PAN 7	150.00	200.00	85.00	225.00

DISNEY VILLAINS COLLECTION
1997-1998

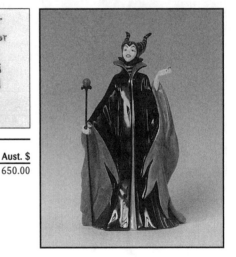

HN 3839
CRUELLA DE VIL™
Style Two

Designer:	Pauline Parsons
Height:	8", 20.3 cm
Colour:	Black dress, white fur coat, red gloves
Issued:	1997 in a limited edition of 2,000
Series:	The Disney Villains Collection

Back Stamp	Doulton Number	Price			
		U.S. $	Can. $	U.K. £	Aust. $
Doulton	HN 3839	400.00	600.00	250.00	650.00

HN 3840
MALEFICENT™

Designer:	Pauline Parsons
Height:	8", 20.3 cm
Colour:	Black and purple
Issued:	1997 in a limited edition of 2,000
Series:	The Disney Villains Collection

Back Stamp	Doulton Number	Price			
		U.S. $	Can. $	U.K. £	Aust. $
Doulton	HN 3840	400.00	600.00	250.00	650.00

HN 3847
THE QUEEN™

Designer:	Pauline Parson
Height:	8 ¾", 22.2 cm
Colour:	Black, white, purple, red and yellow
Issued:	1998 in a limited edition of 2,000
Series:	The Disney Villains Collection

Back Stamp	Doulton Number	Price			
		U.S. $	Can. $	U.K. £	Aust. $
Doulton	HN 3847	325.00	475.00	200.00	525.00

HN 3848
THE WITCH™

Designer:	Pauline Parsons
Height:	7", 17.8 cm
Colour:	Black robes, red apple
Issued:	1998 in a limited edition of 2,000
Series:	The Disney Villains Collection

Back Stamp	Doulton Number	Price			
		U.S. $	Can. $	U.K. £	Aust. $
Doulton	HN 3848	325.00	475.00	200.00	525.00

FANTASIA 2000

FAN1
BUCKETS OF MISCHIEF™

Designer:	Shane Ridge
Modeller:	Shane Ridge
Height:	4 ½", 11.9 cm
Colour:	Brown broom and buckets, blue water
Issued:	2000 in a limited edition of 2,000
Series:	Fantasia 2000

Back Stamp	Doulton Number	Price			
		U.S. $	Can. $	U.K. £	Aust. $
FAN1	8226	100.00	125.00	55.00	135.00

FAN2
FOLLOW ME™

Designer:	Shane Ridge
Modeller:	Shane Ridge
Height:	5 ¼", 13.3 cm
Colour:	Red, purple, black and white
Issued:	2000 in a limited edition of 2,000
Series:	Fantasia 2000

Back Stamp	Doulton Number	Price			
		U.S. $	Can. $	U.K. £	Aust. $
FAN2	8227	175.00	225.00	90.00	250.00

FAN3
NOAH'S™ HELPER

Designer:	Shane Ridge
Modeller:	Shane Ridge
Height:	4", 10.1 cm
Colour:	Brown, white and yellow
Issued:	2000 in a limited edition of 2,000
Series:	Fantasia 2000

Back Stamp	Doulton Number	Price			
		U.S. $	Can. $	U.K. £	Aust. $
FAN3	8228	125.00	150.00	65.00	175.00

FAN4
HEART ON A STRING™
(Pomp and Circumstance)

Designer:	Shane Ridge	
Modeller:	Shane Ridge	
Height:	4 ¼", 10.8 cm	
Colour:	Blue, yellow and white	
Issued:	2000 in a limited edition of 2,000	
Series:	Fantasia 2000	

Back Stamp	Doulton Number	Price			
		U.S. $	Can. $	U.K. £	Aust. $
FAN4	8325	175.00	225.00	90.00	250.00

FAN5
A FLOWER AND HIS HEART™
(Shostakovich's Piano Concerto No. 2)

Designer:	Shane Ridge	
Modeller:	Shane Ridge	
Height:	6 ½", 16.5 cm	
Colour:	Red, white and pink	
Issued:	2000 in a limited edition of 2,000	
Series:	1. Fantasia 2000	
	2. Tableau	

Back Stamp	Doulton Number	Price			
		U.S. $	Can. $	U.K. £	Aust. $
FAN5	8225	350.00	475.00	200.00	500.00

FILM CLASSICS COLLECTION

CN 1
CINDERELLA™ THE DRESS OF DREAMS

Designer:	Shane Ridge
Modeller:	Shane Ridge
Height:	6 ¾", 17.2 cm
Colour:	Pink and white dress
Issued:	2000 in a limited edition of 2,000
Series:	Film Classics Collection

Back Stamp	Doulton Number	Price			
		U.S. $	Can. $	U.K. £	Aust. $
CN 1	–	175.00	250.00	100.00	275.00

FC 1
BAMBI™

Designer:	Martyn Alcock
Modeller:	Martyn Alcock
Height:	4", 10.1 cm
Colour:	Brown deer, yellow spots, black nose and tip on top of ears
Issued:	1999 in a limited edition of 1,500
Series:	Film Classics Collection

Back Stamp	Doulton Number	Price			
		U.S. $	Can. $	U.K. £	Aust. $
FC 1	4440	125.00	175.00	75.00	200.00

FC 2
THUMPER™
Style Two

Designer:	Martyn Alcock
Modeller:	Martyn Alcock
Height:	3 ¼", 8.3 cm
Colour:	Grey, white and cream rabbit, pink nose
Issued:	1999 in a limited edition on 1,500
Series:	Film Classics Collection

Back Stamp	Doulton Number	Price			
		U.S. $	Can. $	U.K. £	Aust. $
FC 2	4432	150.00	200.00	80.00	225.00

FC 3
DUMBO™

Modeller:	Shane Ridge
Height:	4 ½", 11.9 cm
Colour:	Grey elephant, pink inner ears
Issued:	1999 in a limited edition of 1,500
Series:	Film Classics Collection

Back Stamp	Doulton Number	Price U.S. $	Can. $	U.K. £	Aust. $
FC 3	4427	175.00	250.00	100.00	275.00

FC 4
PINOCCHIO™
Style Two

Designer:	Shane Ridge
Modeller:	Shane Ridge
Height:	5 ½", 14.0 cm
Colour:	Yellow shirt and hat, red trousers and shoes, blue bowtie and book
Issued:	1999 in a limited edition of 1,500
Series:	Film Classics Collection

Back Stamp	Doulton Number	Price U.S. $	Can. $	U.K. £	Aust. $
FC 4	4431	175.00	250.00	100.00	275.00

FC5
JIMINY CRICKET™
Style Two

Designer:	Warren Platt
Modeller:	Warren Platt
Height:	4 ¼", 10.8 cm
Colour:	Dark blue jacket and shoes, tan trousers, orange waistcoat, blue hat with orange band, red umbrella
Issued:	2000 in a limited edition of 1,500
Series:	Film Classics Collection

Back Stamp	Doulton Number	Price U.S. $	Can. $	U.K. £	Aust. $
FC 5	3149	125.00	175.00	75.00	200.00

FC 6
TIMOTHY MOUSE™

Designer:	Amanda Hughes-Lubeck
Modeller:	Amanda Hughes-Lubeck
Height:	3 ¼", 8.3 cm
Colour:	Red and yellow suit and hat
Issued:	2000 in a limited edition of 1,500
Series:	Film Classics Collection

Back Stamp	Doulton Number	Price			
		U.S. $	Can. $	U.K. £	Aust. $
FC 6	–	90.00	125.00	50.00	135.00

FC 7
LADY™

Designer:	Shane Ridge
Modeller:	Shane Ridge
Height:	3 ¼", 8.3 cm
Colour:	Tan and brown dog, blue collar
Issued:	2001 in a limited edition of 1,500
Series:	Film Classics Collection

Back Stamp	Doulton Number	Price			
		U.S. $	Can. $	U.K. £	Aust. $
FC 7	–	90.00	125.00	50.00	135.00

FC 8
TRAMP™

Designer:	Shane Ridge
Modeller:	Shane Ridge
Height:	4", 10.1 cm
Colour:	Grey and white dog, red collar, gold dog tag
Issued:	2001 in a limited edition of 1,500
Series:	Film Classics Collection

Back Stamp	Doulton Number	Price			
		U.S. $	Can. $	U.K. £	Aust. $
FC 8	–	90.00	125.00	50.00	135.00

MICKEY MOUSE COLLECTION
1998-2000

MM 1/MM 7
MICKEY MOUSE™
Style Two

Designer:	Warren Platt
Modeller:	Warren Platt
Height:	4 ¾", 12.1 cm
Colour:	Black, red and light brown
Issued:	1. 1998 - 1998
	2. 1999 - 2000
Series:	Mickey Mouse Collection

Back Stamp	Doulton Number	Price			
		U.S. $	Can. $	U.K. £	Aust. $
BK-1 / 70th Anniv.	MM 1	100.00	135.00	60.00	150.00
BK-2	MM 7	100.00	135.00	60.00	150.00

MM 2/MM 8
MINNIE MOUSE™
Style Two

Designer:	Warren Platt
Modeller:	Warren Platt
Height:	5 ½", 14.0 cm
Colour:	Black, blue and red
Issued:	1. 1998 - 1998
	2. 1999 - 2000
Series:	Mickey Mouse Collection

Back Stamp	Doulton Number	Price			
		U.S. $	Can. $	U.K. £	Aust. $
BK-1 / 70th Anniv.	MM 2	100.00	135.00	60.00	150.00
BK-2	MM 8	100.00	135.00	60.00	150.00

MM 3/MM 9
DONALD DUCK™
Style Two

Designer:	Warren Platt
Modeller:	Shane Ridge
Height:	4 ¾", 12.1 cm
Colour:	Blue, white and red
Issued:	1. 1998 - 1998
	2. 1999 - 2000
Series:	Mickey Mouse Collection

Back Stamp	Doulton Number	Price			
		U.S. $	Can. $	U.K. £	Aust. $
BK-1 / 70th Anniv.	MM 3	100.00	135.00	60.00	150.00
BK-2	MM 9	100.00	135.00	60.00	150.00

MM 4/MM 10
DAISY DUCK™

Designer:	Shane Ridge
Modeller:	Shane Ridge
Height:	5 ½", 14.0 cm
Colour:	Blue, white and pink
Issued:	1. 1998 - 1998
	2. 1999 - 2000
Series:	Mickey Mouse Collection

Back Stamp	Doulton Number	Price			
		U.S. $	Can. $	U.K. £	Aust. $
BK-1 / 70th Anniv.	MM 4	100.00	135.00	60.00	150.00
BK-2	MM 10	100.00	135.00	60.00	150.00

MM 5/MM 11
GOOFY™
Style Two

Designer:	Shane Ridge
Modeller:	Graham Tongue
Height:	5", 12.7 cm
Colour:	Red, blue and black
Issued:	1. 1998 - 1998
	2. 1999 - 2000
Series:	Mickey Mouse Collection

Back Stamp	Doulton Number	Price			
		U.S. $	Can. $	U.K. £	Aust. $
BK-1 / 70th Anniv.	MM 5	100.00	135.00	60.00	150.00
BK-2	MM 11	100.00	135.00	60.00	150.00

MM 6/MM 12
PLUTO™
Style Two

Designer:	Graham Tongue
Modeller:	Graham Tongue
Height:	4 ½", 12.1 cm
Colour:	Light brown
Issued:	1. 1998 - 1998
	2. 1999 - 2000
Series:	Mickey Mouse Collection

Back Stamp	Doulton Number	Price			
		U.S. $	Can. $	U.K. £	Aust. $
BK-1 / 70th Anniv.	MM 6	100.00	135.00	60.00	150.00
BK-2	MM 12	100.00	135.00	60.00	150.00

PETER PAN
1953-1965

1301
NANA™

Designer:	Jan Granoska
Height:	3 ¼", 8.3 cm
Colour:	Brown dog, white frilled cap with blue ribbon
Issued:	1953 - 1965
Series:	Peter Pan (Series One)

Back Stamp	Beswick Number	Price			
		U.S. $	Can. $	U.K. £	Aust. $
Beswick Gold	1301	725.00	950.00	400.00	1,000.00

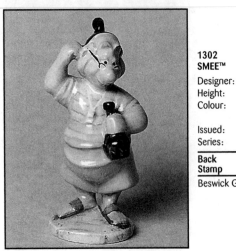

1302
SMEE™

Designer:	Jan Granoska
Height:	4 ¼", 10.8 cm
Colour:	Blue and white shirt, blue pants, red cap, green bottle
Issued:	1953 - 1965
Series:	Peter Pan (Series One)

Back Stamp	Beswick Number	Price			
		U.S. $	Can. $	U.K. £	Aust. $
Beswick Gold	1302	625.00	850.00	350.00	900.00

1307
PETER PAN™
Style One

Designer:	Jan Granoska
Height:	5", 12.7 cm
Colour:	Light green tunic, dark green pants, brown shoes, red and green cap
Issued:	1953 - 1965
Series:	Peter Pan (Series One)

Back Stamp	Beswick Number	Price			
		U.S. $	Can. $	U.K. £	Aust. $
Beswick Gold	1307	900.00	1,200.00	500.00	1,300.00

1312
TINKER BELL™
Style One

Designer:	Jan Granoska
Height:	5", 12.7 cm
Colour:	Light green dress, dark green wings and shoes
Issued:	1953 - 1965
Series:	Peter Pan (Series One)

Back Stamp	Beswick Number	Price			
		U.S. $	Can. $	U.K. £	Aust. $
Beswick Gold	1312	1,200.00	1,600.00	675.00	1,650.00

SLEEPING BEAUTY
2004 TO THE PRESENT

SB 1
BRIAR ROSE SINGING OF LOVE'S DREAMS™

Height:	5 ½", 14.0 cm
Colour:	Pink and purple
Issued:	2004 to the present

Back Stamp	Doulton Number	Price			
		U.S. $	Can. $	U.K. £	Aust. $
Doulton	SB 1	–	–	35.00	–

SB 2
FLORA™, THE NURTURING FAIRY

Height:	4 ¼", 10.8 cm
Colour:	Light purple and pink
Issued:	2004 to the present

Back Stamp	Doulton Number	Price			
		U.S. $	Can. $	U.K. £	Aust. $
Doulton	SB 2	–	–	30.00	–

SB 3
FAUNA™, THE THOUGHTFUL FAIRY

Height:	4 ¼", 10.8 cm
Colour:	Dark and light green and black
Issued:	2004 to the present

Back Stamp	Doulton Number	Price			
		U.S. $	Can. $	U.K. £	Aust. $
Doulton	SB 3	–	–	30.00	–

SB 4
MERRYWEATHER™, THE FEISTY FAIRY

Height:	4 ¼", 10.8 cm
Colour:	Light and dark blue
Issued:	2004 to the present

Back Stamp	Doulton Number	Price			
		U.S. $	Can. $	U.K. £	Aust. $
Doulton	SB 4	–	–	30.00	–

SB 5
MALEFICENT™ "STAND BACK YOU FOOLS"

Height:	6 ¼", 15.9 cm
Colour:	Black, pink and mauve
Issued:	2004 to the present

Back Stamp	Doulton Number	Price			
		U.S. $	Can. $	U.K. £	Aust. $
Doulton	SB 5	–	–	40.00	–

SB 6
WOODLAND WALTZ™

Height:	5 ¾", 14.6 cm	
Colour:	Red, lilac, yellow, green and black	
Issued:	2004 in a limited edition of 1,500	

Back Stamp	Doulton Number	Price			
		U.S. $	Can. $	U.K. £	Aust. $
Doulton	SB 6	–	–	79.99	–

SB 7
LOVE'S FIRST KISS™

Height:	4 ¼", 10.8 cm	
Colour:	Red, pink, yellow and blue	
Issued:	2004 in a limited edition of 1,500	

Back Stamp	Doulton Number	Price			
		U.S. $	Can. $	U.K. £	Aust. $
Doulton	SB 7	–	–	79.99	–

SNOW WHITE AND THE SEVEN DWARFS

BESWICK SERIES 1954-1967

1325
DOPEY™
Style One

Designer:	Arthur Gredington
Height:	3 ½", 8.9 cm
Colour:	Green coat, maroon cap, grey shoes
Issued:	1954 - 1967
Series:	Snow White and the Seven Dwarfs (Series One)

Back Stamp	Beswick Number	Price			
		U.S. $	Can. $	U.K. £	Aust. $
Beswick Gold	1325	225.00	300.00	125.00	325.00

1326
HAPPY™
Style One

Designer:	Arthur Gredington
Height:	3 ½", 8.9 cm
Colour:	Purple tunic, light blue trousers, light brown cap, brown shoes
Issued:	1954 - 1967
Series:	Snow White and the Seven Dwarfs (Series One)

Back Stamp	Beswick Number	Price			
		U.S. $	Can. $	U.K. £	Aust. $
Beswick Gold	1326	225.00	300.00	125.00	325.00

1327
BASHFUL™
Style One

Designer:	Arthur Gredington
Height:	3 ½", 8.9 cm
Colour:	Brown tunic, purple trousers, grey cap, brown shoes
Issued:	1954 - 1967
Series:	Snow White and the Seven Dwarfs (Series One)

Back Stamp	Beswick Number	Price			
		U.S. $	Can. $	U.K. £	Aust. $
Beswick Gold	1327	225.00	300.00	125.00	325.00

1328
SNEEZY™
Style One

Designer: Arthur Gredington
Height: 3 ½", 8.9 cm
Colour: Green tunic, purple trousers,
             brown cap and shoes
Issued: 1954 - 1967
Series: Snow White and the Seven Dwarfs (Series One)

Back Stamp	Beswick Number	Price			
		U.S. $	Can. $	U.K. £	Aust. $
Beswick Gold	1328	225.00	300.00	125.00	325.00

1329
DOC™
Style One

Designer: Arthur Gredington
Height: 3 ½", 8.9 cm
Colour: Brown tunic, blue trousers,
             yellow cap, brown shoes
Issued: 1954 - 1967
Series: Snow White and the Seven Dwarfs (Series One)

Back Stamp	Beswick Number	Price			
		U.S. $	Can. $	U.K. £	Aust. $
Beswick Gold	1329	225.00	300.00	125.00	325.00

1330
GRUMPY™
Style One

Designer: Arthur Gredington
Height: 3 ¾", 9.5 cm
Colour: Purple tunic, red trousers,
             blue cap, brown shoes
Issued: 1954 - 1967
Series: Snow White and the Seven Dwarfs (Series One)

Back Stamp	Beswick Number	Price			
		U.S. $	Can. $	U.K. £	Aust. $
Beswick Gold	1330	225.00	300.00	125.00	325.00

1331
SLEEPY™
Style One

Designer:	Arthur Gredington
Height:	3 ½", 8.9 cm
Colour:	Tan tunic, red trousers, green hat, grey shoes
Issued:	1954 - 1967
Series:	Snow White and the Seven Dwarfs (Series One)

Back Stamp	Beswick Number	Price			
		U.S. $	Can. $	U.K. £	Aust. $
Beswick Gold	1331	225.00	300.00	125.00	325.00

1332A
SNOW WHITE™
Style One
First Version (Hair in Flounces)

Designer:	Arthur Gredington
Height:	5 ½", 14.0 cm
Colour:	Yellow and purple dress, red cape, white collar
Issued:	1954 - 1955

Back Stamp	Beswick Number	Price			
		U.S. $	Can. $	U.K. £	Aust. $
Beswick Gold	1332A		Extremely rare		

Note: Snow White (Style One) was remodelled February 1955.

1332B
SNOW WHITE™
Style One
Second Version (Hair Flat to Head)

Designer:	Arthur Gredington
Height:	5 ½", 14.0 cm
Colour:	Yellow and purple dress, red cape, white collar
Issued:	1955 - 1967
Series:	Snow White and the Seven Dwarfs (Series One)

Back Stamp	Beswick Number	Price			
		U.S. $	Can. $	U.K. £	Aust. $
Beswick Gold	1332B	625.00	850.00	350.00	900.00

SNOW WHITE AND THE SEVEN DWARFS
ROYAL DOULTON SERIES 1997 - 2002

SW 1 / SW 9
SNOW WHITE™
Style Three

Designer:	Amanda Hughes-Lubeck
Height:	5 ¾", 14.6 cm
Colour:	Yellow and blue dress, red cape, white collar
Issued:	SW 1 1997 in a limited edition of 2,000
	SW 9 1998 - 2002
Series:	Snow White and the Seven Dwarfs (Series Two)

Back Stamp	Doulton Number	Price			
		U.S. $	Can. $	U.K. £	Aust. $
Doulton/Disney 60th	SW 1	225.00	300.00	125.00	325.00
Doulton/Disney	SW 9	135.00	175.00	75.00	200.00

SW 2 / SW 10
DOC™
Style Two

Designer:	Amanda Hughes-Lubeck
Height:	3 ¼", 8.3 cm
Colour:	Red tunic, brown trousers,
	yellow hat, green book
Issued:	SW 2 1997 in a limited edition of 2,000
	SW 10 1998 - 2002
Series:	Snow White and the Seven Dwarfs (Series Two)

Back Stamp	Doulton Number	Price			
		U.S. $	Can. $	U.K. £	Aust. $
Doulton/Disney 60th	SW 2	70.00	95.00	40.00	100.00
Doulton/Disney	SW 10	55.00	70.00	30.00	75.00

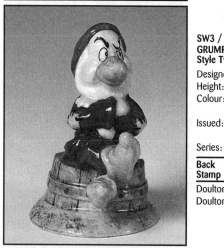

SW3 / SW11
GRUMPY™
Style Two

Designer:	Shane Ridge
Height:	3 ½", 8.9 cm
Colour:	Dark rust tunic and trousers,
	brown hat, light brown basket
Issued:	SW 3 1997 in a limited edition of 2,000
	SW 11 1998 - 2002
Series:	Snow White and the Seven Dwarfs (Series Two)

Back Stamp	Doulton Number	Price			
		U.S. $	Can. $	U.K. £	Aust. $
Doulton/Disney 60th	SW 3	70.00	95.00	40.00	100.00
Doulton/Disney	SW 11	55.00	70.00	30.00	75.00

SW 4 / SW 12
HAPPY™
Style Two

Designer:	Amanda Hughes-Lubeck
Height:	3 ½", 8.9 cm
Colour:	Brown and orange tunic, light blue trousers with black belt and a yellow hat
Issued:	SW 4 1997 in a limited edition of 2,000
	SW 12 1998 - 2002
Series:	Snow White and the Seven Dwarfs (Series Two)

Back Stamp	Doulton Number	Price			
		U.S. $	Can. $	U.K. £	Aust. $
Doulton/Disney 60th	SW 4	70.00	95.00	40.00	100.00
Doulton/Disney	SW 12	55.00	70.00	30.00	75.00

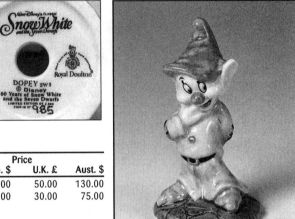

SW 5 / SW 13
DOPEY™
Style Two

Designer:	Shane Ridge
Height:	3 ½", 8.9 cm
Colour:	Yellow coat and trousers, purple hat, black belt
Issued:	SW 5 1997 in a limited edition of 2,000
	SW 13 1998 - 2002
Series:	Snow White and the Seven Dwarfs (Series Two)

Back Stamp	Beswick Number	Price			
		U.S. $	Can. $	U.K. £	Aust. $
Doulton/Disney 60th	SW 5	90.00	120.00	50.00	130.00
Doulton/Disney	SW 13	55.00	70.00	30.00	75.00

SW 6 / SW 14
SNEEZY™
Style Two

Designer:	Warren Platt
Height:	3 ½", 8.9 cm
Colour:	Light brown tunic, dark brown trousers, black belt
Issued:	SW 6 1997 in a limited edition of 2,000
	SW 14 1998 - 2002
Series:	Snow White and the Seven Dwarfs (Series Two)

Back Stamp	Doulton Number	Price			
		U.S. $	Can. $	U.K. £	Aust. $
Doulton/Disney 60th	SW 6	70.00	95.00	40.00	100.00
Doulton/Disney	SW 14	55.00	70.00	30.00	75.00

SW 7 / SW 15
SLEEPY™
Style Two

Designer:	Warren Platt
Height:	3 ½", 8.9 cm
Colour:	Beige tunic, dark brown trousers, green hat and a yellow bottle
Issued:	SW 7 1997 in a limited edition of 2,000
	SW 15 1998 - 2002
Series:	Snow White and the Seven Dwarfs (Series Two)

Back Stamp	Doulton Number	Price			
		U.S. $	Can. $	U.K. £	Aust. $
Doulton/Disney 60th	SW 7	70.00	95.00	40.00	100.00
Doulton/Disney	SW 15	55.00	70.00	30.00	75.00

SW 8 / SW 16
BASHFUL™
Style Two

Designer:	Amanda Hughes-Lubeck
Height:	3 ½", 8.9 cm
Colour:	Dark yellow tunic, light brown trousers, green hat
Issued:	SW 8 1997 in a limited edition of 2,000
	SW 16 1998 - 2002
Series:	Snow White and the Seven Dwarfs (Series Two)

Back Stamp	Doulton Number	Price			
		U.S. $	Can. $	U.K. £	Aust. $
Doulton/Disney 60th	SW 8	70.00	95.00	40.00	100.00
Doulton/Disney	SW 16	55.00	70.00	30.00	75.00

SW 17
DOPEY™ BY CANDLELIGHT

Designer:	Shane Ridge
Height:	3 ½", 8.9 cm
Colour:	Green
Issued:	1998 - 2002
Series:	Snow White and the Seven Dwarfs

Back Stamp	Doulton Number	Price			
		U.S. $	Can. $	U.K. £	Aust. $
Doulton/Disney 60th	SW 17	70.00	95.00	40.00	100.00
Doulton/Disney		55.00	70.00	30.00	75.00

SW 18
BASHFUL'S™ MELODY

Designer:	Graham Tongue
Modeller:	Graham Tongue
Height:	3 ½", 8.9 cm
Colour:	Blue
Issued:	1998 - 2002
Series:	Snow White and the Seven Dwarfs

Back Stamp	Doulton Number	Price U.S. $	Can. $	U.K. £	Aust. $
Doulton/Disney	SW 18	70.00	95.00	40.00	100.00

SW 19
DOC™ WITH LANTERN

Designer:	Warren Platt
Modeller:	Warren Platt
Height:	3 ½", 8.9 cm
Colour:	Red and yellow
Issued:	1999 - 2002
Series:	Snow White and the Seven Dwarfs

Back Stamp	Doulton Number	Price U.S. $	Can. $	U.K. £	Aust. $
Doulton/Disney	SW 19	70.00	95.00	40.00	100.00

SW 20
GRUMPY'S™ BATHTIME

Designer:	Shane Ridge
Modeller:	Shane Ridge
Height:	3 ½", 8.9 cm
Colour:	White, brown, red and yellow
Issued:	1999 - 1999
Series:	Snow White and the Seven Dwarfs

Back Stamp	Doulton Number	Price U.S. $	Can. $	U.K. £	Aust. $
Doulton/Disney	SW 20	200.00	275.00	110.00	300.00

Note: Serial numbered

SW 21
DOPEY'S™ FIRST KISS

Designer:	Disney
Modeller:	Shane Ridge
Height:	5 ¼", 13.3 cm
Colour:	Yellow, blue, red and green
Issued:	2000 in a limited edition of 2,000
Series:	1. Disney Classics
	2. Tableau

Back Stamp	Doulton Number	Price			
		U.S. $	Can. $	U.K. £	Aust. $
Doulton/Disney	SW 21	225.00	300.00	125.00	325.00

SNOW WHITE AND THE SEVEN DWARFS
ROYAL DOULTON SERIES 2004 TO THE PRESENT

SW 22
SNOW WHITE™
(Fairest of them all)

Height:	5 ¼", `3.3 cm
Colour:	Blue, yellow, pink, black, white and green
Issued:	2004 to the present
Series:	Snow White and the Seven Dwarfs (Series Three)

Back Stamp	Doulton Number	Price			
		U.S. $	Can. $	U.K. £	Aust. $
Doulton	SW 22	–	–	45.00	–

SW 23
BASHFULL™
(Aw Shucks)

Height:	4", 10.1 cm
Colour:	Yellow, brown, white and blue
Issued:	2004 to the present
Series:	Snow White and the Seven Dwarfs (Series Three)

Back Stamp	Doulton Number	Price			
		U.S. $	Can. $	U.K. £	Aust. $
Doulton	SW 23	–	–	25.00	–

SW 24
DOPEY™
(Irresistably Lovely)

Height: 3 ½", 8.9 cm
Colour: Yellow, pink, purple and grey
Issued: 2004 to the present
Series: Snow White and the Seven Dwarfs (Series Three)

Back Stamp	Doulton Number	Price			
		U.S. $	Can. $	U.K. £	Aust. $
Doulton	SW 24	–	–	25.00	–

SW 25
DEAR OLD DOC™

Height: 4", 10.1 cm
Colour: Brown, tan, beige, yellow and grey
Issued: 2004 to the present
Series: Snow White and the Seven Dwarfs (Series Three)

Back Stamp	Doulton Number	Price			
		U.S. $	Can. $	U.K. £	Aust. $
Doulton	SW 25	–	–	25.00	–

SW 26
GRUMPY™
(Hmmph)

Height: 3 ½", 8.9 cm
Colour: Red, brown, beige and grey
Issued: 2004 to the present
Series: Snow White and the Seven Dwarfs (Series Three)

Back Stamp	Doulton Number	Price			
		U.S. $	Can. $	U.K. £	Aust. $
Doulton	SW 26	–	–	25.00	–

SW 27
HAPPY™, HAPPY, THAT'S ME

Height:	3 ½", 8.9 cm
Colour:	Blue, browns, yellow and beige
Issued:	2004 to the present
Series:	Snow White and the Seven Dwarfs (Series Three)

Back Stamp	Doulton Number	Price			
		U.S. $	Can. $	U.K. £	Aust. $
Doulton	SW 27	—	—	25.00	—

SW 28
SLEEPY™
(Zzzz)

Height:	2", 5.0 cm
Colour:	White, pink, beige, light brown and green
Issued:	2004 to the present
Series:	Snow White and the Seven Dwarfs (Series Three)

Back Stamp	Doulton Number	Price			
		U.S. $	Can. $	U.K. £	Aust. $
Doulton	SW 28	—	—	25.00	—

SW 29
SNEEZY™
(Aa aa aachoo)

Height:	3 ½", 8.9 cm
Colour:	Light and dark brown, yellow, white and red
Issued:	2004 to the present
Series:	Snow White and the Seven Dwarfs (Series Three)

Back Stamp	Doulton Number	Price			
		U.S. $	Can. $	U.K. £	Aust. $
Doulton	SW 29	—	—	25.00	—

SW 30
EVIL QUEEN™
(Take the Apple, Dearie)

Height:	6", 15.0 cm
Colour:	Black, grey, white and red
Issued:	2004 to the present
Series:	Snow White and the Seven Dwarfs (Series Three)

Back Stamp	Doulton Number	Price			
		U.S. $	Can. $	U.K. £	Aust. $
Doulton	SW 30	–	–	35.00	–

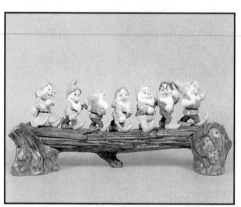

SW 31
HEIGH HO™

Length:	5 ¼", 13.3 cm
Colour:	Browns, yellows, blue, red, green, pink and grey
Issued:	2004 in a limited edition of 1,500
Series:	Snow White and the Seven Dwarfs (Series Three)

Back Stamp	Doulton Number	Price			
		U.S. $	Can. $	U.K. £	Aust. $
Doulton	SW 31	–	–	245.00	–

WINNIE THE POOH

BESWICK SERIES 1968-1990

2193
WINNIE THE POOH™

Designer:	Albert Hallam
Height:	2 ½", 6.4 cm
Colour:	Golden brown and red
Issued:	1968 - 1990
Series:	Winnie The Pooh

Back Stamp	Beswick Number	Price			
		U.S. $	Can. $	U.K. £	Aust. $
Beswick Gold	2193	150.00	200.00	85.00	225.00
Beswick Brown	2193	125.00	175.00	75.00	200.00

2196
EEYORE™

Designer:	Albert Hallam
Height:	2", 5.0 cm
Colour:	Grey with black markings
Issued:	1968 - 1990
Series:	Winnie The Pooh

Back Stamp	Beswick Number	Price			
		U.S. $	Can. $	U.K. £	Aust. $
Beswick Gold	2196	150.00	200.00	80.00	225.00
Beswick Brown	2196	125.00	150.00	70.00	175.00

2214
PIGLET™

Designer:	Albert Hallam
Height:	2 ¾", 7.0 cm
Colour:	Pink and red
Issued:	1968 - 1990
Series:	Winnie The Pooh

Back Stamp	Beswick Number	Price			
		U.S. $	Can. $	U.K. £	Aust. $
Beswick Gold	2214	150.00	200.00	85.00	225.00
Beswick Brown	2214	125.00	150.00	75.00	200.00

2215
RABBIT™

Designer: Albert Hallam
Height: 3 ¼", 8.3 cm
Colour: Brown and beige
Issued: 1968 - 1990
Series: Winnie The Pooh

Back Stamp	Beswick Number	Price			
		U.S. $	Can. $	U.K. £	Aust. $
Beswick Gold	2215	175.00	250.00	100.00	275.00
Beswick Brown	2215	150.00	200.00	90.00	225.00

2216
OWL™

Designer: Albert Hallam
Height: 3", 7.6 cm
Colour: Brown, white and black
Issued: 1968 - 1990
Series: Winnie The Pooh

Back Stamp	Beswick Number	Price			
		U.S. $	Can. $	U.K. £	Aust. $
Beswick Gold	2216	150.00	200.00	80.00	225.00
Beswick Brown	2216	125.00	150.00	70.00	175.00

2217
KANGA™

Designer: Albert Hallam
Height: 3 ¼", 8.3 cm
Colour: Dark and light brown
Issued: 1968 - 1990
Series: Winnie The Pooh

Back Stamp	Beswick Number	Price			
		U.S. $	Can. $	U.K. £	Aust. $
Beswick Gold	2217	150.00	200.00	85.00	225.00
Beswick Brown	2217	125.00	175.00	75.00	200.00

2394
TIGGER™

Designer:	Graham Tongue
Height:	3", 7.6 cm
Colour:	Yellow with black stripes
Issued:	1971 - 1990
Series:	Winnie The Pooh

Back Stamp	Beswick Number	Price			
		U.S. $	Can. $	U.K. £	Aust. $
Beswick Gold	2394	350.00	475.00	200.00	500.00
Beswick Brown	2394	250.00	325.00	135.00	350.00

2395
CHRISTOPHER ROBIN™
Style One

Designer:	Graham Tongue
Height:	4 ¾", 12.1 cm
Colour:	Yellow, blue and white
Issued:	1971 - 1990
Series:	Winnie The Pooh

Back Stamp	Beswick Number	Price			
		U.S. $	Can. $	U.K. £	Aust. $
Beswick Gold	2395	350.00	475.00	200.00	500.00
Beswick Brown	2395	275.00	350.00	150.00	375.00

WINNIE THE POOH
ROYAL DOULTON SERIES 1996 to the present

WP 1
WINNIE THE POOH™ AND THE HONEY POT

Designer:	Warren Platt
Height:	2 ½", 6.5 cm
Colour:	Yellow bear, red jersey, red-brown honey pot
Issued:	1996 - 1999
Series:	Winnie the Pooh and Friends from the Hundred Acre Wood

Back Stamp	Doulton Number	Price			
		U.S. $	Can. $	U.K. £	Aust. $
BK-1	WP 1 / 70th	80.00	100.00	45.00	110.00
BK-2	WP 1	55.00	70.00	30.00	75.00

WP 2
POOH™ AND PIGLET™ THE WINDY DAY

Designer:	Martyn Alcock
Height:	3 ¼", 8.3 cm
Colour:	Yellow bear, pink piglet with green suit, light brown base
Issued:	1996 - 2002
Series:	Winnie the Pooh and Friends from the Hundred Acre Wood

Back Stamp	Doulton Number	Price			
		U.S. $	Can. $	U.K. £	Aust. $
BK-1	WP 2 / 70th	80.00	100.00	45.00	110.00
BK-2	WP 2	55.00	70.00	30.00	75.00

WP 3
WINNIE THE POOH™ AND THE PAW-MARKS

Designer:	Warren Platt
Height:	2 ¾", 7.0 cm
Colour:	Yellow bear, red jersey
Issued:	1996 - 1997
Series:	Winnie the Pooh and Friends from the Hundred Acre Wood

Back Stamp	Doulton Number	Price			
		U.S. $	Can. $	U.K. £	Aust. $
BK-1	WP 3 / 70th	90.00	120.00	50.00	125.00
BK-2	WP 3	80.00	100.00	45.00	110.00

WP 4
WINNIE THE POOH™ IN THE ARMCHAIR

Designer:	Shane Ridge
Height:	3 ¼", 8.3 cm
Colour:	Yellow bear, pink armchair
Issued:	1996 - 1998
Series:	Winnie the Pooh and Friends from the Hundred Acre Wood

Back Stamp	Doulton Number	Price			
		U.S. $	Can. $	U.K. £	Aust. $
BK-1	WP 4 / 70th	80.00	100.00	45.00	110.00
BK-2	WP 4	65.00	85.00	35.00	90.00

WP 5
PIGLET™ AND THE BALLOON

Designer:	Warren Platt
Height:	2 ¾", 7.0 cm
Colour:	Pink piglet, green suit, blue balloon, light brown base
Issued:	1996 - 1998
Series:	Winnie the Pooh and Friends from the Hundred Acre Wood

Back Stamp	Doulton Number	Price			
		U.S. $	Can. $	U.K. £	Aust. $
BK-1	WP 5 / 70th	70.00	95.00	40.00	100.00
BK-2	WP 5	55.00	70.00	30.00	75.00

WP 6
TIGGER™ SIGNS THE RISSOLUTION

Designer:	Martyn Alcock
Height:	1 ¾", 4.5 cm
Colour:	Yellow and black
Issued:	1996 - 2000
Series:	Winnie the Pooh and Friends from the Hundred Acre Wood

Back Stamp	Doulton Number	Price			
		U.S. $	Can. $	U.K. £	Aust. $
BK-1	WP 6 / 70th	70.00	95.00	40.00	100.00
BK-2	WP 6	55.00	70.00	30.00	75.00

WP 7
EEYORE'S™ TAIL

Designer:	Shane Ridge
Height:	3 ½", 8.9 cm
Colour:	Grey donkey with black markings, pink bow
Issued:	1996 - 1999
Series:	Winnie the Pooh and Friends from the Hundred Acre Wood

Back Stamp	Doulton Number	Price			
		U.S. $	Can. $	U.K. £	Aust. $
BK-1	WP 7 / 70th	80.00	100.00	45.00	110.00
BK-2	WP 7	55.00	70.00	30.00	75.00

WP 8
KANGA™ AND ROO™

Designer:	Martyn Alcock
Height:	3 ½", 8.9 cm
Colour:	Dark and light brown kangaroos
Issued:	1996 - 1998
Series:	Winnie the Pooh and Friends from the Hundred Acre Wood

Back Stamp	Doulton Number	Price			
		U.S. $	Can. $	U.K. £	Aust. $
BK-1	WP 8 / 70th	100.00	135.00	55.00	145.00
BK-2	WP 8	55.00	70.00	30.00	75.00

WP 9
CHRISTOPHER ROBIN™
Style Two

Designer:	Shane Ridge
Height:	5 ½", 14.0 cm
Colour:	White and blue checkered shirt, blue shorts, black wellingtons, red-brown hair
Issued:	1996 - 2001
Series:	Winnie the Pooh and Friends from the Hundred Acre Wood

Back Stamp	Doulton Number	Price			
		U.S. $	Can. $	U.K. £	Aust. $
BK-1	WP 9 / 70th	90.00	120.00	50.00	125.00
BK-2	WP 9	55.00	70.00	30.00	75.00

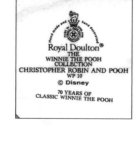

WP 10
CHRISTOPHER ROBIN™ AND POOH™

Designer:	Shane Ridge
Height:	3 ¼", 8.5 cm
Colour:	Light blue shirt and shorts, black boots, reddish brown hair, yellow bear
Issued:	1996 - 1997
Series:	Winnie the Pooh and Friends from the Hundred Acre Wood

Back Stamp	Doulton Number	Price			
		U.S. $	Can. $	U.K. £	Aust. $
BK-1	WP 10 / 70th	135.00	175.00	75.00	200.00
BK-2	WP 10	90.00	120.00	50.00	125.00

WP 11
POOH™ LIGHTS THE CANDLE

Designer:	Graham Tongue
Height:	3 ½", 8.9 cm
Colour:	Yellow bear with white candle and hat
Issued:	1997 - 1998
Series:	Winnie the Pooh and Friends from the Hundred Acre Wood

Back Stamp	Doulton Number	Price			
		U.S. $	Can. $	U.K. £	Aust. $
BK-2	WP 11	55.00	70.00	30.00	75.00

WP 12
POOH™ COUNTING THE HONEYPOTS

Designer:	Martyn Alcock
Height:	3 ½", 8.9 cm
Colour:	Yellow bear, brown honeypots
Issued:	1997 - 1999
Series:	Winnie the Pooh and Friends from the Hundred Acre Wood

Back Stamp	Doulton Number	Price			
		U.S. $	Can. $	U.K. £	Aust. $
BK-2	WP 12	55.00	70.00	30.00	75.00

WP 13
PIGLET™ PICKING THE VIOLETS

Designer:	Graham Tongue
Height:	2 ½", 6.4 cm
Colour:	Pink, light and dark greens
Issued:	1997 - 2000
Series:	Winnie the Pooh and Friends from the Hundred Acre Wood

Back Stamp	Doulton Number	Price			
		U.S. $	Can. $	U.K. £	Aust. $
BK-2	WP 13	55.00	70.00	30.00	75.00

WP 14
EEYORE'S™ BIRTHDAY

Designer:	Martyn Alcock
Height:	2 ¾", 7.0 cm
Colour:	Grey and black
Issued:	1997 - 2002
Series:	Winnie the Pooh and Friends from the Hundred Acre Wood

Back Stamp	Doulton Number	Price			
		U.S. $	Can. $	U.K. £	Aust. $
BK-2	WP 14	55.00	70.00	30.00	75.00

WP 15
EEYORE™ LOSES A TAIL

Designer:	Martyn Alcock
Height:	4", 10.1 cm
Colour:	Pink, yellow, grey, green and brown
Issued:	1997 in a limited edition of 5,000
Series:	1. Tableau
	2. Winnie the Pooh and Friends from the Hundred Acre Wood

Back Stamp	Doulton Number	Price			
		U.S. $	Can. $	U.K. £	Aust. $
Doulton	WP 15	300.00	400.00	165.00	425.00

WP 16
POOH'S™ BLUE BALLOON (MONEY BOX)

Designer:	Shane Ridge
Height:	4 ¼", 10.8 cm
Colour:	Yellow bear, pink pig wearing green suit, white balloon with dark blue rope
Issued:	1997 - 1998
Series:	Winnie the Pooh and Friends from the Hundred Acre Wood

Back Stamp	Doulton Number	Price			
		U.S. $	Can. $	U.K. £	Aust. $
Doulton	WP 16	90.00	125.00	50.00	135.00

WP 17
WOL™ SIGNS THE RISSOLUTION

Designer:	Martyn Alcock
Height:	3 ¾", 9.5 cm
Colour:	Grey and black
Issued:	1998 in a special edition of 2,500
Series:	Winnie the Pooh and Friends from the Hundred Acre Wood

Back Stamp	Doulton Number	Price			
		U.S. $	Can. $	U.K. £	Aust. $
Doulton	WP 17	300.00	400.00	165.00	425.00

WP 18
WINNIE THE POOH™ AND THE PRESENT

Designer:	Graham Tongue
Height:	3 ¾", 9.5 cm
Colour:	Yellow and brown
Issued:	1999 - 2002
Series:	Winnie the Pooh and Friends from the Hundred Acre Wood

Back Stamp	Doulton Number	Price			
		U.S. $	Can. $	U.K. £	Aust. $
Doulton	WP 18	55.00	70.00	30.00	75.00

WP 19
WINNIE THE POOH™ AND THE FAIR-SIZED BASKET

Designer:	Graham Tongue
Height:	2 ¾", 7.0 cm
Colour:	Yellow bear, brown basket
Issued:	1999 - 2002
Series:	Winnie the Pooh and Friends from the Hundred Acre Wood

Back Stamp	Doulton Number	Price U.S. $	Can. $	U.K. £	Aust. $
Doulton	WP 19	55.00	70.00	30.00	75.00

WP 20
THE MORE IT SNOWS, TIDDELY POM™

Designer:	Shane Ridge
Height:	3 ¼", 8.3 cm
Colour:	Yellow, red, pink and green
Issued:	1999-2002
Series:	Winnie the Pooh and Friends from the Hundred Acre Wood

Back Stamp	Doulton Number	Price U.S. $	Can. $	U.K. £	Aust. $
Doulton	WP 20	65.00	85.00	35.00	95.00

WP 21
SUMMER'S DAY PICNIC™

Designer:	Warren Platt
Length:	2 ½", 5.7 cm
Colour:	Blue, yellow and green
Issued:	1998 in a limited editionof 5,000
Series:	1. Tableau
	2. Winnie the Pooh and Friends from the Hundred Acre Wood

Back Stamp	Doulton Number	Price U.S. $	Can. $	U.K. £	Aust. $
Doulton	WP 21	175.00	250.00	100.00	275.00

WP 22
I'VE FOUND SOMEBODY JUST LIKE ME™

Designer:	Martyn Alcock
Length:	5 ¼", 13.3 cm
Colour:	Yellow, black, blue and white
Issued:	1999 in a limited edition of 5,000
Series:	1. Tableau
	2. Winnie the Pooh and Friends from the Hundred Acre Wood

Back Stamp	Doulton Number	Price			
		U.S. $	Can. $	U.K. £	Aust. $
Doulton	WP 22	225.00	300.00	125.00	325.00

WP 23
RABBIT™ READS THE PLAN

Designer:	Martyn Alcock
Height:	4 ½", 11.9 cm
Colour:	Grey rabbit, pink inner ears
Issued:	1999 - 1999
Series:	Classic Pooh

Back Stamp	Doulton Number	Price			
		U.S. $	Can. $	U.K. £	Aust. $
Doulton	WP 23	65.00	85.00	35.00	95.00

WP 24
HOW SWEET TO BE A CLOUD™ (CLOCK)

Designer:	Warren Platt
Height:	4 ½", 11.9 cm
Colour:	Blue, white, yellow and red
Issued:	2000 - 2000
Series:	Classic Pooh

Back Stamp	Doulton Number	Price			
		U.S. $	Can. $	U.K. £	Aust. $
Doulton	WP 24	125.00	175.00	70.00	200.00

WP 25
EEYORE™ NOSE TO THE GROUND

Designer:	Martyn Alcock
Height:	3 ¾", 9.5 cm
Size:	Large
Colour:	Grey and black
Issued:	2000 in a limited edition of 2,000
Series:	Large Size

Back Stamp	Doulton Number	Price			
		U.S. $	Can. $	U.K. £	Aust. $
Doulton	WP 25	135.00	175.00	75.00	200.00

WP 26
PIGLET™ PLANTING A HAYCORN

Designer:	Martyn Alcock
Height:	3 ¾", 9.5 cm
Size:	Large
Colour:	Pink, green and brown
Issued:	2000 in a limited edition of 2,000
Series:	Large Size

Back Stamp	Doulton Number	Price			
		U.S. $	Can. $	U.K. £	Aust. $
Doulton	WP 26	90.00	125.00	55.00	135.00

WP 27
TIGGER™ LOVES TIGGER LILIES

Designer:	Martyn Alcock
Height:	4 ¼", 10.8 cm
Size:	Large
Colour:	Brown, black and red
Issued:	2000 in a limited edition of 2,000
Series:	Large Size

Back Stamp	Doulton Number	Price			
		U.S. $	Can. $	U.K. £	Aust. $
Doulton	WP 27	115.00	155.00	65.00	165.00

WP 28
POOH BEGAN TO EAT™

Designer:	Shane Ridge
Height:	3 ¾", 9.5 cm
Size:	Large
Colour:	Yellow and green
Issued:	2000 in a limited edition of 2,000
Series:	Large Size

Back Stamp	Doulton Number	Price			
		U.S. $	Can. $	U.K. £	Aust. $
Doulton	WP 28	150.00	200.00	85.00	225.00

WP 29
PIGLET AND THE HONEY POT™

Designer:	Amanda Hughes-Lubeck
Height:	2 ½", 6.4 cm
Colour:	Pink, green, grey and yellow
Issued:	2000 - 2002
Series:	Classic Pooh

Back Stamp	Doulton Number	Price			
		U.S. $	Can. $	U.K. £	Aust. $
Doulton	WP 29	50.00	70.00	30.00	75.00

WP 30
TIGGER PLAYS BALL™

Designer:	Warren Platt
Height:	3", 7.6 cm
Colour:	Brown, black and yellow
Issued:	2000 - 2002
Series:	Classic Pooh

Back Stamp	Doulton Number	Price			
		U.S. $	Can. $	U.K. £	Aust. $
Doulton	WP 30	100.00	150.00	60.00	175.00

WP 31
THE BRAIN OF POOH™

Designer:	Amanda Hughes-Lubeck
Height:	4", 10.1 cm
Colour:	Black, grey, yellow and green
Issued:	2000 in a limited edition of 5,000
Series:	Classic Pooh

Back Stamp	Doulton Number	Price			
		U.S. $	Can. $	U.K. £	Aust. $
Doulton	WP 31	300.00	425.00	175.00	450.00

WP 32
CHRISTOPHER READS TO POOH™

Designer:	Shane Ridge
Height:	3 ½", 8.9 cm
Colour:	Yellow, red, white and black
Issued:	2001 (time limited)
Series:	Classic Pooh

Back Stamp	Doulton Number	Price			
		U.S. $	Can. $	U.K. £	Aust. $
Doulton	WP 32	150.00	200.00	85.00	225.00

WP 33
POOH™ AND THE PARTY HAT

Designer:	Amander Hughes-Lubeck
Height:	2 ¾", 7.0 cm
Colour:	Yellow bear, red hat, pale blue ribbon
Issued:	2001-2002
Series:	Classic Pooh

Back Stamp	Doulton Number	Price			
		U.S. $	Can. $	U.K. £	Aust. $
Doulton	WP 33	75.00	95.00	40.00	100.00

WP 34
GOING SLEDGING™

Designer:	Shane Ridge
Height:	4", 10.1 cm
Colour:	Blue, yellow, red, brown, green and grey
Issued:	2001 in a limited edition of 5,000
Series:	Classic Pooh

Back Stamp	Doulton Number	Price			
		U.S. $	Can. $	U.K. £	Aust. $
Doulton	WP 34	200.00	250.00	110.00	275.00

WP 35
WOL™ AND THE HONEYPOT

Designer:	Warren Platt
Height:	3 ¼", 8.3 cm
Colour:	Grey, white, brown and tan
Issued:	2001 - 2002
Series:	Classic Pooh

Back Stamp	Doulton Number	Price			
		U.S. $	Can. $	U.K. £	Aust. $
Doulton	WP 35	65.00	85.00	35.00	95.00

WP 36
UNDER THE NAME MR. SANDERS™

Height:	3", 7.6 cm
Colour:	Yellow bear, brown log
Issued:	2001 - 2002
Series:	Classic Pooh

Back Stamp	Doulton Number	Price			
		U.S. $	Can. $	U.K. £	Aust. $
Doulton	WP 36	65.00	85.00	35.00	95.00

WP 37
ALL THE FLOWERS ARE WAKING UP (Spring)™

Designer:	Warren Platt
Height:	3", 7.6 cm
Colour:	Yellow bear, grey pot with pink flowers
Issued:	2002 to the present
Series:	1. Classic Pooh
	2. Four Seasons

Back Stamp	Doulton Number	Price			
		U.S. $	Can. $	U.K. £	Aust. $
Doulton	WP 37	—	—	25.00	—

WP 38
SUMMER IS FULL OF FLUTTERY SURPRISES (Summer)™

Designer:	Warren Platt
Height:	2 ½", 6.4 cm
Colour:	Pink, green and lilac
Issued:	2002 to the present
Series:	Four Seasons

Back Stamp	Doulton Number	Price			
		U.S. $	Can. $	U.K. £	Aust. $
Doulton	WP 38	—	—	22.50	—

WP 39
LOVE MAKES ALL YOUR BOTHERS DISAPPEAR™

Designer:	Shane Ridge
Height:	2 ¼", 5.7 cm
Colour:	Yellow, red, white and green
Issued:	2002 to the present
Series:	Love and Friendship

HAND MADE AND HAND DECORATED
CLASSIC
POOH
by ROYAL DOULTON
WINNIE THE POOH LOVE & FRIENDSHIP COLLECTION
LOVE MAKES ALL YOUR BOTHERS
DISAPPEAR.   WP 39
2003
©Disney
Based on the "Winnie the Pooh" works
by A.A.Milne and E.H.Shepard
MADE IN THAILAND

Back Stamp	Doulton Number	Price			
		U.S. $	Can. $	U.K. £	Aust. $
Doulton	WP 39	—	—	25.00	—

WP 40
A PRESENT FOR ME? HOW GRAND!™

Designer: Shane Ridge
Height: 3 ¼", 8.3 cm
Colour: Yellow bear, red gift box, purple ribbon
Issued: 2002 - 2002
Series: Birthday Collection

Back Stamp	Doulton Number	Price			
		U.S. $	Can. $	U.K. £	Aust. $
Doulton	WP 40	50.00	70.00	30.00	75.00

WP 41
A LITTLE TREE TRIMMING IS IN ORDER™

Designer: Martyn Alcock
Height: 3 ¾", 9.6 cm
Colour: Yellow bear, blue nightshirt and cap,
             red tree ornament
Issued: 2002 - 2002
Series: Christmas Collection

Back Stamp	Doulton Number	Price			
		U.S. $	Can. $	U.K. £	Aust. $
Doulton	WP 41	50.00	70.00	30.00	75.00

Note: Set with The Most Perfect Tree in all the Wood (WP 42) and Christopher Dresses the Tree (WP 57).

WP 42
THE MOST PERFECT TREE IN ALL THE WOOD™

Designer: Martyn Alcock
Height: 4 ¾", 12.1 cm
Colour: Green tree, red and purple
             decorations
Issued: 2002 - 2002
Series: Christmas Collection

Back Stamp	Doulton Number	Price			
		U.S. $	Can. $	U.K. £	Aust. $
Doulton	WP 42	50.00	70.00	30.00	75.00

Note: Set with A Little Tree Trimming is in Order (WP 41) and Christopher Dresses the Tree (WP 57).

WP 43
SOMETIMES AUTUMN TICKLES
YOUR NOSE™ (Autumn)

Designer:	Shane Ridge
Height:	3", 7.6 cm
Colour:	Tan, black, pink, green and brown
Issued:	2002 - 2003
Series:	Four Seasons

Back Stamp	Doulton Number	Price			
		U.S. $	Can. $	U.K. £	Aust. $
Doulton	WP 43	50.00	70.00	30.00	75.00

WP 44
EEYORE™ MADE A WINTERY WISH (Winter)

Designer:	Shane Ridge
Height:	3 ¼", 8.3 cm
Colour:	Grey, white and pink
Issued:	2002 - 2003
Series:	Four Seasons

Back Stamp	Doulton Number	Price			
		U.S. $	Can. $	U.K. £	Aust. $
Doulton	WP 44	50.00	70.00	30.00	75.00

WP 45
WHO'S CAKE? POOH'S™ CAKE?

Designer:	E. H. Shephard
Height:	3 ¼", 8.3 cm
Colour:	Pink piglet wearing a green suit; pink, white and yellow cake
Issued:	2003 - 2003
Series:	Birthday Collection

Back Stamp	Doulton Number	Price			
		U.S. $	Can. $	U.K. £	Aust. $
Doulton	WP 45	50.00	70.00	30.00	75.00

WINNIE THE POOH
Royal Doulton Series 1996 to the present

(WP1) WINNIE THE POOH AND
THE HONEY POT

(WP2) POOH AND PIGLET
THE WINDY DAY

(WP3) WINNIE THE POOH AND
THE PAW-MARKS

(WP4) WINNIE THE POOH
IN THE ARMCHAIR

(WP5) PIGLET AND THE BALLOON

(WP6) TIGGER SIGNS
THE RISSOLUTION

(WP7) EEYORE'S TAIL

(WP8) KANGA AND ROO

(WP9) CHRISTOPHER ROBIN
Style Two

WINNIE THE POOH

(WP10)   CHRISTOPHER ROBIN
           AND POOH

(WP11)   POOH LIGHTS
         THE CANDLE

(WP12)   POOH COUNTING
         THE HONEYPOTS

(WP13)   PIGLET PICKING
           THE VIOLETS

(WP14)   EEYORE'S BIRTHDAY

(WP16)   POOH'S BLUE BALLOON
         (MONEY BOX)

EEYORE LOSES A TAIL

(WP15)   EEYORE LOSES A TAIL

(WP17)   WOL SIGNS THE
           RISSOLUTION

WINNIE THE POOH

(WP18)   WINNIE THE POOH
         AND THE PRESENT

(WP19)   WINNIE THE POOH AND
         THE FAIR-SIZED BASKET

(WP20)   THE MORE IT SNOWS,
         TIDDELY POM

(WP21)   SUMMER'S DAY PICNIC

(WP22)   I'VE FOUND SOMEBODY
         JUST LIKE ME

(WP23)   RABBIT READS
         THE PLAN

(WP25)   EEYORE NOSE
         TO THE GROUND

(WP26)   PIGLET PLANTING
         A HAYCORN

(WP27)   TIGGER LOVES
         TIGGER LILIES

WINNIE THE POOH

(WP28)   POOH BEGAN TO EAT

(WP29)   PIGLET AND
THE HONEY POT

(WP30)   TIGGER PLAYS BALL

(WP31)   THE BRAIN OF POOH

(WP32)   CHRISTOPHER
READS TO POOH

(WP33)   POOH AND THE
PARTY HAT

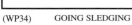

(WP34)   GOING SLEDGING

(WP35)   WOL AND
THE HONEYPOT

(WP36)   UNDER THE NAME
MR. SANDERS

WINNIE THE POOH

(WP37) ALL THE FLOWERS ARE
WAKING UP (Spring)

(WP38) SUMMER IS FULL OF
FLUTTERY SURPRISES (Summer)

(WP39) LOVE MAKES ALL YOUR
BOTHERS DISAPPEAR

(WP40) A PRESENT FOR ME?
HOW GRAND!

(WP41) A LITTLE TREE TRIMMING IS IN ORDER, (WP42) THE MOST PERFECT TREE IN
ALL THE WOOD, (WP57) CHRISTOPHER DRESSES THE TREE

(WP43) SOMETIMES AUTUMN
TICKLES YOUR NOSE (Autumn)

(WP44) EEYORE MADE A
WINTERY WISH (Winter)

(WP45) WHO'S CAKE?
POOH'S CAKE?

WINNIE THE POOH

(WP46)   I LOVE YOU SO
           MUCH BEAR

(WP47)   TOOT TOOT WENT
           THE WHISTLE

(WP48)   ANY HUNNY
           LEFT FOR ME?

(WP49)   A CLEAN BEAR IS
           A HAPPY BEAR

(WP50)   PRESENTS AND PARTIES

(WP51)   A LITTLE SPONGE FOR A
         LITTLE PIGLET

(WP52)   BOUNCY BOUNCY
           BOO-TO-YOU!

(WP53)   A SLEEPY DAY IN THE
         HUNDRED ACRE WOOD

(WP54)   A CLEAN LITTLE
           ROO IS BEST!

WINNIE THE POOH

(WP55/56)   PUSH...PULL! COME ON POOH
(Bookends)

(WP58)   TIGGER'S SPLASH TIME

(WP59)   OH DEAR,
BATHTIMES HERE!

(WP60)   ISN'T IT FUNNY
HOW A BEAR LIKES HONEY

(WP61)   IT'S HONEY ALL
THE WAY DOWN

(WP62)   WHERE DOES THE
WIND COME FROM?

(WP63)   RUM-TUM-TUM WINNIE
ON HIS DRUM

(WP64)   A BIG NOISE FOR
A LITTLE PIGLET

WINNIE THE POOH

(WP65)   TIGGER'S BIRTHDAY
SURPRISE

(WP66)   WITH LOVE

(WP67)   RABBIT'S HARVEST?

(WP69)   PREPARATIONS FOR
CARROT HONEY PIE

(WP70)   THE PERFECT HAT
FOR GARDENING

(WP76)   CHRISTMAS PIGLET

(WP78) PIGLET'S   (WP77) TEA FOR TWO   (WP75) HONEY AND TEA IS
TEA TIME   A VERY GRAND THING

WP 46
I LOVE YOU SO MUCH BEAR™

Designer:	E. H. Shephard					
Height:	4", 10.1 cm					
Colour:	Yellow, pink and green					
Issued:	2003 to the present					
Series:	Love and Friendship					

Back Stamp	Doulton Number	Price			
		U.S. $	Can. $	U.K. £	Aust. $
Doulton	WP 46	–	–	35.00	–

WP 47
TOOT TOOT WENT THE WHISTLE™

Designer:	E. H. Shephard					
Height:	3 ¼", 8.3 cm					
Colour:	Yellow bear, black train, red and black					
	train station, grey train tracks					
Issued:	2003 to the present					

Back Stamp	Doulton Number	Price			
		U.S. $	Can. $	U.K. £	Aust. $
Doulton	WP 47	–	–	30.00	–

WP 48
ANY HUNNY LEFT FOR ME?™

Designer:	E. H. Shephard					
Height:	4", 10.1 cm					
Colour:	Yellow bear, blue and					
	brown honey pots					
Issued:	2003 to the present					

Back Stamp	Doulton Number	Price			
		U.S. $	Can. $	U.K. £	Aust. $
Doulton	WP 48	–	–	30.00	–

WP 49
A CLEAN BEAR IS A HAPPY BEAR™

Designer:	E. H. Shephard
Height:	3 ¼", 8.3 cm
Colour:	Yellow bear and ducks, brown washtub, blue and white bubbles, green towel
Issued:	2003 to the present
Series:	Bathtime Collection

Back Stamp	Doulton Number	Price			
		U.S. $	Can. $	U.K. £	Aust. $
Doulton	WP 49	–	–	30.00	–

WP 50
PRESENTS AND PARTIES™

Designer:	E. H. Shephard
Height:	4 ¼", 10.8 cm
Colour:	Yellow bear, blue hat, green gift box with pink ribbon, white cake
Issued:	2003 to the present
Series:	Birthday Collection

Back Stamp	Doulton Number	Price			
		U.S. $	Can. $	U.K. £	Aust. $
Doulton	WP 50	–	–	30.00	–

WP 51
A LITTLE SPONGE FOR A LITTLE PIGLET™

Designer:	E. H. Shephard
Height:	3 ¼", 8.3 cm
Colour:	Pink piglet wearing green suit, brown washtub, blue and white bubbles, grey bucket
Issued:	2003 to the present
Series:	Bathtime Collection

Back Stamp	Doulton Number	Price			
		U.S. $	Can. $	U.K. £	Aust. $
Doulton	WP 51	–	–	25.00	–

WP 52
BOUNCY BOUNCY BOO-TO-YOU!™

Designer:	E. H. Shephard
Height:	3 ¼", 8.3 cm
Colour:	Orange and black tiger, green, yellow and blue toy box
Issued:	2003 to the present

Back Stamp	Doulton Number	Price			
		U.S. $	Can. $	U.K. £	Aust. $
Doulton	WP 52	–	–	30.00	–

WP 53
A SLEEPY DAY IN THE HUNDRED ACRE WOOD™

Designer:	E. H. Shephard
Height:	4 ¾", 12.1 cm
Colour:	Grey and black donkey, yellow bear, brown and black tiger, pink piglet wearing a green suit
Issued:	2003 to the present

Back Stamp	Doulton Number	Price			
		U.S. $	Can. $	U.K. £	Aust. $
Doulton	WP 53	–	–	70.00	–

WP 54
A CLEAN LITTLE ROO™ IS BEST!

Designer:	E. H. Shephard
Height:	4 ¾", 12.1 cm
Colour:	Brown kangaroos, brown washtub, blue and white bubbles
Issued:	2003 to the present
Series:	Bathtime Collection

Back Stamp	Doulton Number	Price			
		U.S. $	Can. $	U.K. £	Aust. $
Doulton	WP 54	–	–	30.00	–

WP 55/56
PUSH...PULL! COME ON POOH™ (Bookends)

Designer:	E. H. Shephard
Height:	4 ¾". 12.1 cm
Colour:	Left: Grey rabbit, brown, blue, pink and yellow honey pots
	Right: Grey donkey, brown and black tiger, pink piglet
Issued:	2003 in a limited edition of 2,000 pairs

Back Stamp	Doulton Number	Price			
		U.S. $	Can. $	U.K. £	Aust. $
Doulton	WP 55/56	150.00	200.00	80.00	225.00

WP 57
CHRISTOPHER™ DRESSES THE TREE

Designer:	E. H. Shephard
Height:	4 ¾", 12.1 cm
Colour:	Green sweater, blue trousers, red scarf, red and white hat, black boots
Issued:	2003 to the present
Series:	Christmas Collection

Back Stamp	Doulton Number	Price			
		U.S. $	Can. $	U.K. £	Aust. $
Doulton	WP 57	–	–	25.00	–

Note: Set with A Little Tree Trimming (WP 41) and The Most Perfect Tree in all the Wood (WP 42).

WP 58
TIGGER'S™ SPLASH TIME

Designer:	E. H. Shephard
Height:	4", 10.1 cm
Colour:	Orange and black striped tiper, brown washtub
Issued:	2003 to the present
Series:	Bathtime Collection

Back Stamp	Doulton Number	Price			
		U.S. $	Can. $	U.K. £	Aust. $
Doulton	WP 58	–	–	30.00	–

WP 59
OH DEAR BATHTIME'S HERE!™

Designer:	E. H. Shephard
Height:	2 ¾", 7.0 cm
Colour:	Grey and black donkey, brown basket
Issued:	2003 to the present
Series:	Bathtime Collection

Back Stamp	Doulton Number	Price			
		U.S. $	Can. $	U.K. £	Aust. $
Doulton	WP 59	–	–	30.00	–

WP 60
ISN'T IT FUNNY HOW A BEAR LIKES HONEY™

Designer:	E. H. Shephard
Height:	4 ¼", 10.8 cm
Colour:	Yellow bear, blue and purple honey pots
Issued:	2003 to the present

Back Stamp	Doulton Number	Price			
		U.S. $	Can. $	U.K. £	Aust. $
Doulton	WP 60	–	–	25.00	–

WP 61
IT'S HONEY ALL THE WAY DOWN™

Designer:	E. H. Shephard
Height:	4 ¼", 10.8 cm
Colour:	Yellow bear, brown tree trunk
Issued:	2003 to the present

Back Stamp	Doulton Number	Price			
		U.S. $	Can. $	U.K. £	Aust. $
Doulton	WP 61	–	–	30.00	–

WP 62
WHERE DOES THE WIND COME FROM?™

Designer:	E. H. Shephard
Height:	3 ¼", 8.3 cm
Colour:	Yellow bear, red and blue kite
Issued:	2003 to the present

Back Stamp	Doulton Number	Price			
		U.S. $	Can. $	U.K. £	Aust. $
Doulton	WP 62	–	–	25.00	–

WP 63
RUM-TUM-TUM WINNIE™ ON HIS DRUM

Designer:	E. H. Shephard
Height:	3 ¼", 8.3 cm
Colour:	Yellow bear, green, red and blue drum
Issued:	2003 to the present

Back Stamp	Doulton Number	Price			
		U.S. $	Can. $	U.K. £	Aust. $
Doulton	WP 63	–	–	25.00	–

WP 64
A BIG NOISE FOR A LITTLE PIGLET™

Designer:	E. H. Shephard
Height:	3", 7.6 cm
Colour:	Pink piglet, green suit and yellow cymbals
Issued:	2003 to the present

Back Stamp	Doulton Number	Price			
		U.S. $	Can. $	U.K. £	Aust. $
Doulton	WP 64	–	–	25.00	–

WP 65
TIGGER'S BIRTHDAY SURPRISE™

Height:	4 ¼", 10.8 cm
Colour:	Orange and black tiger; yellow balloon, blue and green hat
Issued:	2004 - 2004
Series:	Birthday

Back Stamp	Doulton Number	Price			
		U.S. $	Can. $	U.K. £	Aust. $
Doulton	WP 65	−	−	25.00	−

Note: This was a time limited piece for 2004.

WP 66
WITH LOVE™

Height:	3 ¼", 8.3 cm
Colour:	Pink piglet; green outfit, red scarf with gold fringe, beige heart
Issued:	2004 to the present
Series:	Love and Friendship

Back Stamp	Doulton Number	Price			
		U.S. $	Can. $	U.K. £	Aust. $
Doulton	WP 66	−	−	25.00	−

WP 67
RABBIT'S HARVEST?™

Height:	4 ¼", 10.8 cm
Colour:	Grey rabbit; orange and green vegetables, green and brown baskets
Issued:	2004 to the present

Back Stamp	Doulton Number	Price			
		U.S. $	Can. $	U.K. £	Aust. $
Doulton	WP 67	−	−	25.00	−

WP 69
PREPARATIONS FOR CARROT HONEY PIE™

Height: 3 ¾", 9.5 cm
Colour: Yellow bear; maroon hat, brown basket,
             orange and green vegetables
Issued: 2004 to the present

Back Stamp	Doulton Number	Price			
		U.S. $	Can. $	U.K. £	Aust. $
Doulton	WP 69	—	—	25.00	—

WP 70
THE PERFECT HAT FOR GARDENING™

Height: 3 ¼", 8.3 cm
Colour: Yellow bear; maroon hat, blue honey pot
Issued: 2004 to the present

Back Stamp	Doulton Number	Price			
		U.S. $	Can. $	U.K. £	Aust. $
Doulton	WP 70	—	—	25.00	—

WP 75
HONEY AND TEA IS A VERY GRAND THING™

Height: 4", 10.1 cm
Colour: Yellow bear; brown tree trunk, blue and white
             cup and saucer, red and white napkin
Issued: 2004 to the present
Series: Tea Time Collection

Back Stamp	Doulton Number	Price			
		U.S. $	Can. $	U.K. £	Aust. $
Doulton	WP 75	—	—	75.00	—
				Set price	

Note: Sold as a set with WP 77 and 78.

WP 76
CHRISTMAS PIGLET™

Height:	2 ½", 6.4 cm
Colour:	Pink Piglet; green outfit, yellow parcel, red ribbon and dark green holly
Issued:	2004 to the present

Back Stamp	Doulton Number	Price			
		U.S. $	Can. $	U.K. £	Aust. $
Doulton	WP 76	–	–	22.00	–

WP 77
TEA FOR TWO™

Height:	2 ¼", 5.7 cm
Colour:	Brown tree trunk, red and white table cloth, blue and white tea set
Issued:	2004 to the present
Series:	Tea Time Collection

Back Stamp	Doulton Number	Price			
		U.S. $	Can. $	U.K. £	Aust. $
Doulton	WP 77	–	–	75.00 Set price	–

Note: Sold as a set with WP 75 and 78

WP 78
PIGLET'S TEA TIME™

Height:	3 ¼", 8.3 cm
Colour:	Pink piglet; green outfit, blue and white cup and saucer, red and white napkin, brown tree trunk
Issued:	2004 to the present
Series:	Tea Time Collection

Back Stamp	Doulton Number	Price			
		U.S. $	Can. $	U.K. £	Aust. $
Doulton	WP 78	–	–	75.00 Set price	–

Note: Sold as a set with WP 75 and 77

Tea Time Collection

WIND IN THE WILLOWS

AW1
TOAD™
Style One

Beswick: 2942
Designer: Harry Sales
Modeller: David Lyttleton
Height: 3 ½", 8.9 cm
Colour: Green, yellow
            white and red
Issued: 1987 - 1989

U.S.	$125.00
Can.	$150.00
U.K.	£ 65.00
Aust.	$175.00

AW2
BADGER™
Style One

Beswick: 2940
Designer: Harry Sales
Modeller: David Lyttleton
Height: 3", 7.6 cm
Colour: Black, white and ,
            salmon
Issued: 1987 - 1989

U.S.	$ 90.00
Can.	$125.00
U.K.	£ 50.00
Aust.	$135.00

AW3
RATTY™
Style One

Beswick: 2941
Designer: Harry Sales
Modeller: David Lyttleton
Height: 3 ½", 8.9 cm
Colour: Blue and white
Issued: 1987 - 1989

U.S.	$ 90.00
Can.	$125.00
U.K.	£ 50.00
Aust.	$135.00

AW4
MOLE™
Style One

Beswick: 2939
Designer: Harry Sales
Modeller: David Lyttleton
Height: 3", 7.6 cm
Colour: Dark grey and
            brown
Issued: 1987 - 1989

U.S.	$150.00
Can.	$200.00
U.K.	£ 85.00
Aust.	$225.00

AW5
PORTLY™
(Otter)

Beswick: 3065
Modeller: Alan Maslankowski
Height: 2 ¾", 7.0 cm
Colour: Brown, blue
            green and yellow
Issued: 1988 - 1989

U.S.	$ 725.00
Can.	$ 950.00
U.K.	£ 400.00
Aust.	$1,000.00

AW6
WEASEL GAMEKEEPER™

Beswick: 3076
Modeller: Alan Maslankowski
Height: 4", 10.1 cm
Colour: Brown, green
            and yellow
Issued: 1988 - 1989

U.S.	$325.00
Can.	$425.00
U.K.	£175.00
Aust.	$450.00

WIW 1
ON THE RIVER™ (Mole and Rat)

Designer: Warren Platt
Size: 3 ½" x 6 ½",
            8.9 cm x 16.5 cm
Colour: Yellow, black,
            blue and red
Issued: 2000 in a limited
            edition of 1,908
Series: Tableau

U.S.	$275.00
Can.	$350.00
U.K.	£150.00
Aust.	$375.00

WIW 2
TOAD™
Style Two

Designer: Warren Platt
Height: 4 ¾", 12.1 cm
Colour: Orange-brown,
            browns and grey
Issued: 2000 in a limited
            edition of 2,000
            (C of A)
Comm. by: Doulton-Direct

U.S.	$ 85.00
Can.	$125.00
U.K.	£ 50.00
Aust.	$150.00

WIW 3
BADGER™, Style Two

Designer:	Warren Platt
Height:	5 ½", 14.0 cm
Colour:	Red, blue and white
Issued:	2000 in a limited edition of 2,000 (C of A)
Comm. by:	Doulton-Direct

U.S.	**$ 85.00**
Can.	**$125.00**
U.K.	**£ 50.00**
Aust.	**$150.00**

WIW 4
RATTY™, Style Two

Designer:	Warren Platt
Height:	5", 12.7 cm
Colour:	Mustard, yellow, white and red
Issued:	2001 in a limited edition of 2,000 (C of A)
Comm. by:	Doulton-Direct

U.S.	**$ 80.00**
Can.	**$100.00**
U.K.	**£ 45.00**
Aust.	**$110.00**

WIW 5
MOLE™, Style Two

Beswick:	4039
Designer:	Warren Platt
Height:	4 ½", 11.9 cm
Colour:	Blue, yellow, white and black
Issued:	2001 in a limited edition of 2,000 (C of A)
Comm. by:	Doulton-Direct

U.S.	**$ 80.00**
Can.	**$100.00**
U.K.	**£ 45.00**
Aust.	**$110.00**

WIW 6
WASHERWOMAN TOAD™

Beswick:	4152
Designer:	Warren Platt
Height:	3 ½", 8.9 cm
Colour:	Rose-pink, pink, white, black and brown
Issued:	2001 in a limited edition of 2,000
Comm. by:	Doulton-Direct

U.S.	**$ 80.00**
Can.	**$100.00**
U.K.	**£ 45.00**
Aust.	**$110.00**

WW 1
DELIGHTS OF SPRING, THE™

Height:	4", 10.1 cm
Colour:	Black, white, yellow, brown, green and yellow
Issued:	2004 to the present

U.S.	**–**
Can.	**–**
U.K.	**£25.00**
Aust.	**–**

WW 2
THE OPEN ROAD, THE DUSTY HIGHWAY™

Height:	4 ½", 11.9 cm
Colour:	Green, yellow, blue, red and brown
Issued:	2004 to the present

U.S.	**–**
Can.	**–**
U.K.	**£30.00**
Aust.	**–**

WW 3
NO AMOUNT OF SHAKING™

Length:	6 ¼", 15.9 cm
Colour:	Black, red-brown, green, yellow, blue, white and pink
Issued:	2004 to the present

U.S.	**–**
Can.	**–**
U.K.	**£45.00**
Aust.	**–**

WW 4
PERSUADING RATTY™

Height:	4 ¾", 12.1 cm
Colour:	Black, green, red-brown, yellow, blue, mauve, red and white
Issued:	2004 in a limited edition of 1,000

U.S.	–
Can.	–
U.K.	**£75.00**
Aust.	–

WW 5
SPRAWLING BY THE RIVERBANK™

Height:	2 ¾", 7.0 cm
Colour:	Red-brown, yellow, grey, brown, pink, blue and white
Issued:	2004 to the present

U.S.	–
Can.	–
U.K.	**£30.00**
Aust.	–

WW 6
WHO IS IT THIS TIME?™

Height:	5 ¼", 13.3 cm
Colour:	Black, white, pink, blue, white and brown
Issued:	2004 to the present

U.S.	–
Can.	–
U.K.	**£30.00**
Aust.	–

INDICES

ALPHABETICAL INDEX

MODEL NUMBER INDEX

BESWICK BEARS

BB001	William
BB002	Billy
BB003	Harry
BB004	Bobby
BB005	James
BB006	Susie
BB007	Angela
BB008	Charlotte
BB009	Sam
BB010	Lizzy
BB011	Emily
BB012	Sarah

JILL BARKLEM'S BRAMBLY HEDGE

DBH 1	Poppy Eyebright, Style One
DBH 2	Mr. Apple, Style One
DBH 3	Mrs. Apple, Style One
DBH 4	Lord Woodmouse, Style One
DBH 5	Lady Woodmouse, Style One
DBH 6	Dusty Dogwood, Style One
DBH 7	Wilfred Toadflax, Style One
DBH 8	Primrose Woodmouse
DBH 9	Old Mrs Eyebright
DBH 10A	Mr. Toadflax, Style One, First Version
DBH 10B	Mr. Toadflax, Style One, Second Version
DBH 10C	Mr. Toadflax, Style One, Third Version
DBH 11	Mrs. Toadflax
DBH 12	Catkin
DBH 13	Old Vole
DBH 14	Basil, Style One
DBH 15	Mrs. Crustybread
DBH 16	Clover
DBH 17	Teasel
DBH 18	Store Stump Money Box
DBH 19	Lily Weaver, Style One
DBH 20	Flax Weaver, Style One
DBH 21	Conker
DBH 22	Primrose Entertains
DBH 23	Wilfred Entertains
DBH 24	Mr. Saltapple, Style One
DBH 25	Mrs. Saltapple, Style One
DBH 26	Dusty and Baby
DBH 30	The Ice Ball
DBH 31	Lord Woodmouse, Style Two
DBH 32	Lady Woodmouse, Style Two
DBH 33	Primrose Picking Barries
DBH 34	Wilfred Carries the Picnic
DBH 35	Wilfred and the Toy Chest (Money Box)
DBH 36	Poppy Eyebright, Style Two
DBH 37	Dusty Dogwood, Style Two
DBH 38	Basil, Style Two
DBH 39	Mr. Saltapple, Style Two
DBH 40	Mrs. Saltapple, Style Two
DBH 41	Pebble
DBH 42	Shell
DBH 43	Shrimp
DBH 44	The Bride and Groom
DBH 45	Happy Birthday Wilfred
DBH 46	Mr. Toadflax, Style Two
DBH 47	Mrs. Apple, Style Two
DBH 48	Heading Home
DBH 49	Wilfred's Birthday Cake
DBH 50	Where are Basil's Trousers?
DBH 51	Dusty's Buns
DBH 52	Mrs. Toadflax Decorates Cake
DBH 53	Mr. Apple, Style Two
DBH 54	Lily Weaver, Style Two
DBH 55	Flax Weaver, Style Two
DBH 56	Wilfred Toadflax, Style Two
DBH 57	On the Ledge
DBH 58	Lily Weaver Spinning
DBH 59	Tea at Hornbeam Tree
DBH 60	A Cheerful Blaze
DBH 61	Shooting the Rapids
DBH 62	Old Mrs. Eyebright, Style Two
DBH 63	You're Safe
DBH 64	In the Woods
DBH 65	In the Brambles
DBH 66	Off to Pick Mushrooms
DBH 67	Let's Make a Snowmouse
DBH 68	Hot Buttered Toast for Breakfast
DBH 69	Home for Supper

THE CAT'S CHORUS

CC1	Purrfect Pitch
CC2	Calypso Kitten
CC3	One Cool Cat
CC4	Ratcatcher Bilk
CC5	Trad Jazz Tom
CC6	Catwalking Bass
CC7	Feline Flamenco
CC8	Bravura Brass
CC9	Fat Cat
CC10	Glam Guitar

COMPTON & WOODHOUSE

Teddy Bears

–	Archie
–	Benjamin
–	Bertie
–	Henry

COUNTRY COUSINS

PM2101	Sweet Suzie "Thank You"
PM2102	Peter "Once Upon A Time"
PM2103	Harry "A New Home for Fred"
PM2104	Michael "Happily Ever After"
PM2105	Bertram "Ten Out of Ten"
PM2106	Leonardo "Practice Makes Perfect"
PM2107	Lily "Flowers Picked Just For You"
PM2108	Patrick "This Way's Best"
PM2109	Jamie "Hurrying Home"
PM2111	Mum and Lizzie "Let's Get Busy"
PM2112	Molly and Timmy "Picnic Time"
PM2113	Polly and Sarah "Good News!"
PM2114	Bill and Ted "Working Together"
PM2115	Jack and Daisy "How Does Your Garden Grow?"
PM2116	Alison and Debbie "Friendship is Fun"
PM2119	Robert and Rosie "Perfect Partners"
PM2120	Sammy "Treasure Hunting"

DAVID HAND'S ANIMALAND

1148	Dinkum Platypus
1150	Zimmy Lion
1151	Felia
1152	Ginger Nutt
1153	Hazel Nutt
1154	Oscar Ostrich
1155	Dusty Mole
1156	Loopy Hare

ENGLISH COUNTRY FOLK

ECF 1	Huntsman Fox
ECF 2	Fisherman Otter
ECF 3	Gardener Rabbit, First Variation
ECF 4	Gentleman Pig, First Variation
ECF 5	Shepherd Sheepdog
ECF 6	Hiker Badger, First Variation
ECF 7	Mrs. Rabbit Baking, First Variation
ECF 8	The Lady Pig, First Variation
ECF 9	Hiker Badger, Second Variation
ECF 10	Gentleman Pig, Second Variation
ECF 11	The Lady Pig, Second Variation
ECF 12	Gardener Rabbit, Second Variation
ECF 13	Mrs. Rabbit Baking, Second Variation

ENID BLYTON'S NODDY COLLECTION

3676	Big Ears
3678	Noddy
3679	Mr. Plod
3770	Tessie Bear
—	Noddy and Big Ears

EXPRESS NEWSPAPERS LTD.

Rupert Bear
Beswick Series, 1980 - 1986

2694	Rupert Bear, Style One
2710	Algy Pug
2711	Pong Ping
2720	Bill Badger, Style One
2779	Rupert Bear Snowballing

Royal Doulton Series, 1998 - 2000

—	Bill Badger, Style Two
—	Edward Trunk
—	Podgy Pig
—	Rupert Bear, Style Two
—	Rupert Bear and Algy Pug Go-Carting
—	Rupert with Satchel

Royal Doulton Series, 2004 to date

RB1	Rupert's Toy Railway
RB2	Pretending to by an Outlaw (Edward Trunk)
RB3	Leading the Way (Ping Pong)
RB4`	Rupert Rides Home
RB5	Tempted to Trespass
RB6	Looking Like Robin Hood (Algy Pug)
RB7	Finishing Arrows and Stringing His Bow (Rupert)
RB8	Rupert's Silver Trumpet
RB9	Podgy Lands With a Bump
RB10	Bingo's Huge Firework
RB11	Rupert, Bill and the Mysterious Car

FOOTBALLING FELINES

FF2	Mee-Ouch
FF3	Kitcat
FF4	Dribble
FF5	Thrown In
FF6	Referee: Red Card

HANNA-BARBERA

The Flintstones

3577	Pebbles Flintstone
3579	Bamm-Bamm Rubble
3583	Wilma Flintstone
3584	Betty Rubble
3587	Barney Rubble
3588	Fred Flintstone
3590	Dino

Top Cat

3581	Top Cat
3586	Choo-Choo
3624	Fancy Fancy
3627	Benny
3671	Officer Dibble
3673	Spook
3674	Brain

HARRY POTTER

HP 1	The Remembrall Recovery
HP 2	Harry Casts a Magical Spell
HP 3	Hermoine Studies For Potions Class
HP 4	Ron Follows the Weasley Family Tradition
HP 5	Professor Severus Snape
HP 6	Headmaster Albus Dumbledore
HP 7	Wizard-in-training
HP 8	The Friendship Begins
HP 9	Harry's 11th Birthday
HP 10	Struggling Through Potions Class
HP 11	Slytherin or Gryffindor
HP 12	Ron and Scrabbers
HP 13	Hermoine Learns to Levitate
HP 14	Professor McGonagall
HP 15	Professor Quirrell
HP 16	Hedwig
HP 17	The Birth of Norbert
HP 18	The Mirror Holds the Answer
HP 19	The Journey to Hogwarts
HP 20	Madame Hooch
HP 21	Professor Sprout
HP 22	Harry Potter Playing Quidditch
HP 23	Dobby
HP 24	Dursley Family
HP 25	Whomping Willow
HP 26	Rescue in the Forbidden Forest

THE HERBS

H 1	Parsley the Lion
H 2	Bayleaf the Gardener
H 3	Dill the Dog
H 4	Sage the Owl

HIPPOS ON HOLIDAY

HH1	Grandma
HH2	Grandpa
HH3	Ma
HH4	Pa
HH5	Harriet
HH6	Hugo

Collecting Doulton
& Beswick Collectors Club

The independent magazine for collectors of Royal Doulton and Beswick

If you are a collector of Doulton or Beswick you cannot afford to be without this lively, authoritative and completely independent publication.

If you are a previous subscriber to Collecting Doulton, you may not know how much the magazine has improved over the past few months.

Published six times a year, Collecting Doulton contains articles by leading experts on the wide range of Doulton and Beswick ceramics, including:

- Latest auction results
- Your questions answered
- Collectors' profiles
- Free wants and for sale small ads
- Histories of artists, designers and wares
- Events diary
- News from around the world
- Book reviews

Amongst the subjects regularly covered are Lambeth wares, seriesware, figurines, character jugs, Bunnykins, Burslem wares, Doulton and Beswick animals, commemorative wares, advertising wares, new discoveries, rarities, Beatrix Potter etc etc... *Subscribe today*

Website: www.collectingdoulton.com • Email: barryjhill@hotmail.com

------------------------------ *Please photocopy and mail* ------------------------------

I wish to subscribe to Collecting Doulton magazine.
I enclose my cheque made out to Collecting Doulton Marketing for £21(UK) or £36 (overseas) for six issues.
Please start my subscription from issue No............/the current issue.
Mr/Mrs/Miss/Ms/Dr   First Name...
Surname ....
Address...
....Town ....
Country...Postcode ....
email ....
Please send to: Collecting Doulton Marketing, PO Box 310, Richmond, Surrey TW10 7FU England

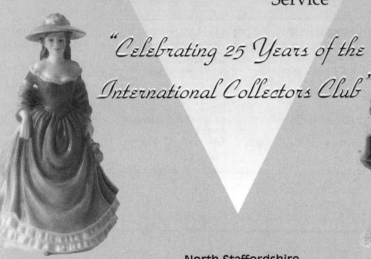

Royal Doulton Stores

ROYAL DOULTON STORES – CANADA

Calgary
Market Mall
C2 - 3625 Shaganappi Trail
NW, Calgary, AB
T3A 0E2

Cookstown
Cookstown Manufactures
Outlet, RR1, Cookstown,
ON L0L 1L0

Dartmouth
Micmac Mall, 21 Micmac
Dartmouth, NS B3A 4K7

Edmonton
West Edmonton Mall
8882 - 170th Street
Edmonton, AB T5T 3J7

Fredericton
Regent Mall
1381 Regent Street,
Fredericton, NB E3C 1A2

London
White Oaks Mall
1105 Wellington Road
London, ON N6E 1V4

Markham
Markville Shopping Centre
5000 Highway #7
Markham, ON
L3R 4M9

Pickering
Pickering Town Centre
1355 Kingston Road
Pickering, ON L1V 1B8

Surrey
Guildford Town Centre
Surrey, BC V3R 7C1

Toronto
Fairview Mall
1800 Sheppard Avenue East
Willowdale, ON M2J 5A7

Waterloo
St. Jacobs Factory Outlet
Mall, 25 Benjamin Road
Waterloo, ON N2V 2G8

Winnipeg
Polo Park Shopping Centre
1485 Portage Ave.
Winnipeg, MA R3G 0W4

ROYAL DOULTON STORES – UNITED STATES

Burlington
Prime Outlets – Burlington
288 Fashion Way, Store #5
Burlington, WA 98233

Cabazon
Dester Hills
Premium Outlets
48650 Seminole Dr.
Building C, Suite 152
Cabazon, CA 92230

Calhoun
Prime Outlets - Colhoun
455 Belwood Rd., Suite 20
Calhoun, GA 30701

Camarillo
Camarillo Premium Outlets
740 Ventura Blvd,
Suite 530
Camarillo, CA 93010

Central Valley
Woodbury Common
Premium Outlets
161 Marigold Court
Central Valley, NY 10917

Ellenton
Gulf Coast Factory Store
5501 Factory Shops Blvd.
Ellenton, Fl 34222

Estero
Miromar Outlets
10801 Corkscrew Rd.
Suite 366, Estero, Fl 33928

Flemington
Liberty Village
Premium Outlets
34 Liberty Village
Flemington, NJ08822

Gilroy
Premium Outlets – Gilroy
681 Leavesley Road
Suite B290
Gilroy, CA 95020

Jeffersonville
Ohio Factory Shops
8150 Factory Shops Blvd.
Jeffersonville, OH 43128

Kittery
Kittery Outlet Center
Route 1
Kittery, ME 03904-2505

Las Vegas
Belz Factory Outlet World
7400 Las Vegas Blvd.
South Suite 244
Las Vegas, NV 89123

Pigeon Forge
Belz Factory Outlet
2655 Teaster Lane
Suite 26
Pigeon Forge TN 37683

Prince William
Potomac Mills
2700 Potomac Mills Circle
Suite 976
Prince William, VA 22192

San Marcos
Tanger Factory Outlet Centre
4015 Interstate 35 South
Suite 402
San Marcos, TX 78666

St. Augustine
Belz Factory Outlet World
500 Belz Outlet Blvd
Suite 80
St. Augustine, Fl 32084

Tannersville
The Crossings Outlet Center
1000 Rte 611, Suite A-
23Tannersville, PA 18372

Vacaville
Factory Stores at Vacaville
336 Nut Tree Rd.
Vacaville CA 95687

Visit our website at:
www.royaldoulton.com

ROYAL DOULTON

Royal Doulton Stores

DOULTON AND COMPANY STORES IN THE UK

Doulton and Company is the new name for Royal Doulton on high street, offering the very best of our three brands plus selected collectables and giftware and homewares from a range of specialist brands.

Doulton and Company Dudley
Unit 52, Merry Hill,
Brierley Hill, Dudley
West Midlands
DY5 1SR

**Doulton and Company Outlet
Superstore Etruria**
Forge Lane, Etrura, Stoke-on-Trent
Staffordshire
ST1 5NN

Doulton and Company Hanley
The Potteries Centre
Hanley, Stoke-on-Trent
Staffordshire
ST1 1PS

Doulton and Company Hereford
19-21 Maylords Street,
Maylord Shopping Centre
Hereford, Herefordshire
HR1 2DS

Doulton and Company HOME
Central 12 Shopping Park
Southport
PR9 0TQ

Doulton and Company Swindon
McArthur Glen Designer Outlet
Great Western, Kemble Drive
Swindon, Wilts
SN2 2DY

LAWLEYS/CHINACAVES

Lawleys Blackpool
Unit 37, Houndshill Shopping Centre,
Fylde, Blackpool
Lancashire
FY1 4HU

Lawleys Carisle
63 Castle Street
Carlisle, Cumbria
CA3 8SL

Lawleys Chelmsford
42 High Chelmer
Chelmsford, Essex
CM1 1XU

**Lawleys Derby
Edwards**
71 St. Peters Street
Derby, Derbyshire
DE1 2AB

Lawleys Peterborough
7 Bridge Street
Peterborough, Cambridgeshire
PE1 1HJ

Lawleys Reading
21 Queen Victoria Street
Reading, Berkshire
RG1 1SY

Lawleys Torquay
38 Fleet Street
Torquay, Devon
TQ2 5DJ

Chinacave Llandudno
94 Mostyn Street
Llandudno, Gwynedd
LL30 2SB

Chinacave Macclesfield
Unit 1, 25 Castle Street Mall
Macclesfield, Cheshire
SK11 6AF

FACTORY SHOPS AND OUTLETS

Factory Shop Burslem
Nile Street, Burslem
Stoke-on-Trent, Staffordshire
ST6 2AJ

Factory Shop Fenton
Disribution Centre, Victoria Road
Fenton, Stoke-on-Trent
Staffordshire, ST4 2PJ

Factory Shop Regent
Regent Works, Lawley Street
Longton, Stoke-on-Trent
Staffordshire, ST3 1LZ

Factory Shop Stourbridge
Crystal Glass Centre, Churton House
Audnam, Stourbridge
West Midlands, DY8 4AJ

Factory Outlet Bridgend
Unit 66, Welsh Designer Outlet
Village, Bridgend, Shropshire
CF32 9SU

*FOR YOUR NEAREST ROYAL
DOULTON DEPARTMENT, PLEASE
CALL ROYAL DOULTON CONSUMER
ENQUIRIES ON 01782 404041*

Factory Outlet Colne
Boundary Mill Stores, Burnley Road
Colne, Lancashire
BB8 8LS

Factory Outlet Dover
De Bradelei Wharf
Cambridge Road
Dover, Kent, CT17 9BY

**Factory Outlet
Ellesmere Port**
Unit 106, Cheshire Oaks
Kinsey Road, Ellesmere Port
Cheshire, L65 9LA

Visit our website at:

ROYAL DOULTON www.royaldoulton.com

342

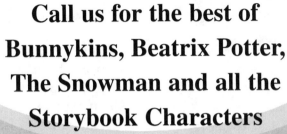